THE POET AS SPY

THE
POET
AS SPY

THE LIFE AND WILD TIMES
OF BASIL BUNTING

KEITH ALLDRITT

AURUM PRESS

First published in Great Britain
1998 by Aurum Press Ltd
25 Bedford Avenue, London WC1B 3AT

A catalogue record for this book is available from the British Library.

ISBN 1 85410 477 2

1 3 5 7 9 10 8 6 4 2
1998 2000 2002 2001 1999

Typeset by ensystems, Saffron Walden, Essex
Printed and bound in Great Britain by
MPG Books, Bodmin, Cornwall

Again, For Joan
With Love and Gratitude

Contents

List of Illustrations ix

Acknowledgements x

Preface xiii

One
Family and Boyhood 1

Two
Leighton Park and Prison 1916–1919 15

Three
The First London Years 1919–1923 23

Four
Paris 1923 31

Five
To Rapallo and Back to London 1924–1928 45

Six
Patronage and Marriage 1928–1930 55

Seven
Rapallo Again 1931–1933 70

Eight
The Canaries and Hampstead 1933–1937 80

Nine
The Years at Sea 1937–1942   92

Ten
A Very Good War and a Lively Peace 1942–1950   101

Eleven
Italy and *The Spoils* 1950–1951   121

Twelve
Paradise Regained and Lost 1951–1952   133

Thirteen
Flight Into Poverty 1952–1957   138

Fourteen
The Years of Obscurity 1957–1965   147

Fifteen
The Years of Eminence 1965–1979   165

Sixteen
The Last Years 1979–1985   187

Notes   202
Bibliography   208
Index   215

Illustrations

1. Basil as a baby with his mother.
2. Scotswood.
3. Basil as a young man.
4. The Literary and Philosophical Society of Newcastle-upon-Tyne.
5. 38 Moorside.
6. Ackworth School.
7. Leighton Park School.
8. Basil aged 23.
9. Ezra Pound.
10. W. B. Yeats and friends.
11. Margaret de Silver.
12. Marian Gray Culver.
13. Basil with his mother and first wife Marian.
14. The Buntings' house near Rapallo.
15. Basil in his early thirties.
16. Louis Zukofsky.
17. Marian with her two daughters.
18. Basil during World War II.
19. Basil's first three children, Bourtai, Roudaba and Rustam.
20. Three Bakhtiari chieftains.
21. The Zagros mountains.
22. Basil in Iran.
23. Tom Pickard.
24. Basil with Sima in Iran.
25. Shadingfield.
26. Basil in the early 1960s.
27. Sima with her mother and mother-in-law in the early 1960s.
28. Basil on a visit to Marian in 1966.
29. Basil with Roudaba and granddaughter Monica in 1966.
30. The Quaker meeting house at Briggflatts.
31. Peggy Greenbank's house at Hope in Shropshire.
32. A family gathering in 1979.
33. Basil's youngest daughter Maria with Roudaba.
34. Greystead.
35. Basil and Bourtai in 1980.
36. The Fox and Hounds, Whitley Chapel.
37. Basil in his last year.
38. Basil and Michael Shayer.

The author and publisher would like to thank the following for permission to reproduce illustrations: plate 9, The Harry Ransome Research Center, Austin, Texas; plate 10, The Huntington Library. Plates 2, 4, 5, 6, 7, 14, 25, 30, 31, 34 and 36 are from originals by the author. The remaining illustrations are the property of Bourtai Bunting Hargrove Nation and Roudaba Bunting Davido and appear here with their generous permission.

Acknowledgements

I wish to thank John Halliday, Basil Bunting's literary executor, for his kind co-operation in granting me access to the unpublished writings of Basil Bunting. All quotations from Basil Bunting's poetry are taken from the *Complete Poems*, published by Oxford University Press.

　　　　　　　so we'll live,
And pray, and sing, and tell old tales, and laugh
At gilded butterflies, and hear poor rogues
Talk of court news; and we'll talk with them too,
Who loses and who wins; who's in, and who's out;
And take upon's the mystery of things,
As if we were God's spies.

　　　　　　　　　　　　King Lear, v, iii

Preface

The writing of this the first book-length biography of Basil Bunting has meant for me travels, meetings and experiences far more varied than those required by my other books. Basil Bunting was a man who travelled much of the globe and I have tried to follow in his footsteps as much as my research funds allowed.

In her house by the fjord known as the Hood Canal under the snow covered peaks of the mountains of the Olympic Peninsula in the State of Washington USA, I came to know Basil Bunting's eldest daughter Bourtai Bunting Hargrove Nation. Sharing the radical social and political views of her father in his early years Bourtai has a busy law practice devoted to helping the disadvantaged. However she took time from her tight schedule to speak to me on more than one occasion of her memories of her father and of her thoughtful insights into his eventful life.

Basil's second daughter Roudaba Davido Bunting is also an idealist who inherited his social conscience. Until her recent retirement she worked as a psychiatric nurse in Washington State. Her house near the lake on the south side of Seattle is always full of animals and children, including her own recently adopted young son. On my visits to her there Roudaba spoke directly, even bluntly, about her father and the times after her mother took the two girls and left him.

In his home at Alston, the stone market-town high atop the Pennines in Cumbria, I visited Tom Pickard who as a teenager worked the great wonder of the literary history of the 1960s by rescuing Basil Bunting from obscurity and neglect and creating a new public and readership for him. Tom answered all my questions with great frankness and most generously loaned me some of his own papers and research relating to Basil Bunting.

In Rapallo on the Italian Riviera I had meetings with Massimo Bacigalupo, Professor of English at the nearby University of Genoa, author of *I Poeti a Rapallo*, and an ardent student of that modernist tradition in the poetry of the English-speaking world to which Basil belongs. Massimo spent time with me climbing the hills above Rapallo in order to identify the house in which Basil and Marian lived. I also met Massimo's father who had been a doctor in Rapallo in the thirties at the time when Bunting, Pound, Yeats and other members of the Rapallo Group lived there.

I have been greatly helped by the three partners who, in the Midlands in the 1960s, constituted Migrant Press and also worked with Tom Pickard to establish Basil Bunting's standing as a writer. From his home in Edinburgh Gael Turnbull sent me letters full of information and kindness. In his seventeenth-century house in a village near Cambridge Michael Shayer, with whom Basil had the last literary conversation of his life, shared many thoughts and insights with me. The third member of Migrant, the poet Roy Fisher, I have known for a number of years; I have learned a great deal about Basil from him on many visits to his home in a small and remote village on the rocky Staffordshire moorlands. His great poem of 1986, *A Furnace*, shows the continuity of the tradition in which Basil Bunting worked. *A Furnace* may look to jazz for its music rather than to the music of Scarlatti that informs Basil Bunting's masterpiece *Briggflatts*; *A Furnace* may also look to the rustbelt in and around Birmingham rather than to the beautiful, rural Northumberland of Bunting's poem, but, in responding to *Briggflatts*, *A Furnace* shows the further possibilities for poetry that Bunting's poem opened up.

A longtime student of this tradition and a friend of Basil Bunting is my colleague of many years, Peter Quartermain. When, in Vancouver, I told him of my decision to write this biography he unhesitatingly and most generously made available to me all the biographical findings which he had been able to assemble.

Another leading scholar in Bunting studies is Rick Caddel of Durham University. I am especially indebted to him for access to a letter written by Basil in Paris in the early 1920s when he was associating with Ernest Hemingway, Ezra Pound, Ford Madox Ford, Constantin Brancusi and the Surrealists and experiencing some of the wildest of the wild times in his life.

Other wild times occurred when Basil was a journalist and a spy in Iran. Of this period in his life it is difficult to write at present since a good deal of information is still concealed and protected by the Official Secrets Act. But such embargoes do not prevent us from observing how Basil's career as a poet was metaphorically as well as literally a matter of spying. In *Briggflatts* after all he described himself, the 'poet appointed', as a spy. The metaphor supplies an excellent way of approaching his art.

And this is what I have sought chiefly to indicate in the title of this book. Perhaps when the government restrictions are lifted, it may be possible to say more about Basil's years in British Intelligence in Iran. His second wife, Mrs Sima Bunting, colourfully recalled some of them when I went to talk to her at her home near Corbridge in Northumberland. An English bungalow on the outside, the interior of her home, particularly the large sitting-room, surprises with its spectacular Iranian decor. Sima, together with her little dog Echo, presides there with great hospitality and charm. The daughter of a quite wealthy family from the tribesmen of western Iran, Sima retains her strong accent and tells her stories in an entertainingly down-to-earth and forthright way.

One bright summer day my wife and I made a most enjoyable visit to Ackworth, the Quaker public school near Pontefract in Yorkshire to which Basil was sent for his secondary schooling. Fred Davies, the archivist of Ackworth School, was most informative and hospitable. I am very grateful to him for making available to me certain of Basil's schoolboy writings. Another kindness I received from Yorkshire was from Jonathan Williams who supplied the photograph of Basil on the front of the jacket.

I should also like to thank my longtime friend Jenny Penberthy for taking time to give me her recollections of Basil and Dave Dillabough for driving me so intrepidly over the Cumbrian hills in thick mist.

I am grateful to many libraries and especially to the Lilley Library at the University of Indiana, the Harry Ransome Humanities Research Center at Texas, the Basil Bunting Poetry Archive at Durham University, the Library of the University of Chicago, Lichfield City Library and the Library of the University of British Columbia.

In London I was the recipient of a great kindness from Esther Whitby who as an editor at André Deutsch for very many years sought to promote quality in English fiction. Like many writers I owe her a great debt, for she it was who helped to facilitate the acceptance of the idea of this biography. I must also thank my editor, Esther's sometime colleague, Sheila Murphy of Aurum Press, for the spirited interest with which she has backed this project.

The many journeys which this book has required cost a good deal of money and I conclude with my thanks to those who have expressed their confidence in me and the subject in financial terms. These are my publishers, Aurum Press, and the Author's Foundation of the Society of Authors which made me a very generous and much appreciated award.

I am also very much indebted to members of my family. My son Benjamin Alldritt has been a kindly and willing consultant; he has an extensive knowledge of the Second World War and has been able to help me with questions I had concerning that period in Basil's life. I am grateful to my daughter Miranda Hardwick Alldritt who drove indefatigably for hundreds of miles on one of my research journeys.

My wife, Joan Hardwick, has most generously assisted me at every stage of the writing. At some cost to her own work on her own books she has travelled with me, participated in interviews, and worked with me in libraries and archives. She helped me to assemble the illustrations, typed the manuscript and assisted me with the editing and improving of the text. My debt to her is immense.

I have taken the decision to refer to my subject as Basil throughout this biography. He was a man who, as he said, liked people with no side on them. And this showed in his attitude to names. Very soon after I first met him in 1970 he was Basil to me as to everyone else whom I knew that knew him. It seems right and proper to refer to him in this way as I attempt to tell the story of his life.

Prologue

On a summer's day in 1980 an old man who was the same age as the
century itself was among the flood of passengers that swept on to the
platform at King's Cross from the Inter City train from Newcastle-upon-
Tyne. He was tidily if a little shabbily dressed, wearing a dark sportscoat
and a loose turtle neck sweater. His heavy black shoes were highly
polished. He was almost bald but had a full grey beard. He made his way
down the platform a little jerkily and slowly, managing his small
travelling bag with some difficulty. His eyes were bright and active; his
thick eyebrows were sharply tufted, mephistophelian.

He was one of the greatest living figures in English literature.
He was also a spectacular instance of the redemption of a career at the
eleventh hour. Fifteen years before, at the age of sixty-five, as
his retirement approached he had been an obscure and overworked
journalist on a Newcastle newspaper. But when he became an old-age
pensioner his life underwent an amazing upswing in fame, fortune and
activity.

A young left-wing poet in Newcastle had been told by an American
that the poet Basil Bunting lived nearby. The young man went and
called on him and was enthralled to hear him read his poetry and speak
of his memories of W. B. Yeats, Ezra Pound, D. H. Lawrence, William
Carlos Williams and T. S. Eliot.

The pensioner was in turn greatly stirred by the young man's
admiration. To his surprise and joy Basil Bunting found himself inspired
to begin another long poem after fourteen years of almost total inactivity
as a poet. The result was *Briggflatts*, *the* poem of the sixties and, as has
often been said, the greatest long poem produced in Britain since *Four
Quartets*. This renewal that came to him after his formal working life was
ended he regarded as something magical.

Leaving the railway station, Basil Bunting made his way to Bayswater.
Here he entered the grand building that housed the Royal Society of
Literature. The main ground-floor room with its dark wooden columns
was crowded with people. Here that afternoon, not long after his eightieth

birthday, Basil Bunting was created a Fellow of the Society. There was enthusiastic and prolonged applause.

It was one of many honours that came to him towards the end of his turbulent life, in his magical old age.

ONE
Family and Boyhood

A native of Northumberland, England's most northerly county, Basil Bunting liked to speak of cattle-rustling ancestors who made raids across the border into Scotland. But his immediate origins were more prosaic. He was born on the first day of March 1900 into a prosperous middle-class family in Scotswood-on-Tyne, now a suburb, but then a colliery village three miles west of Northumberland's largest city, Newcastle-upon-Tyne. It was a township of uniform stone houses built by the mining company, the streets running steeply down to the River Tyne which was here crossed by an early nineteenth-century suspension bridge with granite towers linking Scotswood to the road to Bladon and the famous races. For everyone in Scotswood, including Basil, the Tyne was an inescapable daily presence, so that Basil grew up to think of himself not only as a Northumbrian but more particularly as a Tynesider. He long remembered that as a child, in the days before the river was polluted, he had seen salmon caught at Scotswood and sent on carts for sale in Newcastle. In later life, whenever he was in England, he was not happy unless he was living close to the river which had dominated his childhood.

His mother, born Annie Cheesman, whose maiden name became the poet's middle name, was very much a lady. She was the daughter of Isaac Cheesman, a colliery manager in the small town of Throckley just a few miles further west down the River Tyne. A photograph taken when Annie was about twelve years old shows her father, Isaac, a very substantial figure of a man in a sombre Victorian suit with a waistcoat and watch-chain over his protruding stomach and a heavy bowler hat above his thickly bearded and mustachioed face. His wife, also Annie, wears a black dress with a lace collar. Her hair, parted in the middle, is pulled back very tight and her large, strong jaw, which Basil was to inherit, is set very firm. And her expression, as Basil's could readily be, is at once challenging and sceptical. Basil's mother was one of seven children, having four sisters and two brothers, and this gave Basil a large sense of extended family. Her father was wealthy and owned a good deal of property in the area. His wife's family, the Forsters, were less prosperous; a number of them were colliers. Isaac Cheesman liked to spend and enjoy his money. He helped one of Annie's sisters to assemble a collection of paintings. Basil remembered how one of the walls in her house was dominated by a large work by the once fashionable Northumbrian artist John Martin, the spectacularly melodramatic history painter of the early nineteenth century whose immense canvas, *The Great Day of His Wrath*, hangs in the Tate Gallery. The Cheesmans took culture and education very seriously. And since Annie's family lived in the Newcastle area its members, with their passionate interest in the arts, particularly music and painting, had a greater influence on Basil as a boy and a young man than Dr Bunting's family who lived many miles to the south. Annie herself had been well educated and sent to a finishing school where there was inculcated in her a lifelong perfectionist caring for the proper management of cutlery, tableware, china and all the other things that make for a well maintained and elegant household. To her dismay Basil, both as a boy and a man, was untidy, slovenly and a perpetual threat to the domestic decorum she so much prized. Nevertheless she loved him intensely. In fact she doted on him. And until she died, when she was well into her nineties, she was her son's great stay and support in his various escapades, upheavals, crises and disasters.

Being a Northumbrian was a major part of Basil's sense and definition of himself. However, his father and his father's family were from the Midlands. Thomas Lowe Bunting took his middle name from his mother's family which had lived for several generations in Burton-on-Trent in Staffordshire. He had three sisters: Pollie who died when she was still a child, Sallie (Sarah Anne), a spinster, who was a nurse and a suffragette, and Hettie (Harriet Alice) who had a career in the Post Office and saved a considerable sum of money. On her death in 1957 her substantial legacy to Basil would create a turning point in his life in late middle age. The Lowes had been active in local politics in that beer-brewing town and Thomas Bunting was proud to recall that two members of his family had been mayors of Burton. Thomas's father Joseph Bunting lived a little further north at Heanor in Derbyshire where he had a draper's shop.

In this small town near Ilkeston, at the centre of an area later to become known as 'D. H. Lawrence country', Thomas Lowe Bunting was born in 1868. His father Joseph drank heavily and as a result his business failed. So when Thomas Bunting decided that he wanted to study medicine at the University of Edinburgh which had a famous and highly regarded medical faculty, his father could do nothing to help him financially. Thomas had to approach one of his uncles and ask for a loan. He regarded this dependency on a member of the family other than his father as a humiliation and this seems to have been the reason that Thomas Lowe Bunting, unlike his father and then his son, never touched alcohol.

While he was a student at Edinburgh Thomas came to know the distinguished professor, Patrick Geddes, a man of wide interests who wrote books on both biology and sociology. But he did not confine his attention to academic pursuits. He also involved himself in the city planning movement that developed at the end of the nineteenth century. The example of Patrick Geddes motivated Thomas Bunting always to seek a wider cultural awareness beyond his special expertise as a physician.

When he had gained his medical qualification at Edinburgh Thomas returned to the Midlands to take up an appointment in an asylum near Buxton in Derbyshire. Since he did not have the capital to buy into a practice he had to take a salaried job. He moved to Northumberland when he was offered another salaried position, that of doctor at the Montague Colliery on Scotswood-on-Tyne. When he first arrived in the north in 1895 he lived in a small terrace house at 17 Prospect Terrace in Scotswood. As he socialized and extended his acquaintance with other professional people working in the Northumbrian coalfield, he came to know the wealthy colliery engineer and manager Isaac Cheesman of Throckley with whose beautiful and elegant daughter Annie he fell in love. Their wedding took place on the first day of November, 1898, in St Michael and All Angels, the parish church of Newburn, then a small country town a few miles west of where Dr Bunting lived. The couple subsequently established their home in a modest Victorian house at 27 Denton Road in Scotswood. When Basil was born Annie was twenty-five years old and her husband thirty-one.

On 2 March 1900, the day after Basil came into the world, his father reported his birth at the Registrar's Office in the Subdistrict of Westgate in Newcastle-upon-Tyne. The baby's birth certificate recorded the formal address of the family home in Scotswood as Denton Road, Benwell Urban District. In reporting his occupation Thomas Lowe Bunting merely cited his medical degree.

Marriage and fatherhood did not distract Dr Bunting from his dedication to science. He continued to be a very serious student of medicine and in his spare time he engaged in study and research. In

1904, when Basil was four and his sister Joyce two, their father was awarded a higher degree at the University of Edinburgh. His thesis was on the histology, or tissue formation, of lymphatic glands. For this research he used the bodies of dead animals that he begged from a menagerie in Newcastle. Describing his early childhood Basil recalled how his father worked

> in a tiny surgery with a desk about 2 feet by 18 inches long and a microscope. He managed to compare the histology (Histological structure, cell structure) of the lymphatic glands of very nearly all the mammals, and a good many other creatures too. There was in those days an animal shop in Newcastle and he had an arrangement: when an animal died he would be called at once and go and remove the particular glands he wanted to examine before anything else was done. So he managed to have lions, tigers, leopards, monkeys, all sorts of things on his list beside the small animals he could buy for the purpose. The house was sometimes full of lizards that had escaped from their box in the cellar.[1]

In Dr Bunting's obituary in the *British Medical Journal* the writer noted sadly that although Thomas Bunting had a successful career as a general practitioner, his potential would have been more fully realized, had he been given the opportunity to become a university teacher and an 'investigator of physiology'. His thesis was of a quality to win him the distinction of being elected to the Royal Society in Edinburgh.

Thomas Bunting did not confine himself to his work on his thesis. He also employed his considerable intellectual energy in involving himself in the social and political context of medicine in the north-east. He had great sympathy with the coal miners who constituted a large part of his practice, and deplored the conditions in which the men worked underground. As a doctor he was keenly aware how these conditions damaged the men's health, could lead to serious injuries and even bring about major disasters. Dr Bunting became a member of the Fabian Society, the socialist research organisation founded in 1884 by, among others, George Bernard Shaw and Sidney Webb. In 1900, just a few months after Basil's birth, the Society had become a constituent party of the Labour Party which was founded that year. Another prominent Fabian was the political scientist Graham Wallas who became a friend of Dr Bunting and in later years assisted Basil when he was casting about for a career after leaving school.

The left-wing views that Basil heard argued and repeated in his father's circle had a strong effect on him. Well into middle age Basil was an outspoken critic of the capitalist system. A poem which he published in his early thirties entitled 'They Say Etna' contains lines which recall the harsh conditions and cruel exploitation experienced by the miners in the Northumberland in which he grew up.

> Gear, then, and gear,
> > gritty-grinding.
> The governor spins, raises its arms.
> Two three-inch steel cables scream from the drum
> seventy fathoms.
> We carry lighted Davy lamps,
> stoop along the narrow track.
> Trucks scold tunnel.
> In a squat cavern a
> naked man on his
> knees with a
> pickaxe rips a nugget from the coalface.
>
> Four lads
> > led the pownies
> a mile and a half through rising water,
> lampless because the stife
> asphyxiates lamps,
> by old galleries to the North Shaft.
> The water rose.
> > The others
> came five months later when it was pumped out
> and were buried by public subscription.
> (The widows were provided for.)

Dr Thomas Bunting interested his son in politics; he also interested him in literature. The doctor and his wife were active members of Newcastle's Literary and Philosophical Society. Its president for a time was Sir Walter Trevelyan whose wife, Lady Pauline, had often entertained Pre-Raphaelites such as Dante Gabriel Rossetti, Holman Hunt and Ford Madox Brown at the Trevelyans' Georgian mansion at Wallington. An honorary member of the Literary and Philosophical Society from the other

7

end of the social scale was Joseph Skipsey, a Northumbrian collier poet who was a friend of Dr Bunting and whose life and art had been a triumph over appalling hardship and adversity. Another member of the society who made an impression on Basil was the solicitor R. S. Watson whom Basil remembered as having 'great influence . . . behind the scenes of the radical section of the Liberals' and 'an immense acquaintance ranging from Mazzini to the Pre-Raphaelites, from scholars to cabinet ministers'.[2] Yet another remarkable figure was Thomas Dixon, a cork-cutter from Sunderland who had worked with William Bell Scott to found an art school. Dixon, a self-educated working man, had also engaged in a lengthy correspondence with John Ruskin who held him in high respect.

The 'Lit and Phil' as the Bunting family called the Society was but one of the features of the city that gave it a sense of being an important cultural centre. The architecture and streetscape were impressive. A social historian has noted that:

> In Newcastle-upon-Tyne . . . old and new co-existed, supplying two different ingredients of local pride – tradition and the sense of what a historian of Newcastle called in 1827 'the improving spirit of the age'. Richard Grainger, the builder, John Dobson, the architect, and an intelligent and sensitive town clerk and member of an influential local dynasty, worked out what would now be called a central development plan, completed in 1839, and bequeathed to the city a fine collection of handsome buildings which gave it a distinctive air of dignity and grace. Grey Street, which its admirers preferred to London's Regent Street, was described by Gladstone as the best modern street in Britain.[3]

At the end of the nineteenth century Newcastle also had its own publishing house and one which in terms of British literary history was important. The Walter Scott Company, based at Felling on the eastern edge of the city, had a long and impressive list. The firm's London agent was W. B. Yeats's close friend Ernest Rhys, and in the 1890s the Scott Company published, very successfully, Yeats's *Fairy and Folk Tales of the Irish Peasantry*.

In the Edwardian period, when Basil was growing up, Newcastle-upon-Tyne continued to have a lively literary culture. Through his parents Basil had ready access to it and it clearly had a creative impact on the future poet. So also did the beautiful Northumbrian landscapes outside the big city, the hills and fells where Dr Bunting regularly took his family walking and where he taught his son climbing. The Abraham brothers, who were well-known local rock climbers, often accompanied Dr Bunting to the Lake District where they helped him to coach his son in making the more difficult ascents. One of the places the Bunting family visited was the attractive little village of Capheaton with its row of creeper-covered cottages with low, overhanging roofs. Its great late seventeenth-century baroque hall was the ancestral home of the Swinburne family. Basil later regretted that the poet Algernon Charles Swinburne, then in his seventies, had not been at Capheaton that day. Had he been there, Basil was sure, he would have patted the young lad on the head and given him half a crown, and a poetic succession would have been confirmed. For Swinburne as a child had been taken over to Grasmere and Wordsworth had patted him on the head.

Basil's first experience of Wordsworth, the fellow northern poet whose work would always be most important to him, came through Dr Bunting. Basil's father made a point of taking him climbing in places associated with Wordsworth in and around the Lake District. The doctor also read Wordsworth aloud to his two children. Basil later recalled 'my father used to read poetry to us from the earliest years and included amongst the poems for the children a number of less recondite bits of Wordsworth. It made a great impression on me early in life.'[4]

The Bunting family also took a close interest in the vital musical culture of Newcastle-upon-Tyne during these formative years of Basil's life. Dr Bunting was acquainted with the composer, conductor, organist and scholar William Whittaker, a native of the city who founded the Newcastle Bach Choir and went on to become the first Professor of Music at Glasgow University. Whittaker promoted the compositions of his friends Gustav Holst and Ralph Vaughan Williams and he also performed what was then considered the advanced music of Debussy, Satie and Poulenc. Whittaker himself wrote orchestral works, chamber music and piano pieces. He made numerous arrangements of Northumbrian folk songs and ballads. Until the end of his life Basil kept a copy of Whittaker's *North Countrie Ballads, Songs and Pipe-Tunes*. From this book Basil would sing songs, accompanying himself on the guitar. Another of William Whittaker's great enthusiasms, which he also passed on to Basil, was for the cantatas of Johann Sebastian Bach. Whittaker's two-volume work on them was published posthumously.

Basil had further and closer access to the work of these and other composers through Aunt Jane who was an excellent pianist and often played for him. (She also sang in Whittaker's Bach Choir.) One of Basil's early preferences was for the motets and madrigals of the Elizabethan and Jacobean composer William Byrd. An exciting musical event in the north-east during Basil's youth was the discovery in Durham Cathedral of Byrd's liturgical work *The Great Service*. The discoverer was a friend of William Whittaker, Dr Edmund Fellowes, a musicologist who became choirmaster at St George's Chapel, Windsor. Fellowes passed a copy of the score to Whittaker who with his Bach Choir in Newcastle Cathedral gave the first complete performance of the work for three centuries. Basil often sat at the back of the cathedral and listened carefully to the way his father's friend conducted rehearsals.

Because of his father's intellectual powers and wide-ranging interests Basil was given a considerable education long before he received any formal schooling. This began when he was six and was sent to a private nursery school outside the predominantly working-class Scotswood and closer to the centre of Newcastle. It was rather a long journey and he was accompanied by the housemaid. They had to walk about a mile and a half to the tram terminus and then travel some distance into the city. The school, essentially an old-fashioned dame school, was run by an old lady, Miss A. M. Bell at 24 West Parade, Rye Hill in Newcastle. Miss Bell taught the children the alphabet and how to copy pothook hand-writing into exercise books. Those who made mistakes had their knuckles rapped. The old lady also stressed good manners. An important part of these, she insisted, was that the children eat up everything that was put before them at lunchtime. This led to the first of Basil's many conflicts with authority. A good deal of tapioca was served at the school and Basil simply could not eat it. His plateful was left in front of him until the middle of the afternoon and then, for leaving it still untouched, he was spanked.

The old lady had an assistant, Miss Winny, a young woman with long black ringlets. In her class the young Basil spent much of his time reading the Bible. Another figure in Basil's early education was Miss Wraith who served as governess to Basil and his sister Joyce in their home in Scotswood. Born in 1902 and two years younger than Basil, Joyce was a more stolid child than her brother. After her schooldays she followed in her father's footsteps and qualified as a doctor. In adulthood she and Basil quarrelled a good deal. She was ever a harsh critic of his Bohemian way of life and unsympathetic to his misfortunes. Already, in his days in the family nursery as at school, Basil was often in trouble. He considered Miss Wraith a nice woman but a stern disciplinarian; she 'kept a cane and used it fairly frequently'.

Dr Bunting was by now developing a lucrative private practice and he readily spent money on the education of both Basil and Joyce. Around the time of his eleventh birthday Basil went on to the Royal Grammar School in Newcastle-upon-Tyne. Not long afterwards his sister Joyce was sent to Newcastle Central High School, but like her brother she soon moved to a boarding-school – in her case, St Leonard's in the university town of St Andrew's in Scotland. In September 1912 at the age of twelve and a half, Basil was sent to the public school where he was to remain for almost four years, by far the greater part of his school days. Ackworth was a Quaker boarding-school in the West Riding of Yorkshire, just south of Pontefract and about a hundred miles away from his home in Scotswood-on-Tyne. Originally erected in 1758 as a foundling hospital and then purchased by the Quakers to use as a school some forty years later, Ackworth is an imposing piece of eighteenth-century architecture. The main block is thirteen bays long and has a large three-bay pediment and a pedimented doorway. Nearby there are courtyards and other substantial buildings including a spacious Quaker meeting house.

Neither Bunting's father nor his mother were members of the Society of Friends, but one of his uncles was and Basil's parents seem to have been extremely sympathetic to the Society and its beliefs. Basil once remarked that he 'was brought up entirely in a Quaker atmosphere'. Fabian Dr Bunting and his wife may also have been influenced in their choice of school by the thought that at Ackworth their son could receive the quality of education offered by a public school without also encountering the snobbish, conservative and hierarchical attitudes that pervaded non-Quaker boarding schools.

Within weeks of entering Ackworth Basil drew still closer to Quakerism. On the enrolment register he was unable to name a Quaker meeting place which his parents attended but he quickly became friends with a boy who could. John Allen Greenbank was just over eight months older than Basil and his name appeared on the admittance register immediately after Basil's. Along with his name was entered the information that John's family attended the Quaker meeting at Sedbergh. The Greenbanks lived very close to this small, stone-built town on the remote western edge of Yorkshire. Their house was in a small hamlet, Briggflatts, across the road from a famous early Quaker meeting house bearing the date 1675 on its simple porch. John Greenbank's father, also a John, had a stonemason's business close to the Quaker burial ground at Briggflatts. As Basil approached his thirteenth birthday he was invited by young John, his schoolmate, to spend some of the holidays with his family at Briggflatts. Basil accepted the invitation and at Briggflatts met John's sister Peggy. And so began the love story on which his poetic masterpiece is founded. *Briggflatts* is its title and Peggy is its dedicatee, the girl who is poignantly remembered both at its beginning and at its close.

The two young people quickly fell in love with each other that spring. Peggy was eight years old, four years younger than Basil. This was the first of a number of occasions on which he would become involved with someone far less mature than himself. At the outset their intense love for each other was pre-sexual. But, *Briggflatts* suggests, it did not end that way. But even at this time of their innocent beginnings Basil was sophisticated enough to see that, in order not to give offence to Peggy's parents, and to be sure of being invited back, it would be a good idea, as he later put it, to 'sweetheart' her mother.[5] And this he did assiduously. Also each time he returned to the Greenbank home he brought Peggy's younger sister Jean a box of Edinburgh rock which was her special favourite. Such tactics worked. As he told his French translator Jacques Darras many years later, he spent 'at least half of every holiday' at Briggflatts until his schooldays came to an end.

Peggy was a most attractive girl with full lips and a heart-shaped face and deep-set eyes full of kindliness and candour. She and Basil went out cycling together exploring the fells and dales close to Briggflatts. They rode to the deep glaciated valley of Mallerstang and up to Pendragon Castle which reputedly had belonged to King Arthur. His beloved and her landscape were inextricably linked for the city boy from Newcastle. More than half a century later, in a letter to a friend, he continued to remember his first love and the beautiful place in which she lived. 'Peggy Greenbank and her whole ambience, the [River] Rawthey valley, the fells of Lunedale, the Viking inheritance all spent save the faint smell of it, the ancient Quaker life accepted without thought and without suspicion that it might seem eccentric.'[6] For more than six years he made the train journey across the Pennines to spend his holidays with his sweetheart. During one of his later holidays when he was about seventeen and Peggy thirteen, they crept into the old whitewashed meeting house with its heavy mullioned windows and under the wooden gallery inside went through a pretend Quaker marriage ceremony together. It was an occasion he remembered long after he had discontinued the relationship.

During the years in which his relationship with Peggy developed Basil was academically successful at Ackworth School. On the honour board in what was formerly the school assembly hall his name is inscribed as top pupil for the year 1915. What Basil himself remembered most about his education at Ackworth was the amount of Bible study the school insisted on. He later recalled: 'Every morning you had to get a large lump of the Bible by heart before breakfast. At breakfast the Bible was read to you. At dinner the Bible was read to you again. And on Sunday there were *very* large lumps of the Bible, besides Scripture lessons in between.' But looking back in old age, the poet was glad that he had had this 'grounding in the Holy Scriptures' and had come to know so intimately 'the authorized version of Job, of the Song of Songs, some of the Prophets, all the extraordinary narrative skill of some of the chapters of the Book of Kings.'

At Ackworth Basil's career as a writer began. The school still preserves one of his earliest literary efforts, a short story of some fifteen pages. It has the peculiar title 'T versus N'. A preparatory note explains that 'N' was Napoleon's monogram and 'T' was the symbol of the Tagenbund, a German political society opposed to the French. The historical tale is related by Baptiste Rénaud who, as Basil himself would become, is a secret agent. His mission is to deliver confidential despatches to Napoleon from Marshall Ney. Rénaud's journey takes him across a battlefield full of the dead and the dying. He then saves a damsel in distress. He fights and defeats another secret agent, a member of the Tagenbund. The secret despatches which Rénaud removes from the man's body and delivers to Napoleon help to save the French army. Basil's story ends with his hero receiving the cross of the Legion of Honour from his grateful emperor.

Owing a great deal to Alexander Dumas but also showing Basil's early fascination with the secret service, the story suggests a young author who has a keen interest in history, enjoys narrative and is happy to thrill, horrify and generally entertain his readers. His style has a confidence and an authority unusual in someone of his age.

The evidence suggests that Basil's schooldays at Ackworth were happy ones. He certainly was not lonely or isolated as some poets have been when at school. John Allen Greenbank was not his only close friend. Perhaps even more important to Basil was Ernest Cooper Apperley

Stephenson who came from nearby Leeds. Their relationship was joyous and stimulating to both. When Ernest Stephenson, despite his Quakerism, went off to the First World War and there lost his life, Basil experienced intense grief and misery. He never forgot his friend. Some seventy years on, not long before he died, Basil planned to write a memoir of Stephenson. But the project was never embarked upon.

The headmaster of Ackworth at that time later remembered Basil and two other pupils requesting a conversation with him. The three boys were concerned what they should do when the time came for them to be called up to fight in the war in France. Basil and his two friends, under the influence of their Quaker education, were already considering declaring themselves pacifists. As they walked the green lawns around Ackworth School with their headmaster they discussed the consequences of taking such a position. This was the first of very many occasions when history impinged problematically upon Basil's life.

In his final year Basil's first poem to be printed appeared in the Ackworth School magazine. It too suggests a happy author, a pupil who has greatly enjoyed being at the school and who leaves with affection for it. Entitled 'The Song of the Ackworth Clock', the poem has five stanzas evoking various aspects of schoolboy life which the old school clock has witnessed. The final stanza looks forward with pleasure to future class reunions.

> when at Easter's happy time
> Old scholars here from every clime
>   Make a lordly show;
> When Tommy B. meets Johnny A.,
> When aged fogeys leap and play,
> When all the world feels young and gay.
>   Is this what you know?
>   Aye, this is what I know;
> Tick tock, tick tock, all of this I know,
> Tick tock, tick tock, tick tock, slow.

This first published poem was his farewell to his beloved school. Under the title he styled himself 'Basil C. Bunting. Leaver, July 1916'.

Two
Leighton Park and Prison
1916–1919

As the time approached for Basil to enter the sixth form his parents decided to transfer him from Ackworth to another school. They hoped and believed that he had the ability to win a scholarship to a university. Ambitious on their son's behalf, they had in mind Oxford or Cambridge. They were also persuaded that his chances of achieving this would be greatly improved if he went south to Leighton Park, a new Quaker boarding-school near Reading in Berkshire which had quickly established an academic reputation and which charged high fees. It was, Basil later recalled, one of the 'public schools for the rich – the kind of place in which Cadburys and Frys get their education'.[1]

Basil entered the lower sixth at Leighton Park in September 1916 at the time when the terrible battle on the River Somme was being fought in France. He was halfway through his seventeenth year and, from the outset, was not at all happy as a new boy at the school. Within weeks his distress turned to panic. In the first week of October he wrote despairingly to his father, 'I think I am going mad here. I can't work, nor anything – just dream of home.' Basil doubted his ability to go to the headmaster and discuss the situation without losing his composure and breaking down. So he wrote out a list of reasons for his misery and took it to the Head's study. The statement began, 'I think I ought to leave this school at once for several reasons.' The first was that he saw some 'great underlying difference between North and South'. As a Northumbrian he felt thoroughly uncomfortable with all the southerners in this expensive school in the Thames valley. His second cause of complaint was the bullying that he had witnessed. He instanced an occasion on which 'the whole school turned on one helpless little chap'. Thirdly, Basil reproached the headmaster for boasting in an address to the assembled pupils that Leighton Park 'had public school fees so as to get the public school class of men'. In Basil's view this Quaker school had at the same time 'borrowed from the public schools all that is bad and vile'. He gave one example of the hazing that went on. 'There is a system of making new boys sing in the dormitories.' One wonders whether this happened to Basil himself. If it did, his indignation eventually cooled for he conceded, 'There is no real harm done, and it would be excusable in a school with long traditions but Leighton Park School is too young to have traditions.' But his anger and anxiety return as he lists his fourth and final complaint charging that his schoolmates 'have no respect whatever for property'. His writing becomes nervous as he describes the thieving that goes on. One of the least wealthy pupils, he wonders what he would do if his own coat were to be stolen.

This statement presented to his headmaster demonstrates two features of Basil's character that would endure throughout his life. First, there is his uncompromising determination to speak up forthrightly and clearly for principles in which he believes. And second, there is his propensity for strong, even violent, emotional reaction to people and situations. His father alluded to this latter characteristic in his reply to a letter from the headmaster reporting Basil's troubles at school. On 26 October 1916, some six weeks after his son had arrived at Leighton Park, Dr Bunting wrote to him: 'I certainly agree with most that you say of him. There is a brain storm, or hysteria, with intervals of what is probably nearly normal thought; though he may perhaps regard the intervals as having been periods of self-suppression.' The doctor also commented to the headmaster on what he saw as Basil's tendency to role-playing: 'I think too there is some self-conscious posing. I can't help feeling that in the midst of it he stands outside of himself and admires his own attitudes.' These, Dr Bunting concluded, 'may nevertheless be quite sincere.'

A photograph of Basil and his father taken one sunny winter's day in this same year suggests that the doctor, despite the complex reservations expressed to the headmaster, also felt great admiration for his son. The body language in the snapshot, most likely taken by Mrs Bunting, is very revealing. Sixteen-year-old Basil in a three-piece suit and tie faces the camera with a slight and somewhat aggressive smile. He clearly regards himself as the centre of attention. But there is also tension in his confident stance. His hands are clenched nervously and held awkwardly beside the pockets of his jacket. Dr Bunting in semi-profile stands to the side, very much the secondary figure in the dual portrait. He seems to be waiting respectfully for his son's next words. The same height as his son, the doctor is bald with a grey moustache and beard. He also wears a suit with a waistcoat. But his appearance is that of an older generation of the middle class. He wears a winged collar and a pince-nez. Below the knee his trousers are tucked into gaiters. He is far more relaxed than his son.

The doctor stands with his hands in his pockets regarding Basil with a smile that radiates affection. The picture indicates that, despite his emotional volatility and his readiness to clash with authority, Basil grew up with a father who did not conceal the loving pride he took in him.

Denied his father's permission to leave the school, Basil quickly overcame his fit of revulsion and became reconciled to Leighton Park. He did well at arts subjects and became a capable swimmer, winning the bronze medallion of the Royal Life Saving Society. But literature and politics interested him more than athletics. One of the roles that he assumed at the school would surely have pleased his father. He presented himself as the school socialist. At the end of the second week of November, about a month after his crisis of homesickness, he read a paper entitled 'The Relation of the State and Individual Liberty and Law' to the school's literary and philosophical club which was called the Senior Essay Society. The members listened attentively to his insistent, rhetorical, somewhat truculent speech. They saw a stocky, slightly plump boy with rich dark hair neatly parted, a heavy forceful jaw and eyes that burned intensely behind his steel-rimmed spectacles. He proclaimed the need for a 'Social Revolution' which would have as its watchwords 'Equality; Freedom of Conscience . . . Collectivism and Mercy'.

Under capitalism, he maintained, man had become a 'covetous machine'. Basil, however, associated himself with 'those who would return to the teachings of Christ: the communism of our forefathers: the times before limited companies and the policy of laisser-faire had produced the "covetous machine"'. He deplored an England which had 'fallen from the simple teaching of Christ and from the high poetic feeling of Shakespeare; from the communist ideals of More's Utopia, and from the greatness of Cromwell's autocracy'. The roster of names of radical figures in English history is extended as Basil again recalls the Civil War and declares that 'the precedents of Pym and Hampden show that conscience has an absolute veto on any law'.

In his talk Basil goes on to relate this fundamental Quaker principle to another one, the pre-eminence of the spirit of the law and morality over the letter. This was a principle that never ceased to inform his thought and his art. At the beginning of his talk he asked, 'what profit we if the spirit of the law is liberty while the letter of it is not so? It is by the letter of the law that the Englishman is ruled; and letters may be differently read.' In a ringing final paragraph he urged a return to the spirit as a way of building a less oppressive social order. He declared:

'Everywhere the spirit is right. It is the letter of the law, the current practice of Christianity, the abuse of Individualism, that have brought the workers to misery. Let us return to the spirit. That may lighten the burden of the poor.'

The school magazine, the *Leightonian*, reported that the audience had listened to the talk with interest but there had been no time left for discussion of such a large subject as socialism. A few months later the magazine noted that B. C. Bunting read an essay on Blake 'whom he admired as a prophet rather than a poet'. Some weeks later Basil read yet another paper, this time on Kerensky, the moderate socialist who became Prime Minister of the provisional government that took over in Russia in 1917 after the toppling of the Czar. In November of that year, the month in which Kerensky's government collapsed before the Bolshevik revolution headed by Lenin, Basil presented to the Senior Essay Society a literary rather than a political offering. His title was 'A Revival of a Forgotten Art – A Romantic Allegory'. It was a story reminiscent of the medievalizing tales of William Morris; Basil told of an enchanter who had studied his art with Merlin and who lived with his young apprentices, male and female, in a remote 'vale more beautiful than man has ever dreamed'. When he needs a special plant for his spells, the wizard sends the two youngest apprentices, a boy and a girl, out into the world beyond the vale to find the weed for him. Once away from the wizard and his community the two young people feel happier, more alive. They meet a gaunt Christian hermit and decide to live with him. But the wizard comes to claim them. The couple refuse to return. The wizard says he will come again and compel them. As the story ends, the young man is putting on armour in which to fight his former master on his promised return.

The story is an allegorical assertion of the beliefs which Basil had spoken about explicitly in his first talk on politics. The wizard is a man of concepts, a seeker of sensations and a materialist; he offers to teach the two young people geometry, Arabic and 'incantations for the abstract beauty of their wording, alchemy to broaden the mind and spells for the attainment of riches'. The hermit on the other hand wins the young couple by offering to instruct them in 'the art of living and the law of liberty . . . the colours of the rainbow, the music of the rain. I will teach them God.'

Not long after writing this story Basil contributed a poem to the *Leightonian*. It is in the style of Rudyard Kipling, then at the zenith of his literary career and reputation, and the poem asserts the patriotic feeling that intensified throughout the country in the last year of the war as victory over the Kaiser became a possibility. The poem, entitled 'Keep Troth', takes an imperative and inspirational tone. It reads:

> When Algebra is done, boys,
> And Latin is no more;
> And when the war is won, boys, –
> When boyhood's past and o'er –
> What will you do for England,
> Who's done so much for you?
> Keep troth, speak true, for England,
> Be straight, keep troth, speak true.
>
> And while we're still at school, boys,
> The principle's the same;
> Stick to the golden rule, boys,
> Play up, and play the game.
> What do you do for England
> Who does so much for you?
> Keep troth, speak true for England,
> Be straight, keep troth, speak true.
>
> And when you're growing old, boys
> And sinking to your grave,
> You'll find that it will nerve you,
> The rule the Captain gave, –
> What have you done for England?
> How will you answer, you?
> I've lived a Man for England,
> Kept troth, and spoken true.

A schoolboy poem, it speaks the orthodoxies of its time; it is conventional in its attitudes, commonplace in its wording; its metre and rhyming are mechanical. But at school Basil also began that literary education that was to make him one of the most sophisticated and technically adroit practitioners of poetry. One day in the Ackworth school library he had come upon an early edition of Walt Whitman's *Leaves of Grass*. Long unread, it had been pushed behind a shelf of other books. This was the beginning of Basil's interest in American poetry and in a prosody not based on preconceptions, (such as the iambic pentameter) but rather on the open, *non a priori*, cadenced line which would later affect his own art and, as the years went by, set him apart, disadvantageously, from the poets and reputation makers in his own country. As a schoolboy Basil was entranced by Whitman. He wrote an essay on him which won a prize in a national publication.[2]

But Basil's literary skills did not prove adequate to ensure his long-term objective in transferring to Leighton Park. His ambition (and that of his parents) was now settled; he should try to win a scholarship to Cambridge University. The college he approached was Peterhouse and at the beginning of the year he went there to sit the scholarship examinations. He was entirely unsuccessful. The admissions tutor singled out Basil's writing as especially defective. He reported that 'his English essay made a very unfavourable impression for its lack of taste and even of sense'. The tutor granted that Basil's 'work in Ancient History and Medieval European History was very promising'; but in 'the paper of General Questions there were signs of immaturity and a certain recklessness'. Basil's abilities with languages did not impress the Cambridge examiners. 'His French was fair, in Latin he only just qualified.' The tutor concluded that there could be no possibility of awarding him a scholarship.

Basil's schooldays thus ended, early in 1918, with a sense of failure. But worse was to come. The war was still going on and on his eighteenth birthday on 1 March he was legally required to register for military service. But Basil refused to do so. For all the patriotism expressed in 'Keep Troth' he declared that he was a conscientious objector and would not fight in the war. His schoolfriend John Greenbank, Peggy's brother and a Quaker, was also a conscientious objector; but he solved the moral problem conscription presented to him by volunteering for and being accepted into the Red Cross. But Basil was utterly intransigent. He refused to participate in the war in any way. Such uncompromising adherence to principle, be it ethical, political, intellectual or literary, would remain an important part of his character. In 1918, as on later occasions, he would pay a high price for his obduracy. Basil first stated his position before the Military Service Representative whose office was in Northumberland Street in Newcastle. Here he was ordered to appear before the local Military Tribunal. His hearing, held on 17 April 1918, was, to the embarrassment of his parents, who could not support his stand, covered in the press. The *North Mail* reported that Basil 'carried himself with great self possession' and that 'the lad' declared that in refusing to serve 'he was doing his duty as a citizen of the world'. Asked whether he was prepared to see 'the German hordes overrun England', Basil answered that he was. The Tribunal recommended that Basil do agricultural work in lieu of military service. But Basil refused, maintaining that such a step meant sending another man to fight in his place, and asked leave to appeal to the Northumberland Appeal Tribunal. His appeal was heard at the Education Offices in Newcastle on 20 June 1918 and turned down.

Police appeared at the Bunting residence at 38 Moorside, the large pleasant house on the well-to-do western edge of Newcastle to which the family had moved a few years earlier. The officers took Basil away to the guard room at nearby Fenham Barracks. Years later Basil remembered this as 'a large, crowded, underheated eighteenth-century-style room'. Many of his companions there were pickpockets and thieves. Most of the prisoners were grown men and rough, not middle-class boys of eighteen. There were a few blankets for which the prisoners fought. One prisoner, a large angry man, managed to get hold of two blankets and gave one of them to Basil. It turned out that his benefactor, the only person in the room to treat Basil with kindness, had committed a double murder. He had poisoned two women.[3] The authorities dealt roughly with Basil and in later years he did not like to speak much about this period in his life. The four long years of war had created a mood of intense and intolerant patriotism in British society, and also of militarism. On the streets women would hand the white feather to men of an age to serve in the armed forces who were not in uniform. Conscientious objectors like Basil were disparaged and sneered at as 'conchies'. His sufferings at this time were exacerbated by the terrible news that his closest friend at Ackworth School, Ernest Stephenson, had been killed in action in France. Stephenson, who had rejected pacifism, had been recently commissioned as a Second Lieutenant in the Royal Flying Corps.

Basil was sentenced to be taken south to serve 112 days in Wormwood Scrubs, the dark Victorian prison on the west side of London. Here, he reported in a letter to the *Leightonian*, he was compelled to do hard manual labour, 'making mailbags and twisting ships' fenders'. At first he did the required work and started to pile up remission days; but one morning he flared up against his jailers, refused to continue his hard labour and all his remission was lost. It was not until January of 1919 that he was released from Wormwood Scrubs. At this time it was discovered that he had developed a septic ulcer and he was sent to a military hospital on Salisbury Plain. Here he was under the jurisdiction of the army. Again he refused to obey an order and was immediately court-martialled. He was sent to do a year's hard labour in Winchester Prison.

Here Basil went on hunger strike. With the war now over the prison authorities were no longer so hostile to the conscientious objectors who still had time to serve. Also, after the scandal of the force-feeding of the suffragettes in prison before the war, the governor of Winchester Prison felt unable to physically compel Basil and other conscientious objectors on hunger strike to eat. In later life Basil often repeated the story of how the governor sent the guards to tempt him with the most succulent of roast chicken. But in vain. Basil became an embarrassment to the authorities. They offered him release days which he accepted. After one such period outside Basil simply did not go back. Apparently no one took the trouble to pursue him and return him to prison. In its edition of July 1919 the *Leightonian* reported: 'On June 24th ... B. C. Bunting visited the school in person and informed us cheerfully that he was now living in London and avoiding the police.'

THREE
The First London Years
1919–1923

After making up his mind not to return to Winchester jail Basil took up residence in a room in a small hotel in central London. He was supported financially by his parents. He also helped to feed himself by going to the common room of the Fabian Society of which he had been a member since he was sixteen. The Society's common room was above its shop in Westminster and here Basil was able to live on free toast and tea whilst at the same time meeting all the prominent Fabian socialists of the day. However, he spent most of his time in Bloomsbury and the area of Soho north of Oxford Street. He was by now a keen drinker as his grandfather had been before him. The pub he most regularly frequented was the Fitzroy Tavern on the corner of Charlotte Street and Windmill Street. It was a spacious pub with a sawdust-strewn floor and well known as a meeting place for artists and writers. It was run by Papa Judah Kleinfeldt, a Russian emigré who became famous in the arts world of London for his generosity and his readiness to help his clients when they were having difficulties selling their canvases or manuscripts.[1] Papa Kleinfeldt, a former tailor who had been a guardsman in the czarist army, liked to say that his pub was the 'Rendezvous of all the World'. In Kleinfeldt's congenial surroundings Basil found his entry into literary London. Although always keen to emphasize that he was a Northumbrian, from 1919 on he spent a number of years, off and on, trying to make his way as a writer in London. He was no longer simply a provincial. As the opening lines of the second section of *Briggflatts* indicate, he also came to know well the Grub Street of his day.

> Poet appointed dare not decline
> to walk among the bogus, nothing to authenticate
> the mission imposed, despised
> by toadies, confidence men, kept boys,
> shopped and jailed, cleaned out by whores,
> touching acquaintance for food and tobacco,
> Secret, solitary, a spy, he gauges

lines of a Flemish horse
hauling beer, the angle, obtuse,
a slut's blouse draws on her chest,
counts beat against beat, bus conductor
against engine against wheels against
the pedal, Tottenham Court Road, decodes
thunder, scans
porridge bubbling, pipes clanking, feels
Buddha's basalt cheek
but cannot name the ratio of its curves
to the half pint
left breast of a girl who bared it in Kleinfeldt's.

The process of entering the literary life of London got underway when, most probably in the Fitzroy Tavern, Basil began an important friendship. This was with the artist Nina Hamnett, a regular at the pub. Some ten years older than Basil, Nina knew just about everyone in the arts in both London and Paris, and after the war moved continually to and fro between the two cities. Though born into a middle-class family and with a colonel for a father, Nina quickly entered Bohemia via art schools in Dublin and London. By the time she was thirty and met Basil, Nina had had many adventures. She had done paintings for, and then quarrelled with, Yeats's great enemy, the diabolist and magician Aleister Crowley. With the French sculptor Gaudier-Brzeska she had stolen marble so that he could make a carving of her shapely torso which she was always ready to uncover and display on social occasions. The sculpture was eventually purchased for the Victoria and Albert Museum. Nina was very proud to be displayed there. When Dylan Thomas first introduced her to a friend in the Fitzroy she declared: 'You know me, m'dear – I'm in the V and A with me left tit knocked off.'[2] In London the womanizing Augustus John was Nina's close friend; in Paris Modigliani. She wore unusual clothes and had a vast collection of brightly coloured stockings such as 'ladies' of that time definitely did not wear. Nina was a great lover of alcohol. She was friendly, outgoing, amusing and there were few with whom she would not readily have a drink or go to bed.

Nina was in a position to introduce Basil to, among others, the writers and artists who were his near neighbours in Bloomsbury. She had worked for Roger Fry at the Omega workshops and knew well other people associated with the Bloomsbury Group, including the painters Dora

Carrington and Mark Gertler. By 1919, the year Basil started living in London, the word Bloomsbury was beginning to have a cultural as well as a topographical meaning. That year Maynard Keynes published *The Economic Consequences of the Peace*, his celebrated attack on the Prime Minister Lloyd George and British policy at the Versailles Peace Conference. Virginia Woolf, who with her husband Leonard had recently founded her own publishing company, the Hogarth Press, successfully brought out her second novel *Night and Day*. Lytton Strachey had provoked outrage and controversy the year before with his sequence of irreverent biographical essays, *Eminent Victorians*, and was now working on his life of Queen Victoria. Bloomsbury's leading art critic and impresario, Nina's friend Roger Fry, was completing his influential work on aesthetics, *Vision and Design*, which would be published in the following year, 1920.

When introduced to Fry and other fashionable Bloomsbury writers Basil felt ill at ease. They evidently patronised the rather nervy young man from the north. Throughout his life Basil would speak of them with resentment. Like H. G. Wells, who called the members of the Bloomsbury set 'genteel whigs', Basil found them extremely snobbish. He said that 'they were all of that well-to-do middle class, bordering on country gentry who felt that if you couldn't afford to live in Bloomsbury or Regent's Park or some similar, desirable, but very expensive part of the world, well, poor devil, there wasn't much to be expected from you'. Basil wearied of being drawlingly condescended to by members of the Group. Himself a student of economics he was especially uneasy with Bloomsbury's famous economist. There was, he said, 'a certain cocksureness which in particular made me distrust Maynard Keynes'.[3]

After some months of hanging around Bloomsbury and Fitzrovia, Basil was ready to try something else. He decided to set off to Russia to see, and perhaps to write about, how the new Soviet regime was faring. He clearly retained the interest in the Russian revolution that he had expressed to the Senior Essay Society at school. His destination was Leningrad but in northern Norway he got into trouble. As on several subsequent occasions he went to a bar, had too much to drink, became obstreperous and was arrested by the police. The Norwegian authorities quickly shipped him back to England.

His parents were concerned about him. They tried to persuade him to end his months of idling and drifting and to resume his education. And finally, in 1920, he enrolled at the college created towards the end of the nineteenth century by members of the Fabian Society to further socialist thought, the London School of Economics, now assimilated into the University of London. Situated on what had recently been a slum on the north-eastern side of the Aldwych, the School was then largely made up of converted army huts. The deafening noise created by the construction of Bush House, a vast building just to the south, made it extremely difficult for the lecturers to make themselves heard. Nevertheless there was an intellectual vitality in the School during these immediately post-war years that inspired great enthusiasm in its students. One of Basil's friends and contemporaries there, Lionel Robbins, a highly successful academic, later ennobled as Lord Robbins, recalled what the London School of Economics had meant to him as a young man. 'For me, at least, this was an entry to a new world. Here was really first-rate intellect. Here was free discussion of the great problems of man in society. Here, with no abatement of personal conviction was integrity and a search after truth.' Robbins treasured 'the atmosphere of intellectual adventure and serious purpose which informed the tradition of the institution of Webb's creation. This was something I had not known before but something which, almost at once, I felt to be the spiritual home for which I had been searching.'[4]

Basil had memorable learning experiences at the School. He remembered especially the lecturing skills of his father's friend Graham Wallas of whom Robbins wrote, 'he surpassed anyone I have ever known. In the lecture room he was unique. His delivery was easy and informal, utterly free from any tricks of rhetoric or declamation. Yet from the moment he began to speak, he held audiences fixed as, I suppose, the greatest preachers held their congregations in the ages of faith; all the stops of intimate argument and persuasion were at his command.'[5] Basil shared his friend's intense admiration of Wallas. More than forty years after hearing him lecture Basil told Jonathan Williams that Wallas 'could make any subject interesting. The result was that if they had to get across something which nobody on earth could be expected to take any interest in, they gave it to Graham Wallas to teach. And he would begin with a class of five and by the end of the first term he would have a hundred fighting to get in the room. I remember a series of lectures on the history of the internal organisation of the War Office which began and ended that way!'[6]

As an undergraduate Basil met other founding Fabians of an earlier generation. Late in life he recalled actually speaking to a Fabian Society meeting and receiving the congratulations of George Bernard Shaw. He also knew Beatrice and Sidney Webb and he met seventy-three-year-old Annie Besant, friend both of Yeats and of Shaw and a prominent and redoubtable figure in both left-wing and occultist circles in late Victorian London.

In this lively intellectual milieu Basil seems to have been academically successful without expending a great deal of effort. Lord Robbins later recalls how in 1921 immediately before an examination his 'fellow student, Basil Bunting the poet, who having been distracted by other matters during the greater part of the session, borrowed my notes at the end and, having read them intensively for three or four days, lying on the grass in Green Park opposite Buckingham Palace, emerged from the ordeal triumphant'.[7]

The 'other matters' distracting Basil at this time included the erotic and the literary. At this period he was sexually very active, his principal relationship being with Helen Moore. She remains a shadowy figure of whom little is known and about whom Basil was never very forthcoming in later years. It would seem that for a time they lived togethr in Nina Hamnett's London flat during one of Nina's prolonged stays in Paris. Basil remembered Nina's room with its numerous drawings on the walls and a little marble mask, all done by Henri Gaudier-Brzeska, the French sculptor who, before his death early in the war, had worked innovatively with elemental forms and about whom his friend, the flamboyantly avant-garde poet Ezra Pound, had written the first book-length study.

Basil was introduced to Pound's poetry in these first months in London and also to that of Pound's close literary associate T. S. Eliot. The young provincial was much impressed by the radical renewal that these two American expatriates, a generation older than he, had effected in English poetry. He felt special admiration for Pound's free-verse adaptation from the Latin, the twenty-two-page *Homage to Sextus Propertius*. Years later he told an interviewer that *Homage to Sextus Propertius* was 'the first poem which is consciously using the rhythmic material of music in the manner in which it was used, in a small number of his best poems, by Walt Whitman, but possibly with greater skill, and shows a rhythmic variety which is very pleasing and very important to my mind'. Most critics were taken with the irony in the poem but for Basil its musical quality was its chief distinction; 'the thing that is important is a change in the view of rhythm and the use of rhythm'.[8] Basil was also intrigued by T. S. Eliot's sequence entitled 'Preludes' because the musical analogy suggested in the title and the wording of the poem were possibilities for poetry that he himself had been considering. He had, he told Carroll Terrell some sixty years later, 'been thinking along similar lines'.[9] Here was a means of rescuing the art form from its current sterility as exemplified by the, for the most part, mechanical nature poetry in the successive editions of the *Georgian Anthology* compiled by Winston Churchill's secretary, the literary conservative Edward Marsh, which was celebrating nearly a decade of successful publication when Basil was a student at the London School of Economics.

The resemblance between Chopin's preludes and those of T. S. Eliot might not be profound, but Basil was greatly reassured, as he later told Barbara Lesh, 'to discover that there were actually people doing what I had merely worked out in my head was the kind of thing that ought to be done'.[10] This was the beginning of a lifelong concern with, and insistence upon, the close and indissoluble relationship between poetry and music.

Basil's calling as a poet was now becoming more audible to him. His developing interest in poetry and also in music and the other arts led him to neglect his formal studies in economics. He came to find the subject boring and after three terms he gave up the London School of Economics without completing his degree. He had already begun to try to develop a literary career. He sought out London editors offering to write articles and reviews. A. R. Orage, the editor of *The New Age* who, years before, had sustained Ezra Pound, was one of the first to help him.

At the same time Basil's education in classical music was further advanced when, again in Kleinfeldt's Fitzroy Tavern, he met two of the most colourful and controversial figures in the musical world of London in the early 1920s. One was the Scots composer and critic Cecil Gray, some five years older than Basil and then engaged in writing his successful *Survey of Contemporary Music*. (Gray went on to become music critic for the *Nation and Athenaeum*, then for the *Daily Telegraph* and finally for the *Guardian*.) The other was Gray's flamboyant, hard-drinking friend and ally in the acrimonious politics of London music, Philip Heseltine, who composed and wrote music under the pseudonym Peter Warlock. Always involved in bitter polemics about music, Warlock was known for his caustic wit and his obscene limericks. However he also had a gentler, even soft, side and it is this aspect of his personality that his sometime friend, and current enemy, D. H. Lawrence reveals in the character of

Halliday in *Women in Love* who is based on Warlock. (Legal threats from the composer compelled Lawrence to alter the portrait in subsequent editions). At the time he first met Basil Peter Warlock was beginning work on his *Capriol Suite*, a sequence based on sixteenth-century French dances that was to enjoy great popularity. He had just completed his song cycle *The Curlew*, a series of settings of some early poems by W. B. Yeats. Likewise, there were strains between Yeats and Warlock in connection with *The Curlew* and Yeats contemplated legal action.

But Basil seems to have had a pleasant and stimulating relationship with the emotionally unstable Peter Warlock (who later did him an important personal kindness) and the tough minded Cecil Gray. These two musical enthusiasts, just a few years older than Basil, greatly assisted his development as a poet who looked to music. Peter Warlock and Cecil Gray were especially knowledgeable in the music of the sixteenth century, at that time by no means so widely known and performed as it is today. Basil remembered the many beer-drinking sessions at Kleinfeldt's with Warlock and Gray as occasions on which he received a thorough grounding in Tudor music.

But although he was progressing in his awareness of music and poetry he was still unable to sustain himself as a writer. For a brief period he had a job as secretary to Harry Barnes, a Liberal MP who represented one of the Newcastle constituencies and was a friend of Basil's father. But Basil was no more inspired by Westminster politics than by his studies in economics. In later life he would speak scathingly of the Liberal–Tory coalition government that ruled Britain after the snap election of 1919 which the Prime Minister David Lloyd George called in order to profit from his popularity as 'the man who won the war'.

After four years in London without advancing himself very much, Basil felt that he needed a change. A photograph taken in 1923 shows an unsmiling young man, with a heavy moustache, looking out with quiet defiance through his round-lensed metal spectacles. Certainly, as he decided to leave London there was little for him to smile about. He had become a heavy drinker, a brawler and a university drop-out. He continued to display the same kind of emotional volatility and problematical temperament about which his headmaster had written at Leighton Park. He was not at all sure how to pursue a career as a writer and a poet. However, Nina Hamnett and others of his acquaintance in and around the Fitzroy Tavern had captured his imagination with their many entertaining stories of the liveliness of the art scene in Paris. Nina was in fact so taken with Paris that she now regarded it, rather than London, as her home. So, as his twenty-third birthday came and went, that is where the young would-be poet decided that he too would go.

FOUR
Paris
1923

One summer's day in 1923, with very little money on him Basil took the boat train from Victoria to the Gare du Nord in Paris. He rented a dingy room high up in a cheap hotel. He then went out and found himself a job as a labourer in a construction gang working on a road-building project just outside Paris. In his free time he hung around the cafés on and around the Boulevard Montparnasse hoping to bump into Nina Hamnett and her friends and perhaps even to make contact with some of the artists and writers from all over the world who had exiled themselves to this corner of Paris just south-west of the Jardin de Luxembourg. For this was the time when a large number of painters and would-be painters and writers and would-be writers congregated in the cafés and brasseries on the busy left-bank boulevard between the Avenue de l'Observatoire in the east to the intersection with the Rue de Rennes in the west. There was the Closerie des Lilas, the Dôme, the Select, the Nègre de Toulouse and the Jockey, where Basil later managed to obtain work as a part-time barman.

At this moment this part of Paris was home to some of the most innovative writers of the English-speaking world: James Joyce, Ford Madox Ford, Gertrude Stein and Ezra Pound. It was a major turning point in Basil's life when one day he fell into conversation with Ezra Pound at a boulevard café. The encounter marked the beginning of a literary apprenticeship for him and also a lifelong friendship. Basil's most vivid memory of that important occasion at the café in Montparnasse was of the poet he so admired, the author of *Homage to Sextus Propertius*, 'playing a swashbuckling kind of chess'. Now in his thirty-eighth year and fifteen years older than Basil, Pound had an air of great assurance; he also had trenchant, often amusingly expressed literary opinions and a strong American accent. His truculent manner gave way to kindliness as he sensed the awe and admiration his new young acquaintance felt for him.

Very much the Bohemian poet, Pound wore a green jacket with blue square buttons. He had a mass of dark golden hair with a reddish cast;

his beard and moustache were thick and heavy. He had piercing grey eyes. He lived with his English wife Dorothy in a small apartment just a little to the north of the busy Boulevard Montparnasse at 70 bis Rue Notre-Dame des Champs. He had been based in Paris for nearly three years now and was becoming tired of it. Prior to Paris he had lived for a decade and more in London where he had gone from being a literary unknown to a leading and celebrated figure in the great modernist movement in literature that occurred in the decade of the First World War.

The only child of middle-class parents in Philadelphia, Pound had studied Romance literatures at Hamilton College and the University of Philadelphia. As a student he was already a practising poet and had friends, Hilda Doolittle and William Carlos Williams, who had similar literary ambitions. In 1908, when he was twenty-two, Pound had gone to Venice, a city that always fascinated him, and there privately published his first collection of poems titled with a funereal phrase from Dante, *A Lume Spento* ('With tapers quenched'). He then went on to London where he energetically set about introducing himself into the literary world. He made contact with W. B. Yeats and became a regular at the Irish poet's 'Mondays', his weekly evening open house in his flat in Woburn Walk on the northern edge of Bloomsbury. Pound courted Dorothy Shakespear, the daughter of Olivia Shakespear, Yeats's sometime mistress. And in 1914, after (and before) a number of affairs Pound married Dorothy. Well known as a sexual predator in cultural and artistic circles in London, Pound also made a name as the leading figure in a literary movement known as imagism, an early impulse towards the making of modernism in English poetry. In 1910 the newcomer to London relied on the literary hospitality of such as Ford Madox Ford, the idealistic editor of the *English Review* in which Pound was published alongside older writers, Thomas Hardy, Joseph Conrad and Henry James, as well as his contemporaries, Wyndham Lewis and D. H. Lawrence. But as the years went by Pound became sufficiently established in literary London to assist others whose work he admired such as James Joyce and T. S. Eliot.

During the war decade of the 1910s, most of which time Bunting was still a schoolboy, Pound was also producing major works in the new modernist mode; he completed his fine work of creative translation, his *Homage to Sextus Propertius*, and began the first sections of his life's work, the *Cantos*. He was a prolific and energetic writer of literary criticism, expounding in numerous essays the new poetics that he and his associates were developing. He also promoted his ideas in the lecture hall, speaking and giving readings all over the country. Perhaps at that first meeting with Basil in Paris Pound may have recalled how he gave a lecture on the troubadours at the Newcastle Literary and Philosophical Society in November 1919, when Basil was already living in London.

As the First World War dragged on, Pound became increasingly disillusioned with social, political and literary life in England. At the end of 1920, as D. H. Lawrence had done, he abandoned England for ever. He and Dorothy moved to France. By April of 1921 they were installed in Paris in a two-room studio in the Hotel Pas de Calais, just a little to the south of the Boulevard Saint Germain. This was round the corner from the home of the wealthy American hostess and flamboyant lesbian, Natalie Barney, who soon recruited Pound to her extensive circle. Pound also came to know Jean Cocteau and Gertrude Stein. To Pound's hotel studio in 1921 came his American friend from the London years, T. S. Eliot, now in the grip of a mental breakdown and on his way to a sanatorium in Switzerland. Eliot entrusted Pound with the first draft of the manuscript which, after being edited by Pound, would be published as *The Waste Land*. In time for Christmas Pound and Dorothy moved itno their flat on the quiet, curving Rue Notre-Dame des Champs, and Pound immediately set about carpentering chairs with which to furnish it. Among their first visitors in the New Year were the recently arrived Ernest Hemingway and his wife Hadley, followed by Yeats and his difficult muse, Maud Gonne. James Joyce and his family were also now settled in Paris, and Pound became good friends with the great Romanian sculptor Constantin Brancusi.

During the early months of 1923 Pound and Dorothy travelled in Italy. Then they returned to Paris where Pound's American friend William Bird was preparing to publish an edition of the first sixteen of Pound's *Cantos*. Bird's Three Mountains Press was one of several little presses in the English-speaking community in Paris in the 1920s. Another prospect which greatly excited Pound was the production of the opera on which he had been working for some time, *Le Testament de Villon*. It was based on the life and writings of the imprisoned fifteenth-century French poet and Pound wrote both the libretto and the music. For Basil Bunting with his recent experience of prison, Villon, his poetry and the opera were readily interesting subjects of conversation. Undoubtedly at that first meeting in the boulevard café Pound, the colourful literary celebrity, fired his rather shy but very admiring young acquaintance with his exuberance about the project.

Basil was quickly received into the Pound circle in Paris. Some of its members were young people of his own age. Pound's beautiful lover, Olga Rudge, a gifted violinist and expert on Vivaldi, who was greatly interested in the composition of the *Villon*, was still in her twenties. George Antheil was exactly the same age as Basil; he also assisted Pound with the music for the opera. This very short, baby-faced pianist and composer from New Jersey thrived on the excitement of the avant-garde in the arts in Paris in the early 1920s. His compositions called for aeroplane propellers, car horns and the like. When he performed he would take a revolver on to the concert platform in order to intimidate any conservative critics in the audience. George Antheil later recalled a concert he gave just a few months after Basil Bunting arrived in Paris.

On October 4, 1923, I played in Paris for the first time . . . My little group of piano pieces, the 'Mechanisms', the 'Airplane Sonata', and the 'Sonata Sauvage' were to go on as a prelude to the opening of the brilliant Ballets Suedois . . . The Theater, the famous Champs Elysées Theater, was crowded with the most famous personages of the day, among others Picasso, Stravinsky, Auric, Milhaud, James Joyce, Erik Satie, Man Ray, Diaghileff, Miro, Artur Rubinstein, For Maddox Ford [*sic*], and unnumbered others. They had not come to hear me, but to see the opening of the ballets.

My piano was wheeled out on the front of the stage, before the huge Leger cubist curtain, and I commenced playing. Rioting broke out almost immediately. I remember Man Ray punching somebody in the nose on the front row. Marcel Duchamps was arguing loudly with somebody else in the second row. In a box near by Erik Satie was shouting, 'What precision! What precision!' and applauding. The spotlight was turned on the audience by some wag upstairs. It struck James Joyce full in the face, hurting his sensitive eyes. A big burly poet got up in one of the boxes and yelled, 'You are all pigs!' In the gallery the police came in and arrested the surrealists who, liking the music, were punching everybody who objected.

It was a full twenty minutes later, when I had finished playing, that order was finally restored . . . But from October 4, 1923, everybody in Paris knew who I was. I represented the anti-expressive, anti-romantic, coldly mechanistic aesthetic of the early twenties.[1]

But George Antheil was also schooled in traditional classical music, particularly that of the Post-Romantics. It has been suggested that his contribution to Pound's opera was the Stravinsky-like colouring to the final motet, 'Frères humains qui après nous vivez', sung by the prisoners awaiting execution.[2]

Pound communicated to Basil Bunting as he did to George Antheil his strong feeling for Villon. When Basil was ten years old Pound had written, in his first volume of literary criticism, *The Spirit of Romance*, that 'Villon holds his unique place in literature because he is the only poet without illusions'.[3] This poet of medieval Paris who was 'thief, murderer, pander, bully to a whore' had a wisdom which was 'the wisdom of the gutter'. 'In Villon filth is filth, crime is crime; neither crime nor filth is gilded.'[4] Pound concludes that 'Dante is many men, and suffers as many. Villon cries out as one. He is a lurid canto of the Inferno, written too late to be included in the original text.'[5] The work of this poet to which Pound now introduced Basil was to have a profound effect on the young man. It is clear that Villon's poetry about crime, the underworld and the gutter, his sense of being, albeit anachronistically, the *poète maudit* appealed strongly to a side of Basil's nature. Villon became an early model and reference for his own poetic practice. Not long after their first meeting, Ezra Pound was to be surprised and touched when he unexpectedly discovered how his enthusiasm for Villon had captured his new young friend.

One member of Pound's acquaintance with whom Bunting quickly struck up a friendly relationship was Constantin Brancusi, a man of high artistic ideals and dedication. The Romanian sculptor had a primitive studio in a back alley at number 11 Impasse Ronsin. He was well known for serving simple, but memorably delicious food. In this dusty little workshop of a home, littered with stone fragments ('shapes to carve and discard') Basil saw some of the sculptor's current pieces, the Leda in burnished bronze, the Torso of a Young Man in maplewood with a polished limestone base, and the bronze Bird in Space which, two years later, United States customs would notoriously refuse to regard as an abstract work of art and on which they would seek to impose duty as a piece of polished metal.

Not long after meeting Pound Basil spent a memorable evening with Brancusi. The two went out together and ate fresh oysters and drank white wine. They continued to eat and drink as the forty-seven-year-old sculptor talked on to his young companion about the art of carving and the nature and qualities of materials. They kept ordering more oysters and more white wine. All through the night. Only when the dawn came did they decide to part and set off home. Basil was so drunk that he found it immensely difficult to stay upright and find his way.

Some days later he again got drunk, but this time with serious consequences. A friend from Britain had been sent a hundred pounds from home and he invited Basil and another friend to go on the town and celebrate. Around midnight the other friend gave up but Basil and his host kept on drinking far into the early hours of the morning. When they finally separated Basil was too drunk to stand up and had to have a taxi to take him back to his hotel. As he recalled, years later:

> The Paris streets laid out in the time of the Empire often had four corners that looked exactly alike, so that my hotel on one corner looked like the one on the next corner. My taxi driver drove up in front of one which I took to be mine. I got in and found my room but the damn key wouldn't work! That got me quite frustrated and furious. Finally, I had to relieve myself on the wall of the stairs, but I went back and tried to knock the door down. Eventually the noise aroused the concierge whose husband appeared. He's never seen me before so concluded I was a burglar and had broken in. I'd never seen him before, and couldn't imagine what he was protesting about or why he should be trying to kick me out of my own hotel. Finally, he threatened to call the cops if I wouldn't leave quietly. I invited him to do so.

Basil went on to claim that whilst the man was telephoning, he, Basil jumped into bed with his wife who though fairly old showed a great deal of enthusiasm. It caused him great

> chagrin and surprise, right at the height of my own enthusiasm, to be dragged out of bed by the police, who for some mysterious reason wanted to take me to jail. Well, now, as an innocent man, it was my duty to refuse to go. I was outnumbered, but while they were trying to restrain me, I managed to give one of them a good swift kick in the pants. In the end, they overpowered me. By this

time I could be charged with a number of crimes: minor ones such as disturbing the peace, but also serious ones such as resisting arrest and what the French call 'rebellion'.[6]

After a night in the cells Basil was sent to a courtroom to await his appearance before the magistrate. In what was for Basil an astonishingly significant coincidence it was the same room in which Villon had waited to face his accusers some four hundred years before. 'The next day I was herded into the Grande Salle along with a flock of petty thieves, pickpockets, prostitutes, pimps, and other assorted characters. I happened to have a copy of Villon in my pocket, so while waiting my turn, I sat on a bench reading him quite aware of the ironies. For Villon himself, centuries before, had sat in this same salon and waited his turn before the magistrate.' Basil sent a note to Ezra Pound appealing for help. He also gave the name and address of Pound as someone who would vouch for him. Pound duly appeared at the Santé prison and was greatly touched to see that his young friend had bought a copy of Villon's poems and was intently studying them. Immediately Pound went into action to help. Basil recalled: 'He was always interested in helping young writers in trouble; but I think it was seeing me reading Villon that really got him. After he had heard my story, he rushed away to get lawyers and money or whatever to get me off and see justice done.'

When the case came to trial, Basil was sentenced to two weeks in jail, a far lighter punishment than he had feared. When he got out of prison towards the end of September he left Paris for a while. Peter Warlock (Philip Heseltine) had kindly supplied him with an introduction to his uncle Arthur Heseltine who lived in the village of Marlotte not far from the forest of Fontainbleau, some eighty kilometres south of Paris. Sixty-eight-year-old Arthur Heseltine (Uncle Joe) was a painter and engraver who was especially interested in doing pictures of nude males. While staying in Uncle Joe's house Basil wrote a letter to a poet friend in England, one J. J. Adams, mentioning that posing for an artist had been one of his recent jobs; it seems probable that elderly Uncle Joe, who allegedly 'had a streak of latent homosexuality',[7] had been the painter in question. In the same letter Basil reported that he had also done some 'charing' and, best of all, tutoring 'to a lovely girl of fourteen . . . a ravishing Juliet'. He had also sought work in Paris as a tram conductor but had been rejected because he was not a French citizen. He looked back on his first months in Paris with some resentment, even bitterness;

'impromptu', he sent his friend a three-stanza poem which he termed an mocking Parisians and their pretensions to sophistication and wit. The poem was an impromptu because, Basil claims, he had no intention of writing verse when he began the letter. It is clearly inspired by a good deal of anger; the second stanza runs:

> Perhaps you wouldn't notice it.
> They do not always show their wit –
> Their conversation's often boring
> Their faces, too, are reassuring,
> Placid and flat, debauched and bleary
> Their deeds and thoughts and looks are dreary.
> Their learning is not evident.
> Their work is heavy, tho' well meant,
> Both flatulent and constipated,
> Pompous, pious and inflated;
> Or else loose-bowelled and ecstatic
> Or too much-labored-empty-Attic.
> Yet they themselves aver they've wit
> And that's strong evidence of it.

Basil's disenchantment with French life and culture extended to French literature too. He excepted Stendhal's *De L'Amour* which he had just been reading and which he thought a wonderfully written book. And grudgingly he allowed Rabelais and Maupassant to be Stendhal's nearest rivals. Racine and Villon, he declares were France's only poets 'with a half-exception for over-rated Baudelaire'. Otherwise there was nothing. He much preferred poetry in English and German to that in French and Latin. In years to come he would acknowledge Malherbe and Horace as major influences in his development as a poet, but in his present state of youthful frustration and anger he was in favour, he told his friend, of sticking 'French and Latin where the monkey put the nuts'.

Basil was disillusioned not just with the French but also with the international *émigrés* he had known on the Left Bank. He wrote that 'most of the "artistic" bunch of Montparnasse are bores'. Among the few he exempted from this category were Nina Hamnett and Ezra Pound.

Years later Basil recalled his acquaintance with the French surrealists whose movement, both in poetry and in painting, was growing ever more dynamic and influential at this time. He remembered an afternoon he spent with Tristan Tzara creating poems in various bizarre ways. The surrealists, he told an interviewer forty years later, sometimes wrote poems 'without words. Just any damn sound like Grrrrr! and Arrrrr! and Brrrrr! . . . and managed to palm them off on highbrow papers as serious efforts.'[8] Such occasions must have been among those in Basil's mind when in his 'Autobiography', *Briggflatts*, he observed that 'Poet appointed dare not decline/to walk among the bogus'.

Announcing his imminent return to Paris from Marlotte, Basil gave his English friend Nina's apartment as the address at which he could at first be contacted in the city. Nina was living at 8 Rue de la Grande Chaumière, Montparnasse, with her current lover, a Polish artist, Waclow Zawadowski who was a close friend of Modigliani. Their apartment, which had once been Modigliani's, was on the top, third floor of a dark rickety wooden building. The entrance to their rooms was at the head of a steep and narrow winding staircase. Zawado, as everyone called him, was a calming influence on the exuberant Nina, and Basil took a liking to him. He admired his humour, his generosity and his common sense. 'Zawado', he told his friend Adams, 'is a very nice (and very funny fellow) [*sic*]'.

On one entertaining occasion, when Basil was with Nina and Zawado, Nina's friend, the famous Polish pianist Artur Rubinstein, and a companion decided that they wanted to go to the traditional annual student ball, the Bal des Quatz' Arts. They were not eligible to attend and so had to disguise themselves completely in fancy dress, the stipulated theme that year being Greek. Rubinstein and his friend, Nina remembered,

> decided to go to the Bon Marché and buy suitable material and that I would make them clothes at the studio. I went home and waited for them, collecting needles, cotton, and scissors. They came back with yards of tussore silk, with red and blue swastika patterns on it, bunches of imitation grapes for headdresses, and sandals and ribbons to put round their waists. I cut the silk in half and sewed each side up, leaving only a hole for the head, and holes each side for the arms. The ribbon was tied round the middle under the armpits. I made two wreaths of the grapes and the vine leaves, and helped them to paint their faces. They looked very fine and were extremely proud of themselves.[9]

Thus outlandishly disguised, the two managed to gain entry into the students' ball. Afterwards they all went to a night club in Montmartre where Rubinstein, still with a painted face, played Hungarian dance duets with the Russian violinist Jascha Heifetz who was the same age as Basil. Some sixty years later Basil told Jonathan Williams how he had helped Nina to dress up Rubinstein: 'I remember in the 1920s painting his arse gilt for the Bal des Quatz-Arts in Paris.'[10]

Life in Montmartre was not, however, entirely a matter of fancy dress balls and parties. On his return Basil faced the problem of finding a job and making enough money to live on. But Ezra Pound was again on hand to help him. He had been involved in opening one more bar in Montparnasse; it was called the Jockey Club Bar and the decor suggested a Wild West saloon. Among the nine founders were the Dada poet, Tristan Tzara, Jean Cocteau and the artist photographer Man Ray whose famous model and lover, Kiki, was one of the attractions that made the Jockey a success. Pound got Basil a job as bartender at the club. He also found him a new home. This was in the ménage of Ford Madox Ford, Pound's friend of some fifteen years, who had also exiled himself to France and who was now in the process of beginning another literary venture, the periodical, the *transatlantic review*. Eight years before Ford had published his great and best novel, *The Good Soldier*, a study of the passing of the English gentleman.

Ford was close to his fiftieth birthday when he took in the young ex-prisoner. A famous figure in literary London, he had now become one of the distinctive characters on the Boulevard Montparnasse. Here is how a young American exile remembered him:

> Ford moved ponderously, with his feet at right angles to each other. His hair was white, his teeth imperfect. His head resembled Humpty-Dumpty's except for the walrus moustache and the rosy complexion of a retired officer of the Indian Army ... He spoke with a slight, sibilant hesitation, as if he suffered from asthma. I was not favourably impressed. Yet after he sat down and we had talked a while, I felt drawn to him. Something of his spirit, courage and generosity came through.[11]

Ford's current mistress and the mother of his three-year-old daughter, Esther Julia, was the young Australian painter, Stella Bowen. At this time Ford was also becoming involved in an affair with his literary protégée Jean Rhys, a young woman whose career as a writer would describe a curve remarkably similar to Basil's. After some success as a novelist in the 1920s and 1930s she fell into obscurity and poverty. Then in the 1960s just after Basil completed *Briggflatts*, Jean Rhys also enjoyed success and critical acclaim on the appearance of her thematically dense yet delicately crafted masterpiece *Wild Sargasso Sea*. In the early 1920s Jean Rhys's life had much in common with Basil's. Her husband was serving a jail sentence and she knew prison life in Paris; she had no money and had been homeless. Like Basil she was a latterday figure from the world of Villon. Of the gifted young writer who caused the ending of her relationship with Ford, Stella Bowen remembered, 'When we met her she possessed nothing but a card-board suitcase and the astonishing manuscript. She was down to her last three francs and she was sick'. 'Jean Rhys', Stella continued, 'took the lid off the world she knew, and showed us an underworld of darkness and disorder, where officialdom, the bourgeoisie and the police were the eternal enemies and the fugitive the only hero . . . She regarded the law as the instrument of the "haves" against the "have nots" and was well acquainted with every rung of that long and dismal ladder by which the respectable citizen descends towards degradation.'[12]

Back up such a ladder the kindly Ford now helped Basil Bunting. To earn his keep in the Ford household the former student of finance and economics helped Ford's assistant, the highly efficient American Marjorie Reid, to do the accounting for the *transatlantic review*.[13] But his responsibilities quickly increased. In a radio interview of 1974 he remembered

> Besides the obvious duties of an assistant editor I did all sorts of other things . . . I corrected not only the proofs of the magazine but those of the current novel which was *Some Do Not*, and some of Conrad's work. Finally, when there was nothing else that needed doing, I would sometimes bath the baby . . . I occupied a room on one side of the studio, Ford and his wife [*sic*] were in rooms on the other side.[14]

Ford also required Basil to escort his numerous literary acquaintances when they visited Paris. For instance, Ford wrote to the successful short story writer A. E. Coppard: 'If you let us know the route you are coming by and the time of the train we will either meet you or have you met by Bunting – a dark youth with round spectacles, in a large Trilby hat and a blue trench coat with a belt who shall hold up a copy of the *transatlantic review* towards passengers arriving at the barrier and smile.'[15]

In return for these various and numerous services as general factotum Basil was given only very cramped accommodation in the apartment at

65 Boulevard Arago, close to the Observatoire, where Ford and Stella were living. Stella recalled that Basil 'slept in a damp little store-room beyond our kitchen and was kept on the run by Ford for eighteen hours a day. He endured much in the cause of Literature, and indeed everybody seemed ready to be overworked and underpaid in the good cause – rather in the same fashion as in a theatrical production.'[16] With such poor living conditions and all the pressures that went with running an English literary periodical in a foreign city, the problems of financing, editing, printing, advertising and of distribution, it was inevitable that Basil with his quick temper should finally quarrel with Ford. And around the time of the publication of the first edition dated 24 January he did. Basil packed up his few things and returned to England. Ernest Hemingway, whom Basil regarded as a bully and a vulgarian, took over his job on the magazine.

Later in life Basil explained the parting in very kindly terms. He told an interviewer,

> I left for a reason which it is a little difficult to explain. The great drawback to working with Ford at all times was that he was overcome so easily by little worries. Small things would go wrong, they would pile up and instead of doing a little general cursing and getting on with it as most folk would do, Ford would weep on your shoulder. It's very uncomfortable for a young man of twenty-two to have someone a generation older than himself and very heavy weeping on his shoulder and in the end I couldn't put up with it and moved on.[17]

Despite this incompatibility and his walking out, Basil subsequently came to appreciate the importance to him as writer and man of having known Ford Madox Ford. Fifty years later in what was clearly an act of literary homage Basil edited and wrote the introduction to a selection of Ford's poems. The qualities which he here identified in Ford were 'his kindness to young men and men in distress, his readiness to talk to them at length, without being patronising or pedantic, his willingness to consider everything, the tolerance in his frivolity, his care for living English, his generosity, his fun'.[18] Basil here also defended Ford against the criticism made by Ernest Hemingway in his memoir of Paris in the 1920s, *A Moveable Feast*, published in 1964. Bunting's immediate successor at the *transatlantic review* wrote mockingly, even contemptuously, of his middle-aged English boss. His first impression of Ford was of someone 'breathing heavily through a heavy, stained moustache and holding himself upright as an ambulatory, well-clothed, up-ended hogshead'.[19] Hemingway went on to speak of the 'wheezing ignoble presence of Ford'. Bunting responded sharply to the 'unlaughable caricature' which Hemingway set out to create and remarked on Hemingway's own failings, particularly the 'chronic fantasy' which had brought him 'readers and prosperity', the 'unusually vulgar' fantasy of 'a magnanimous bully'.

In conversation with Jonathan Williams in the 1960s Basil again emphasized his good memories of Ford. Anyone who knew Basil will see that in praising Ford Basil was describing some of his own characteristics, especially his love of reminiscing and of telling stories that he made sure were entertaining even if they were not invariably truthful. Basil said of his mentor in the art of the anecdote:

> He liked eating and drinking expensively and well and he wanted somebody to talk to meanwhile. Now Ford may have been the biggest liar you like. No doubt he was quite a considerable one, but he was always exceedingly entertaining and the untruths were there not for the sake of untruth but for the sake of turning a mediocre story into a very good one. To feed in his company while he talked was always a pleasure. I'd say he was a kind hearted man.[20]

One example of his kindness to Basil was a dance that Ford organized. Basil was

> fairly sure that the root reason behind a large party he gave that year was not so much that he was anxious to entertain his literary friends as that he thought it a good opportunity for me to dance with the daughter of one of his American colleagues whom I suddenly had a fancy for. Unfortunately he didn't ask me beforehand whether I could dance! It was rather a failure.[21]

In no way a failure was Ford's contribution to Basil's education as a writer. The accomplished craftsman who had written *The Good Soldier* and who had been close to such highly self-conscious artists as Joseph Conrad and Henry James communicated to the younger man a belief in literature as a demanding craft or métier and a dedication to *le mot juste* and to the scrupulous management of the medium of literary art. Basil never forgot 'his care for living English'. In these ways Ford's influence on the aspiring young poet was second only to that of Ezra Pound.

At the time Basil left Paris Pound too was preparing to leave. The city was intellectually alive and highly stimulating; 'an immense seething cauldron (that) bubbled and overflowed', Ford called it.[22] But for Pound it was becoming too much of a good thing. He came to the conclusion that the social life of the cafés of Montparnasse and the endless visitors to his apartment in the Rue Notre-Dame des Champs were distracting him from his proper work as a writer, the composing of the *Cantos*. In recent years he and Dorothy had travelled a good deal in Italy and had developed a liking for the small harbour town of Rapallo on the coast some miles north of Genoa. Now, early in 1924, they decided to settle there permanently. When Basil Bunting came to announce his return to England, Pound gave him his address in Rapallo. Basil was urged to come to see him, should he find his way to Italy.

After a week or two back in Newcastle-upon-Tyne Basil decided that he could not let the invitation go unaccepted and forgotten. As he approached his twenty-fourth birthday Basil felt compelled, fascinated, inspired by the famous and dynamic writer whom he had come to know in Paris. With Pound's encouragement and assistance he had already begun work on 'Villon'. His first long poem to be published, the work derived from those first exciting conversations with Pound in Paris in the latter part of 1923. In Newcastle Basil missed him. Pound was glamorous, energetic, confident. He was a dedicated artist, an inspiring teacher, a vitalizing companion, a model to follow. Pound always attracted to himself a circle of lively, creative people. Basil wanted to be of such company. In February of 1924 he set off for Italy.

FIVE
To Rapallo and Back to London
1924–1928

Much smaller than it is today, Rapallo was a town of sun-whitened buildings on the Italian coast some seventeen miles south of Genoa. Its setting is spectacularly beautiful. Immediately to the landward side of the town there rise up sheer mountains covered with woods, vines and olives. Near the summit of one of them is the little village of Sant' Ambrogio in which Olga Rudge, who had followed the Pounds to Italy, leased the upper half of a house. Her view from atop the steep mountainside was magnificent. The town guidebook for English visitors, which went into its fifth edition towards the end of Basil's stay, observed:

> From the Piazza of S. Ambrogio Rapallo looks beautiful as it lies below encircled by the bay, the castle standing up from the water . . . The whole appears like some picture by an old master wherein he had delighted to trace each village and remote hamlet in perfect perspective, but almost as if there were no atmosphere to lend to distance a softening veil. This thinness of atmosphere on certain days is very noticeable in Riviera landscapes.[1]

The most direct way down into Rapallo from Sant' Ambrogio was a disconcertingly steep mule path or *salita*. Ford Madox Ford's mistress Stella Bowen remembered a hair-raising climb up this *salita* after attending one of the musical occasions arranged by Olga and Ezra in Rapallo. Olga

> asked me to spend the night with her after one of her concerts. She warned me to wear stout shoes and to bring the smallest possible luggage. We left the light of Rapallo at midnight, and as soon as we were outside the town, Olga changed her slippers, hitched up the skirt of her evening dress, and slung her violin-case on a strap over her shoulder. Then we began the slow, steep ascent of a cobbled, zig-zag mule track through the pitch-black olive terraces, losing our way, stumbling on invisible steps, and bumping into someone's silent cottage. It was a long way up, lonely and ghostly

45

and dark, but Olga, who made that journey by herself twice a week, declared that she had long ago stopped being nervous.

Once she had completed the long, steep climb Stella was captivated by the view from Olga's rooms. 'They looked out into a huge black silence, with stars above and festoons of light defining the harbour below.'[2]

The harbour at Rapallo was a busy one. There was a very active fishing fleet that included *paranzelle*, small boats with coloured wing-like sails that seemed to hover like butterflies on the surface of the bright blue sea. Also picturesque were the large, slow-moving haulage boats, the *barcaccie*, with their triangular, lateen sails. On this mountainous coastline the ocean was the best means of transporting heavy goods. The *barcaccie* brought great wooden vats of wine from Sardinia, coal from down the coast and sand from Livorno and Viareggio. The striking manner in which the bronzed crew unloaded the large baskets of sand gained a mention in the guidebook. 'Running along the planks with an elastic pace, the men swing the baskets from their shoulders with a deft twist of the body, and quickly return with them empty, for another load.'[3] Soon after his arrival in Rapallo Basil got a job as a deckhand on one of the *barcaccie* and worked alongside these men.

He had had difficulties in reaching Rapallo. When he broke his journey in Genoa he was involved in a drunken disturbance and arrested by the police. Apparently Basil wrote to Ford to tell him that he had been put in jail in Genoa. Ford passed on the news to his assistant, Ernest Hemingway, who in a letter to Pound offered to write to Italian officials on Basil's behalf.[4] However Basil seems to have obtained his own release. But when he finally arrived in Rapallo, he had another setback. When he enquired about Ezra and Dorothy Pound at the Hotel Mignon where he had confidently expected them to be, he was told that they had left town. Disappointed, he hung about the seafront bars and cafés. He also climbed some of the *salitas* to enjoy the famous views. Near the top of one of these narrow winding mule tracks was a tiny inn. Just as Basil plodded on past it he had a memorable experience. As he later told Carroll Terrell, 'As I passed the inn somebody rushed out of the doorway and began shouting "Bunting! Bunting!" And I looked around and there to my astonishment was Ezra Pound, followed almost immediately by Dorothy, running after me up the mountain.' It was from this moment that Basil dated the evolution of his acquaintance with Pound into a friendship.

'Ezra was very pleasant, and it was from that meeting that I can say that I became one of Pound's friends.'[5]

During the first three months of 1924 the two men saw a great deal of each other, Basil frequently calling at the Hotel Mignon for afternoon tea. From April until October the Pounds went travelling in Italy and spent time in Paris, but in the autumn they returned to the Mignon. Early in 1925 they moved out of the hotel into a permanent home, an apartment high up and overlooking the sea at 12 Via Marsala. That was also the year in which Basil, with Pound's assistance, completed his 'Villon', the first of his major poems. Bunting later recalled that Pound 'did for my "Villon" exactly what he'd done for Eliot in *The Waste Land*. He took a blue pencil and scratched out about half the poem, though it's true when he came to Part IV he sighed and said, "I don't know what you young men are up to."'[6] Bunting does not say why Pound was uncertain about the final section of 'Villon'. But five years later, in a letter to Louis Zukofsky, Pound using his own distinctive spelling called the 'ending possibly too universul'.[7] Certainly there is at the last a straining for philosophical utterance that is unsuccessful. The last lines contrast with the richly imagistic lines of the third section, lines which Pound considered 'remarkable'. The third section as a whole contrasts with its two predecessors. It is a highly textured evocation of a Mediterranean landscape and seascape reminiscent of Rapallo, whereas the two previous sections evoke the dark and the discomfort of the prison life that Villon and Bunting had known in the dark, cold north. 'Villon' depicts the two locations in which Bunting began his poet's apprenticeship with Ezra Pound.

It is an ambitious poem, more than a hundred and sixty lines long and in places a homage to Villon resembling Pound's homage to Propertius. Bunting offers some skilfully managed versions from Villon but he also introduces a voice that speaks vividly of his own experience of prison. The second section of the poem moves on to take up larger issues such as mental and artistic imprisonment. It mocks the crude, restrictive and reductive positivism dominating the twentieth century just as it criticizes the delimitations imposed on Villon and his art by later French poets such as Marot and Ronsard. These destructive restraints upon life and art as presented in this section, which ends with Villon's image of criminals' dead bodies hanging from a gibbet, are challenged in the final section by the sunny openness and Mediterranean brightness of Rapallo and the Italian Riviera. The conclusion commends an art that is not confining, that respects 'wilderness' and 'vagueness' and 'the name-less'. Basil's Quaker background shows itself as he alludes to that which cannot be finally known or articulated, that which art may modestly and tentatively seek to clarify and show cohering:

> precision clarifying vagueness;
> boundary to a wilderness
> of detail; chisel voice
> smoothing the flanks of noise;
> catalytic making whisper and whisper
> run together like two drops of quicksilver.

As the work of a twenty-five-year-old 'Villon' is a remarkable poem. It is a substantial piece of English containing a large variety of verbal textures and prosody. It is intellectually serious and profound; though it has to be said that the thinking about art and life and death in the last eighteen lines contains obscurities that show a young man's lack of surety. In his extended essay on the poem Kenneth Cox was right to conclude that ' "Villon" is a masterpiece not in the conventional but in the original sense of the word: work done by an apprentice to demonstrate his mastery of the craft, though as man as yet unformed.'[8]

Shortly after he had completed the final version of 'Villon' in Rapallo, dismaying news disrupted Basil's life. Word came from England of his father's deteriorating health; he had long suffered from a painful heart condition. Basil decided he had to return home. He did not know then that he would not see Ezra Pound again for nearly five years.

Dr Thomas Bunting's last months seem to have been melancholy ones. Forty years later, when reviewing his own life in a letter to a friend, Basil spoke of himself as 'an old man revisiting the scenes of his youth, casting up accounts, as my father did in the few months before he died'.[9] Soon after Basil's return to Newcastle-upon-Tyne, in February 1925, Dr Bunting died of a heart attack. He was fifty-six years old and died after a long period of pain. Basil attended his father's funeral at Jesmond Old Cemetery, not far from 6 Portland Terrace, a substantial house with a view to which Dr Bunting and his wife removed around the time of Basil's imprisonment in 1918. The doctor left money to his sisters Sarah Anne and Harriet Alice; what remained was bequeathed to his wife Annie. Was it disapproval of his son that caused him to exclude Basil from his will? Basil's twenty-two year old sister Joyce also received no legacy; so it may be that the doctor thought that the older members of his family were in greater need.

In the weeks and months following the funeral Basil remained with his mother in the north-east. He managed to make a little money giving lectures at Lemington Settlement, a working men's college in Northumberland. Basil got the job through family connections. The Adult School, as the college was called locally, had been founded in 1913 by his uncle, Andrew Messer, who had married Annie Bunting's sister Elizabeth. Like Basil's father, Andrew was a public-spirited doctor with a great interest in helping and educating the poor in the local mining communities. To his friend Adams, to whom he had written the mocking letter about Paris, Basil confessed that he feared that for two pounds a week he was merely confusing the minds of the working men by explaining the technicalities of the money market.[10] His other subjects were currency and anthropology.

Living and working close to the miners of his native region, Basil became caught up in the events that made 1926 the most turbulent year in the history of industrial relations in Britain. A bitter miner's strike and the intransigence of the colliery owners precipitated in May a General Strike throughout the country. There were acts of violence in which Basil later reported some involvement. He told Ezra Pound that he 'stuck a knife in the tyres of a government strike-breaking lorry and tried unsuccessfully nearly every paper in the country to get the scandalous faked benches of magistrates who condemned the strikers to years of hard labour shown up'.[11] Certainly he was a passionate supporter of the strikers. His poem 'They Say Etna' is a harsh indictment of the colliery owners and of the larger capitalist system.

But politics was not his prime concern; his ambition was still to be a writer. To achieve this, he realized, he needed to be in London. During the early months of 1926 he travelled down repeatedly. On Pound's suggestion he visited T. S. Eliot at Faber & Faber. But Eliot could do little to help him. It seems to have been in the October of 1925 that Basil also went to meet D. H. Lawrence who had been a friend of Ezra Pound in the days of the *English Review* in London before the war. Lawrence, who after years of deprivation was beginning to prosper as a writer, was now briefly in London en route from Mexico to Germany and then Italy. The forty-one-year old novelist and the twenty-six-year old poet were both provincials and from coal-mining backgrounds but they did not get on well. When I last talked to Basil in 1980 I asked him about his meeting with Lawrence. As a strong and longstanding admirer of Lawrence's work I was disconcerted by Basil's four-word reply to my question. 'He was a jerk', was all he said.

In 1926 Basil served for a while as London correspondent for the Italian publication, the *Revista di Romos*, but abandoned this work when no payments were sent him. At last he managed to persuade the editor of the conservative weekly *The Outlook* to let him contribute articles on a fairly regular basis. This meant settling in London. By early November of 1926 he found himself a flat at 5 Osnaburgh Terrace, just north of the Euston Road and what could be termed the northern edge of Bloomsbury. His struggle to establish himself in London literary life now began. His first success was as a music critic.

In later years one of Basil's often repeated stories was about how he became music critic for *The Outlook*. One evening when he was drinking in Kleinfeldt's Fitzroy Tavern he was unexpectedly called to the telephone to speak to the American Otto Theiss, the literary editor of the weekly. He asked Basil if he knew anything about music. 'Not a damn thing!' was the reply. But Theiss told him that he'd better find out quickly because he was *The Outlook*'s new music critic. This is a good story but for dramatic effect Basil slightly adjusted the facts. In actuality Basil's involvement with *The Outlook* had begun before this telephone exchange took place. His old friends and sponsors Ford Madox Ford and Ezra Pound had both published in the periodical a good deal in previous years and it seems likely that one or both of them supplied Basil with letters of introduction. Each was fully aware of the fact that Basil had learnt a great deal about music as a boy in Newcastle. His career with the periodical began in the third week of February 1927, not as music critic but more modestly with a lighthearted little piece on the current state of journalism. Then a week later he supplied a rather nostalgic essay on costermongers or Cockney street-traders as an endangered species in London life. His feeling for London also showed itself in a review of a little pamphlet put out by the London Society, *London Squares and How to Save Them*.

He reviewed a number of books for *The Outlook* including *Hymen, or the Future of Marriage* by the Australian sexologist Norman Haire, who a few years later performed the Steinach operation for sexual rejuvenation on the seventy-year-old W. B. Yeats. But the twenty-seven-year-old reviewer is sceptical about Haire's sexual utopianism. When Haire poses questions about the consequences of 'open marriage', Basil replies: 'The reviewer is not to answer the questions he asks, thank goodness! He is neither philosopher nor prophet, and finds his own very simple love affairs embarrassment enough without undertaking to regulate those of the world at large.'[12]

Basil's lyrics of this time confirm his difficulties with love. A year earlier the poem 'I am agog for foam' had referred in its dedication to a new girl friend, Peggy Mullett. But to 1927, the year he reviewed Haire, he also attributed a poem inscribed to his much earlier love Helen Moore, now married to someone else. The very long, slow lines convey a sense of loss and waste. The poem is informed by regret that their experiences together have not been properly commemorated. He ends with a prayer to the muse of heroic poetry to assist him in doing this. The last line is a wish that Helen and he 'respond bringing the savour of our sadness or delight again'. Clearly the complexities of love are very much on his mind whether he writes as a journalist or as a prosodically erudite poet calling for the aid of Polyhymnia.

The short feature articles that Basil contributed to *The Outlook* reveal an extensive culture on the part of such a young journalist. For instance, he writes a piece in praise of his old friend Nina Hamnett in which, showing considerable knowledge, he situates her art and achievement in relation to that of a wide range of artists such as Daumier, Rowlandson, and Cruickshank. He regards her, David Bomberg and Wyndham Lewis as the only artists free of the conspicuous derivativeness characterizing contemporary British painting, especially that produced by the artists of the Bloomsbury Group. He regrets that Nina is better known as 'a social figure' than an artist. With a mild jest that mentions himself he concludes: 'The rich and great enjoy her company (so do sailors and journalists and others of the poor) but seldom purchase her drawings.'

Basil shows an altogether different area of expertise in his admiring account of the great English ballerina of the day, Lydia Munnings, who danced under the name Sokolova. The article suggests that Basil may have known her personally. But it is the nature and context of her art that Basil knowledgeably discusses in his essay. He considers her relations as a dancer with Massine and Nijinsky. He evokes her performances dwelling especially on the qualities that most impressed him. He stresses her intense dedication to her craft, her hard work and, above all, the impersonality, the austerity in her performances. With excited admiration Basil recalls her dancing in *Le Sacre du Printemps*, the first and once highly controversial modern ballet, with music by Stravinsky and choreography by Nijinsky. Sokolova had, Basil recalls, a 'lofty and complete absorption in the moment'; she 'filled us with genuine awe'. 'The audience paid her the tribute of a deeper silence than is common in theatres.' Her secret, Basil concludes, is her ability to transcend self. 'She is always willing to spare us the details of her own personality.' She 'eschews that rather spurious charm and dances with a dryness acceptable to the connoisseur'.[13]

Three months after writing this piece on the ballet, months in which he wrote on a wide range of subjects from William Blake to Bolshevism and criminology to the economics of smallholdings, Basil settled down as the music critic for *The Outlook*. This was at the end of October 1927. From then on, until the periodical had to close down as a result of a lawsuit in the summer of the following year, he regularly contributed essays on musical subjects or reviews of concerts. Taken as a whole these writings constitute an impressive body of work that can be ranked in terms of quality with that of music critics such as Charles Burney and Bernard Shaw.

The essays are forceful; they are never hesitant. Their style ranges from the colloquial to the elegantly formal; sometimes, for humorous effect, his writing contains elements of pastiche. There is a good deal of humour. Here, for example, is his playful account of an all female chamber orchestra which gave a concert that included the *Capriol Suite* by his friend Peter Warlock.

> Unfortunately Miss Erhart's ladies were not unanimous. A certain waywardness, doubtless very attractive in their private lives, showed in their playing. Every fiddler had her own idea of how the music should be played, regardless of her companions and of the conductress, so that differences were constantly occurring, giving rise to a number of short involuntary solos, and several ladies were true enough to their sex to try to have the last word, which gave a devastatingly ragged, jagged, and saw-like edge to every pause of silence.[14]

His criticism can be far harsher. Of the composer Arnold Bax and his *Fantasy Sonata* Basil writes: 'That he should ever have written this dull work betrays his crucial fault – a strained, mechanical, and often trite invention used to cover an embarrassing lack of imagination.'[15] Bax is again a target when Basil in a piece of mocking rhetoric exclaims: 'Alas! We ask for Thucydides and are given – Strachey! We search for Rubens and find – Grant! We listen for an echo of Beethoven and hear – Bax.'[16]

As a music critic Basil is by no means awed by established reputations. Liszt, for instance, was 'one of the greatest virtuosi; but he had not the ultimate gift of creation. He could not work in a void. He could make splendid, dazzling music from the most intractable and unpromising material but he could not make it, like Bach or Mozart, out of nothing at all. He required a stimulus . . . he found his stimulus in literature or philosophy or religion.'[17] Nor will Basil accept the conventional wisdom about Beethoven as a tortured romantic genius. He sees sentimentalities in this view and dismisses them with a magisterial certitude and in antithetical sentences which alike recall that great arbiter Dr Johnson.

> Beethoven was a gross person, of peasant mentality, tempestuous egotism, suspicious and tyrannous inclination, tortuously shady habits of business and boisterous strength. He lived without refinement in constant quarrels and incivility, never perceiving that politeness might be distinguished from toadyism or forbearance from weakness. He exacted a deference he denied to others, and the loneliness of which he complained was of his own procuring. He never restrained his mostly unamiable emotions and impulses, but was ruled by pique as other men by pride.[18]

This arresting and provocative opening paragraph is characteristic of Basil as a music critic. But it is but one part of his critical method. From this same essay and some others it is clear that, despite the startlingly unflattering character sketch, he remains an admirer of Beethoven. And generally he is by no means a negative critic. There is much that is commendatory in this sequence of essays covering a year of musical life in London. Some performers such as the pianist Artur Schnabel, the soprano Elisabeth Schumann and the guitarist Segovia receive warm, carefully formulated praise. Some of the essays commend and even seek to promote certain new composers. Chief among these is Arnold Schoenberg, then not well known in England. This composer's *Gurrelieder*, a setting of Danish poems translated into German, required five soloists, a speaker, three male choirs, a mixed choir and an orchestra. The work had been first performed in Schoenberg's native Vienna in 1913. It was not heard in England until 1928 when it was broadcast from the Queen's Hall by the six-year-old BBC. Basil listened to the programme and became an immediate admirer of *Gurrelieder*. He published an account of the work in *The Outlook* speaking of its 'wonders undreamt of by the multitude'; he wrote of 'its alternate loveliness and force'.[19]

Basil's musical criticism shows a concern with the social context of serious music. He knows a good deal about the economics and the politics of the concert and recital circuit in London. He supplies an ironic perspective on the doings of the most flamboyant and controversial impresario and conductor of that time, Sir Thomas Beecham. Like Beecham, Basil sought to educate public taste. In one of the last essays he wrote prior to the demise of *The Outlook* he urged a larger repertoire than that then prevailing in London. He regretted that 'In spite of the researches of . . . Mr Heseltine the Elizabethans remain outside the limited canon of the classics.' He also argued for other composers then suffering from neglect: 'Palestrina and Byrd, Monteverdi, Lully, Purcell'.[20]

Basil's writings on music in *The Outlook* were well received. Editors of other publications, such as the *Musical Times* and *The Times*, gave him the occasional opportunity to do music criticism for them. His articles for *The Times* began a relationship which continued intermittently for nearly a quarter of a century. But when *The Outlook* ceased publication Basil lost his financial mainstay. His occasional work for other newspapers was not enough to sustain him in London. In the summer of 1928 he became desperate for money. It was a painful experience that would recur in his life.

But then, as would also happen again to him, his fortunes improved suddenly and dramatically. On this occasion a lady who enjoyed playing the role of fairy godmother unexpectedly entered his life.

SIX
Patronage and Marriage
1928–1930

Eleven years older than Basil, Margaret Burnham came from a prosperous Quaker family in Philadelphia. In 1907, whilst on vacation with her family at Lake George, just before she became an undergraduate at Vassar she met eighteen-year-old Albert de Silver, the only child of an extremely wealthy couple from Brooklyn Heights, New York. A pen friendship subsequently developed between the two young people; both were deeply interested in the social and political issues of the day. During his years at Yale the tone of Albert's letters grew ever more loving; he took to using the Quaker pronoun 'thee' as he corresponded with her. Margaret was far more radical than he and deeply committed, as he was not, to the women's movement. She was a staunch feminist and suffragist. Nevertheless they became engaged in 1910 and were married in 1913. The marriage was made possible by the death that year of Albert's father who left him a large inheritance. Also in 1913 Albert completed his graduate work at Columbia University, gained his law degree and joined a well-to-do New York law firm. He and Margaret quickly started a family. Harrison was born in 1914. Anne, the dedicatee of Basil's odes 'Not to thank dogwood', followed in 1917. And their third and last child, George Burnham de Silver, was born in 1919.

Albert de Silver was essentially a conservative. A close friend remembered him as 'wise, jolly and fat. He had inherited wealth and a sharp legal mind; he had a conscience and a Quaker wife. But he himself was not a Quaker or even a pacifist; he was simply stirred by the attacks on freedom of speech and press and conscience.'[1] These attitudes came from America's super-patriots who, particularly after the United States' entry into the war in 1917, could brook no dissent. The suppression of various publications, such as the radical weekly *The Masses* and the persecution of individuals said to be part of the Red Peril offended Albert de Silver's patrician sense of fair play. He became a leading figure in the organization that evolved into the American Civil Liberties Union.

In November 1924 the career of this wealthy lawyer and dedicated proponent of civil rights ended prematurely and in tragedy. Albert and

Margaret had driven to New Haven to watch the Yale-Harvard football match. They took the train home to New York and a few days later returned by rail to Connecticut to recover their car. While Albert was walking down the corridor of the fast-moving express train looking for the smoker there came a sudden sharp bend in the track and Albert was catapulted through an open door and killed instantly. He was thirty-six-years old.

Margaret, the widowed mother of three, inherited her husband's large fortune in its entirety. She was extremely generous with her new wealth. She funded individuals whom she considered creative and deserving. She was lavish in her support of various radical and left-wing causes. She also engaged in a series of love affairs; for though she was heavily built, she was attractive to men. Her friend the literary critic Edmund Wilson once observed that 'women can get quite fat and still be all right – as in the case of Margaret de Silver'.[2] She finally settled into an extended relationship with the Italian anarchist Carlo Tresca who was based, and finally assassinated, in New York City. In 1933 Margaret came very close to identifying herself with the American Communist Party by joining a committee organized by the Friends of the Soviet Union to welcome a delegation from Moscow.

Just over three years into her widowhood Margaret decided to spend some time in London. As a lover of the arts and a wealthy patroness she was welcomed into Bloomsbury circles and here she met Basil. They took to each other and apparently had an affair. In later years Margaret's attitude to Basil would be marked by fits of jealousy.

They had a good deal in common. Both had a Quaker sensibility, firm principles and strong left-wing sympathies. Margaret quickly became interested in Basil's literary ambitions. As well as poetry, he wanted to write a book on one of his favourite authors, Charles Dickens, stressing the novelist's powers as a stylist and master of form. Basil also had in mind both a history of English music halls, which he enjoyed frequenting and to which he doubtless took Margaret, and a book about prisons. But none of these plans could be worked on while he had no dependable income and had to hurry around London begging editors to allow him to contribute the occasional piece of journalism.

Margaret was impressed by Basil's abilities and by the sincerity and dedication that he brought to his writing. She decided to subsidize him so that he might have time to work. Shortly after her visit to England ended and she had embarked for New York, Basil heard from Otto

Theiss, the former literary editor of *The Outlook*, that Margaret had asked him to administer a fund she had created for Basil. Theiss informed Basil that he was to receive two hundred pounds a year for two years.

Overjoyed with this good fortune Basil decided to leave London and to go and live quietly and inexpensively in the country. He returned to Northumberland and found himself lodgings in a shepherd's cottage in the Simonsides, a remote and unspoiled area of high and dramatic moorland in the north of the county. Wanting to get as far away as possible from civilization Basil settled for a spot seven miles south of the nearest centre of population. This was Rothbury, a picturesque little town surrounded by numerous ancient earthworks and promontory forts cut into the hilltops of the rolling sandstone moors.

The remote cottage was known as Coldside Farm and was the home of Ned Wilson who tended the sheep for a tenant farmer, Matty Milburn of Lordenshaws. Here, as in the coalfields, Basil lived close to poverty and hardship. Ned Wilson was ill and could not properly do his job; to support his family his wife had to take in lodgers. The couple had a six-year-old daughter who was both impressed by and in awe of this new member of the small household. The little girl was much intrigued by his bushy moustache, his smoky pipe and by the fact that, unlike any other man she knew, he spent his days in his room reading and writing.

Basil set to work on improving his Italian through a close study of Dante's *Divine Comedy*. He stayed some six months in this place of near isolation. He did, however, make the long walk to the cigarette shop and the pub and became interested in one of the local country crafts, the training of sheepdogs. In *Briggflatts* nearly forty years later he remembered and paid tribute to the art and skill of some of the well-known local trainers such as Wilson and Telfer, 'fell-born men of precise instep/ leading demure dogs/from Tweed and Till and Teviotdale'. In the Rothbury sheepdog trials in October 1928, during the time when Basil was in the Simonsides, J. M. Wilson (who was not related to Basil's landlord) captured the championship from Walter Telfer who had held it in previous years.

Basil's months in the country apparently inspired no other writing that has survived, but his period of retreat seems to have made him ready to take on a big city again. At the end of the year he set off for Berlin. He used to say later that *The Times* sent him there. And certainly there was much to report on in the German capital at that time. The stability of the Weimar Republic was threatened by street fighting between the

Communist and Nazi paramilitaries. The German economy, just a few months before the great financial crash on Wall Street, was running out of control. And some of the entertainments and night clubs in Berlin were then the most bizarre in the western world. They were especially attractive to homosexuals. W. H. Auden and Christopher Isherwood were among those who went there, the latter vividly evoking the atmosphere and peculiarities of the city in his two novels *Mr Norris Changes Trains* and *Goodbye to Berlin*.

Basil did not like Berlin at all. His perceptions of the place are clearly expressed in his two-page poem 'Aus Dem Zweiten Reich' which, like 'Villon', he classified as a 'sonata' and which he completed in, and datelined, 1931, some two years after his visit to Berlin. The poem emphasizes both the efficiency and the vulgarity of the city. The 'I' of the poem is wearied by the heavy, obvious pornography in a film he sees. He is similarly put off by the brash sexual advances of the girl who is accompanying him. A German who offers to show him 'the naked cabarets in Jaegerstrasse' remarks 'Berlin is very shocking to the English' and asks 'Are you shocked?' On the evidence of the poem as whole it is plain that Basil was scornful rather than shocked. It is because the tone and feeling in the work do not range beyond scorn and condescension that this poem about Berlin, however interesting in historical terms, is the slightest of the six long poems he classed as sonatas.

But 'Aus Dem Zweiten Reich' does have some biographical significance in that within the carefully datelined sequence of poems that constitute Basil's oeuvre, his *Collected Poems*, it is the first of the several reportage poems. A recurrent method in Basil's poetry is to supply a detailed report on a reality that he sees and hears before him and then file and refer it to powers and authorities elsewhere in the world, or sometimes, as a result of his Quaker beliefs, beyond this world. At times he is the moral spy, at other times God's spy. This method of verbal proceeding is evident in his two major long poems, *The Spoils* and *Briggflatts*. It is also there in lyrics such as 'The Orotava Road', 'Search under every veil' and 'Under sand clay. Dig, wait' These poems range in setting from the Iranian desert to North Africa to the Canary Islands. A condition of this kind of philosophical espionage was that Basil should take on, along with other forms of poethood, the role of travel poet. Paris, Rapallo, Berlin were his first destinations.

In 1929 Basil seems to have been back in London for a short time, or at least friends expected him there. At his old haunt, the Fitzroy Tavern, the Kleinfeldt family kept an autograph book. And on 29 May of that year Donald Calthorpe, a successful film actor of the day, wrote a greeting in it to his Fitzroy friends including Basil. Basil's interest in sailing, dating from his stay in Rapallo, seems to have been developing at this period; for Calthorpe addressed him with the words 'To all Mariners – particularly Naval mariners and especially good "Buntings" '.[3]

But by the time these words were written Basil was no longer in England. Margaret de Silver's allowance permitted him to go where he chose. And when he gave up on Berlin he decided to return to Rapallo and experience again the stimulating company of Ezra Pound and the group around him. He had long hankered to go back there. A letter of April 1926 expresses his enduring affection for the place and for his friend. 'I am delighted to write to Rapallo – you for the moment are Rapallo. The fact that you are there sanctions my enthusiasm. I should never have left the place if my father hadn't begun to die. I would have starved there sooner than seek a living elsewhere'.[4] Basil was back in Rapallo by the beginning of March 1929. He then visited the city of which Pound spoke so much, Venice. Here he took a room in a pension with a view on to the Campanile in the Piazza San Marco. On Corpus Christi Sunday in 1929 Mussolini's blackshirts held a large and elaborate rally in the square. There was much operatic marching up and down to loud popular music supplied by a military band. As he watched the display Basil happened to glance up at the balcony of his hotel. And there was a most beautiful red-haired girl. When he smiled at her she spoke to him tentatively in English. Seeing that he understood she asked him what the demonstration was all about. He called up his explanation but then decided it would be easier if he joined her on the balcony. And so began his relationship with the young woman who in a year's time would become his wife.

Marian Gray Culver, who was twenty-six when she met Basil, was from the small town of Eau Claire in rural Wisconsin. A grandfather had been a Presbyterian minister and her father, who had begun life humbly as a shoe salesman, had gone on to make a good deal of money in real estate. Marian and her five brothers had been brought up in very comfortable circumstances. A keen student of English literature Marian had left the Middle West to go to New York City where she had recently completed an MA in Englsh at Columbia University. Her trip to Europe had been financed by her father as a graduation gift. Before coming to Venice she had been in Vienna visiting one of her brothers who was studying medicine there.

A couple of days after Basil joined her on her balcony, they became lovers. Marian was entranced by his excited talk of poetry and poets and by his passionate commitment to his art. Their relationship was intense and made all the more memorable to each of them by the beautiful city which they explored together. But Marian's passage back to America had been booked long before. Their summer affair had to end and Marian had to leave. Both felt a sense of loss and it seems likely that Basil promised to do all he could to follow after and join her in New York City where she was to teach English in a high school. After their goodbyes Basil returned to Rapallo.

It was intellectually exciting to be back with Ezra Pound and his circle that winter of 1929–30 and Basil's literary activity increased markedly. Six of the poems in his *First Book of Odes*, published in 1965, are datelined 1930; within the carefully dated sequence this was an unusually large number for one year. They range from poems of political protest such as 'Gin the Goodwife Stint' and 'The Complaint of the Morpethshire Farmer' to one of Basil's profoundest lyrics, the meticulously lineated meditation on consciousness, art and thought beginning 'Nothing/substance utters or time/stills'. This year he also undertook other kinds of writing. One day on a trip up the coast to Genoa he was browsing among the bookstalls on the harbour quays and came upon an Italian translation of the Japanese prose work the *Ho-Jo-Ki* by Kamo-no-Chomei. Basil admired what he later called the author's 'urbane sceptical and ironical temper'. Sharing Pound's belief in the necessity to translate and assimilate world literature into English Basil set about doing a version. He did it as a ten-page poem which he completed in 1932 and entitled 'Chomei at Toyama'. Chomei, a member of the minor nobility of Japan and a civil servant, reviews the vicissitudes of his life. They include fire and drought, cyclone and floods, poverty and corruption. The poem is about an old man's resignedness; here are some characteristic lines:

> The dew evaporates from my sixty years,
> I have built my last house, or hovel,
> a hunter's bivouac, an old
> silkworm's cocoon:

ten feet by ten, seven high: and I,
reckoning it a lodging not a dwelling,
omitted the usual foundation ceremony.

I have filled the frames with clay,
set hinges at the corners;
easy to take it down and carry it away
when I get bored with this place.
Two barrowloads of junk
and the cost of a man to shove the barrow,
no trouble at all.

Since I have trodden Hino mountain
noon has beaten through the awning
over my bamboo balcony, evening
shone on Amida.
I have shelved my books above the window,
lute and mandolin near at hand,
piled bracken and a little straw for bedding,
a smooth desk where the light falls, stove for bramblewood.
I have gathered stones, fitted
stones for a cistern, laid bamboo
pipes. No woodstack,
wood enough in the thicket.

The tone throughout is one of stoical undeludedness. The language is frequently and successfully informed by imagist technique. This piece of literary *japonaiserie* is the most subtle of Basil's contributions to English literature as a translator/adaptor.

'Chomei at Toyama' had a mixed reception from Basil's fellow poets. To Harriet Monroe, the editor of *Poetry* of Chicago in which the adaptation was first published (or partly published), Basil reported that 'Ezra likes it and so does Yeats, but Eliot speaks ill of it because I haven't been in Japan which seems irrelevant, and because he says it echoes Pound, which, if true, would be a count against it. But Pound supposes it to contain certain echoes of Eliot. I'm not aware of echoing anybody. Except Chomei: his book was in prose and four to five times as long as my poem. But I think everything relevant in Chomei has been got into the poem.'[5]

Basil was dismayed that the associate editor of *Poetry*, Morton Dawen

Zabel, insisted on printing what he saw as the highlights of the poem rather than its totality. He wrote to Zabel: 'I hate to see Chomei cut up, because I think it depends mainly on the balance of parts throughout and the picking out of four somewhat "poetical" bits rather misrepresents the very simpatico ole Jap.'[6] In a note to the poem in *Poetry* Basil again insisted on 'the careful proportion and balance of the parts'. His adaptation of the *Ho-Jo-Ki* was a careful condensation of the original. Basil's greatest achievements were in the long poem; in his adaptation of the book which he picked up on the quays of Genoa he clearly advanced his skills in mastering the principles of concision and economy in what can easily become a rambling form.

On the same quays at Genoa Basil also came upon a battered copy of a French translation of the *Shah na Meh* of Firdusi, the Persian epic poet of the tenth century. Basil took it back to Rapallo and read it aloud to Ezra and Dorothy. All three of them were immediately fascinated. The *Shah na Meh* or 'Book of Kings' is a vast poem, comprising nearly sixty thousand couplets. In it Firdusi, versifying a prose original, tells, in epic terms, the history of the kings of Persia from mythical times right down to the reign of Khosrow II who died in 628 AD. Firdusi also added on the story of the overthrow of Persia's Sasanian dynasty by the Arabs around the middle of the seventeenth century. There are also verses dealing with the career of the prophet Zoroaster. Basil was especially interested in Firdusi's account of the activities of Alexander the Great in Iran. And, like Matthew Arnold, he was much taken by the story of Sohrab and Rustam. Dorothy, Ezra and Basil were disappointed, when they got to the end of the book, to find that they were still in the middle of the story. But they hit upon a solution to the problem. Pound bought Basil a three-volume edition of the *Shah na Meh* in Persian and Basil set about learning the language in order to translate the epic into English. He worked hard and the *Shah na Meh* became an important influence on his future development as a poet, but he despaired of doing justice, in English, to the verbal and prosodic complexities of Firdusi's original. In a letter to Pound a year or so later he promised to send 'a lump of Firdusi before long' but added: 'As to onomatopaeic accompaniment, which is the marvel of the whole thing, internal rhymes, contrapuntal arrangements of stress against stress against ictus against succession of longs, it is a hopeless task for anybody except Homer translating Firdusi or Firdusi translating Homer'.[7] However, it was a literary initiative that in ten years' time created a major turning point in his life. When the Second World War came and Basil, the former conscientious objector, determined to join up and fight against Hitler, the RAF decided they could make use of his knowledge of the Persian language. They sent him to Iran as translator and interpreter for a squadron based there. He was made an officer and had the experience, which surprised him, of successfully leading and managing men. In Iran he met and married his second wife. And there also, he began his career with British Intelligence.

But in the early thirties Basil thought that his future lay in Italy. Busy with his various literary projects Basil wrote to his mother in England saying that he intended to make Rapallo his permanent home. Mrs Bunting made up her mind that she would join him there and had all her furniture sent out. She took an apartment close to the seafront. Another new resident of Rapallo was someone Basil had known in his Paris days, the pianist and avant-garde composer George Antheil. They spent a good deal of time together in the cafés enjoying the lively conversation of yet another new member of Pound's Rapallo group, W. B. Yeats, who had recently arrived with his young wife George. Antheil was composing musical settings for Yeats's plays *At the Hawk's Well* and *On Baile's Strand*. The young American had continually to be restrained in matters of instrumentation. At one point in his setting of Yeats's *Oedipus at Colonus*, performed at the Abbey Theatre in Dublin, twelve pianos played simultaneously.

Now in his sixty-fifth years, and a Nobel prize winner, Yeats was spending his second winter close to Ezra Pound whom he had first known in London some twenty years before. The relationship had become closer when in 1914 Ezra married Dorothy, the daughter of Yeats's former mistress, Olivia Shakespear. When Yeats met Basil in Rapallo the Irish writer was engaged in writing *A Packet for Ezra Pound*, a three-part prose work that assesses his complex literary and personal relationship with the author of the *Cantos*. With Basil Yeats was at first uneasy. To Olivia Shakespear he described the young man as 'one of Ezra's more savage disciples'. He goes on: 'He got into jail as a pacificist and then for assaulting the police and carrying concealed weapons and he is now writing up Antille's [*sic*] music.' The second imprisonment Yeats mentions may well have occurred during Basil's pro-union activities during the General Strike in Britain in May 1926. In any event Yeats and his wife were clearly fearful of Basil's capacity for violence and intransigence.

Yeats adds: 'George and I keep him at a distance and yet I have no doubt that just such as he surrounded Shakespeare's theatre, when it was denounced by the first puritans.'[8]

A photograph of Basil taken at Rapallo at this time conveys the aggressiveness about which Yeats wrote. The deep-set eyes behind the steel-rimmed spectacles are challenging, and the wide, bushy moustache and the jutting beard, an imperial, suggest a truculence that is confirmed by the way his arms are folded. In his old age Basil was quickly dismissive and scornful of anything that smacked of cant. In his early thirties such responses must have been stronger and more violent. One can easily imagine him abetting Ezra Pound in the American's notorious colourfully worded irreverences. And one can also imagine the elderly and ailing Yeats being disconcerted by Basil's harsh, scoffing intransigence on literary, political and spiritual matters.

Gradually, however, Yeats's distrust gave way and the two poets became good friends. Years later, in 1973, in a lecture to the Yeats Society at Sligo Basil remembered appreciatively the older man's kindness to him and the way 'he put up with the presence of Antheil or myself at times when he must have found us intrusive, merely because the young learn from the old and the old must let them. Now that I am old myself I realise how much kindness was necessary to show such tolerance.'[9] Basil was astonished by one act of courtesy on Yeats's part; at a social gathering the older poet stood up and recited from memory one of Basil's poems. He had it word perfect, though the recitation, Basil remembered, made the poem 'almost unrecognisable in his hieratic chant'.[10]

During the latter weeks of 1929 Yeats became extremely unwell. He was suffering from a glandular disease known as Maltese fever, so called in those days because the Maltese were said to catch it from drinking goats' milk. At Christmas time Yeats was so ill that his wife felt she could not leave his bedside and go to Switzerland to bring their two children home from their boarding school for the holidays. She asked Basil to go and fetch them and he agreed. Ten-year-old Anne and her eight-year-old brother Michael were somewhat uneasy with the young man who came to collect them, Anne Yeats told me, when years later she recalled that Christmas journey across the Alps. Inexperienced with young children Basil was extremely shy and awkward with his two charges. However, their relations improved at Milan where they had to change trains. Basil led them out of the station so they might visit a large toyshop which with its sumptuous Christmas decorations the two children thought wonderful.

On Christmas Eve Yeats was so ill that he thought he was about to die. With a struggle he wrote a brief, one sentence will leaving all his assets to his wife for the rearing of their children. Frantically George sought out Basil and Ezra Pound and asked them to come and witness the will. This they did, Basil giving as his address his London rooms at 5 Osnaburgh Terrace.

When Yeats's health improved Basil found him an entertaining companion. His conversation was occasionally about the technical side of poetry but more often just gossip. Yeats took a particular pleasure in employing vicious invective in his many stories about his sometime friend in the Irish literary renaissance, the novelist George Moore. Yeats who, according to Antheil, was 'a veritable expert on seeing ghosts in broad daylight' was also prone to josh his respectful young friends as they sipped their drinks together at the sidewalk cafés. Antheil later remembered:

> We would often sit together discussing our project, when suddenly he'd say: 'Hello, William', and he'd tip his soft felt sombrero.
>
> I'd follow his look and, seeing nobody within fifty feet of our table, I'd ask him, not without astonishment, where William was.
>
> 'Right in the chair alongside of you; he's the ghost of my indigestion', Yeats would say.
>
> Yeats would sometimes talk quite a bit to William and also to other Irish spirits who had been kind enough to come all the way from Ireland to see him.[11]

Basil remembered that Yeats at his more serious liked to talk 'about religion and the wilder sort of metaphysics'.[12] But Basil, still mindful of his Quaker inheritance, was not impressed by Yeats's notions of the religious or the occult. Early in 1930 he had an experience that greatly widened his understanding of the spiritual. He travelled to Siena to look at some of the paintings in the cathedral there. The visit also made Basil aware of the writings of St Catherine. He was much impressed by them and attributed to that 'very hardheaded and formidable lady' the same degree of religious understanding that he saw in the founder of the Quaker movement, George Fox. In 1973 Basil observed that 'Compared with these, Yeats's mysticism was trivial.'[13] Basil's own mysticism was something he was prepared to speak of at any length only in his last years. An important statement is his *A Note on Briggflatts* which was published posthumously in 1989. Here Basil rejects hierarchy and order, 'the virtues of the neo-Platonic quasi-religion' which were also prime virtues to 'Yeats, Pound and Eliot'. Basil regarded hierarchy and order not as virtues but as mere 'expedients that chafe almost as vilely as the crimes they try to restrain'. The philosophers with whom Basil had greatest sympathy were Lucretius and his masters who were 'content to explain the world an atom at a time'. Basil could also sympathize with Spinoza 'who saw all things as God, though not with his wish to demonstrate that logically; and with David Hume, the doubter'. Basil sensed that as a young man in Rapallo learning the art of poetry from the likes of Pound and Yeats he was somehow wrongfooted. For they saw the world differently from he. 'Both Pound and Yeats fancied the dreary notion of a history that repeats itself, not as the Buddhists see it, nor as Toynbee, but the cruder Spengler, and that too is part of the neo-Platonic outlook.' What Basil sought to articulate was something that George Fox and St Catherine of Siena concerned themselves with and which Basil termed 'the pulse of God's blood in our veins'. He wrote: 'In silence, having swept dust and litter from our minds, we can detect the pulse of God's blood in our veins, more persuasive than words, more demonstrative than a diagram. That is what a Quaker meeting tried to be.'[14]

Not long after his visit to Siena Basil found himself compelled to leave Italy. Apparently Margaret de Silver abruptly discontinued his allowance long before the agreed termination date. Could it have been that in his letters he had told her of his feelings for Marian Culver and that this had angered Margaret? In any event he now felt it necessary to return to London to earn an income by resuming his activities as a journalist. Before he left he arranged for a private printing of a volume of his poems. He may well have done this in order to prove to Margaret de Silver that her financial support had produced something. In a brief preface he thanks her 'for bailing me out of Fleet Street'. He adds that 'after two years convalescence from an attack of journalism I am beginning to recover my honesty'. He gave the thin paper-bound volume the jokey title of *Redimiculum Metallanum* ('A necklace of chamber pots'). The little book appeared in Milan in March 1930. The print run was small and the book itself flimsily bound. The few copies that have survived are now extremely valuable.

By this time Basil was back in London struggling ineffectually to make a living. He had great difficulties. In the aftermath of the 1929 crash on Wall Street had come the terrible depression. Unemployment soared. In Britain a soon miserably familiar sight was that of the jobless, shabby and hungry, queueing in long lines outside the labour exchanges waiting for the dole. The number of homeless increased dramatically. This was the year when Basil's near contemporary George Orwell was doing the research for his aptly titled *Down and Out in Paris and London*. In the economic circumstances of the day Basil found that he could make but little money and when he could not beg a bed from friends in London he had to sleep alongside the down and outs on Primrose Hill and the Embankment. It was one of the most painful and difficult periods of his life. In a letter to Ezra Pound he described his condition as one of 'dire poverty'.

He wanted above all to go to New York. He wanted to see Marian again and he wanted to become reconciled with his patroness, Margaret de Silver. After some miserable, poverty-stricken weeks his wish was granted. In June with a sum of money advanced to him either by his mother or Margaret de Silver he was able to pay his passage to America. Just before he embarked for New York he gave his mother and his friends his next address as c/o Margaret de Silver, 98 Joralemon Street, Brooklyn.

From New York he went up to Rhode Island to stay with Margaret de Silver at one of her several large homes. They had convivial times together. And when the drink ran out Margaret sent Basil to a speakeasy to get more. (Prohibition was still in force in the United States.) Basil later claimed that he did not go as far as Margaret had told him; he just stopped a cop and asked where the nearest booze was to be found and the cop said he could bootleg some for him.

In New York City Basil's reunion with Marian was joyous. In less than three weeks they got married. The ceremony took place on 9 July at Riverhead, Long Island. The couple then lived together in Marian's apartment at 63 Montague Street in Brooklyn. On learning of the marriage Margaret de Silver announced that she would make no further payments to Basil. Contact between them was suspended.

Four days after the wedding Basil initiated another important relationship. He sent a postcard to the New York poet Louis Zukofsky saying: 'Ezra Pound says I ought to look you up. May I?' Zukofsky responded enthusiastically and thus began a friendship which both in literary and personal terms Basil came to regard as being as important as his friendship with Ezra Pound. Four years younger than Basil, Louis was twenty-six when they first met. He had been brought up on the Lower

East side of Manhattan; his parents were poor Jewish immigrants from western Russia. Yiddish was the only language Louis knew until he went to school, but he was very gifted and proceeded to graduate in English at Columbia University. Already a dedicated poet in his teens, Louis went on to publish progressive poetry in little magazines where it attracted the attention and admiration of Ezra Pound. The year he met Basil Louis wrote the first extended essay on Pound's *Cantos 1–27*; it was published in the French periodical *Echanges*.

Basil also came to know others who were active in the arts in New York. He met William Carlos Williams, the doctor poet who had been a friend of Pound's ever since the pair of them had been students together at the University of Pennsylvania over twenty years before; René Taupin, the French critic and scholar who was especially interested in the modernist movement in poetry; and the Hungarian composer Tibor Serly who had studied with Béla Bartok and who completed some of his teacher's unfinished compositions.

Pound had provided Basil with letters of introduction to various editors in New York. Years later when Marian no longer loved and admired her husband so fervently as she did in this first year of marriage, she would blame him for not presenting the letters and for not working hard enough to establish himself as a writer in New York. He did, however, manage to place a few articles in newspapers and magazines. But he found difficulty in getting published and the pay was low. In America as in Britain there was deepening economic depression which the administration of President Hoover was unable to control. It would be another three years before the urbane Franklin Delano Roosevelt, then Governor of New York State, entered the White House promising a 'New Deal' to end the depression.

For the most part Basil had to live on the money Marian earned as a teacher. Finding his writing unsaleable he spent more and more time in the apartment working on his Persian. Marian had bought him a large Persian dictionary. He also began to teach himself Greek. He grew increasingly and bitterly frustrated by the literary scene in New York. Marian remembered that he had a lunch with the influential journalist and editor Malcolm Cowley. It was a disaster and provoked Basil on his return home to deliver to Marian a lengthy, violent, frightening tirade against journalists and all those who sold their talents for money. To make matters worse, on a visit to Wisconsin in the summer, Basil had come to dislike Marian's very conventional family.

68

When a letter arrived from Ezra Pound containing the observation that if Basil had to be unemployed it would be better to be so in sunny Rapallo rather than in wintry New York City, Basil though the idea convincing. But how to pay for the steamship tickets for their voyage across the Atlantic? He went to Margaret de Silver and appealed to her for the money. She finally consented. Marian was uneasy about abandoning her teaching job at this time of heavy unemployment. She was always more cautious than her husband and came to regard him as rash and headstrong. But about Rapallo he was insistent. They gave up their home in New York and with absolutely no sure prospects of work or income set off for the place and the company in which Basil had always been happy.

SEVEN
Rapallo Again
1931–1933

They were back in Italy by January 1931. With money which the New York school system had returned to Marian from her retirement fund they took a lease on a house high up in the side of Montallegro overlooking the rooftops of Rapallo and the bright blue waters of the harbour.

Basil was delighted to be back and living close to Ezra and Dorothy Pound. He visited them at least twice a week in their hotel apartment right above the centre of the seafront. Basil took a keen interest in the surroundings and lifestyle of his older friends. He wrote to a correspondent: 'Ezra has a queer flat, like a couple of parallel corridors cut into sections. Unfinished wall decorations. Drawings by (Wyndham) Lewis, sculptures by Brzeska, etc. His wife's excellent watercolours everywhere. View of the whole gulf.' Basil clearly pondered a great deal on his relationship with his mentor who, he said, was 'the pride of the town'. Basil continued:

> You go up to tea and talk, very fragmentary, ('politics of literature' J. J. Adams says), but good things in it. He is very quick, I'm slow as the deuce. Small magazines lying about. Not very many books. There is no alternative to the homemade chairs. The ungenteel, lively side of Bloomsbury Bohemia (whatever he says about Bloomsbury), nothing particularly American except his bodily restlessness and sometimes his accent. Alcohol is rare and almost solely for visitors. He bursts with American energy, part of it, I think, truly American, that is, almost objectless, but usually useful and pointed.[1]

In the spring of 1931 Basil and Marian took photographs of their own mountainside house and surroundings with the spectacular views. They pasted the photographs into a small album about seven inches by four and pencilled in more than thirty explanatory captions. The album was then mailed back to Eau Claire, presumably as a way of reassuring Marian's parents and brothers and demonstrating that she had not given up her job in New York for no good alternative.

An early caption describes the approach to their home. 'You turn left by the ancient castle of Rapallo and follow the road by the torrent almost dry for nine months of the year.' The next entry describes the steep, stepped road. 'You turn up the mountain by this road . . . 330 of these steps with about a mile of path bring you to our house, here seen through vines and olives and cypresses. The cement steps are for men, the grassy ones for mules.' A picture of the vines has a caption that jokes about Prohibition in America: 'Vines. Some grapes eaten. Some converted into an ILLEGAL BEVERAGE.' Later comes the comment, 'Better than a speakeasy'. Under the photograph of Basil in a state of undress behind a clump of roses is the observation: 'The rosetree is trying to hide B.B.'s Bacchic posture.' One photograph taken 'from above where Mrs Bunting Senior's house' is situated shows the mountain on which Marian and Basil live, Montallegro, 'sacred once to Apollo, then to the Virgin'.[2]

One of the portraits in the album is admiringly identified as Francesco Monotti who 'sometimes writes for the New York Times'. He also wrote for the local weekly newspaper in Rapallo, Il Mare, and was a friend of Ezra Pound. Monotti was closely connected with the substantial English-speaking community in Rapallo. Wounded in the First World War he had been befriended by a wealthy American woman, Miss North of California. She had brought him to her luxurious home at Zoagli, just south of Rapallo, in order that he might recover his health. A man of wide literary interests Monotti was steadily building his career and influence as a journalist and soon helped to make Il Mare a platform for the opinions of Basil Bunting and Ezra Pound. A local literary magazine L'Indice, which was published at nearby Genoa, also accepted their work.

How much Marian's parents were reassured by the photographs sent to them is unknown. But they certainly felt it necessary to send an allowance of thirty-five dollars per month to sustain their daughter and her unemployed husband. Basil, like his friend Ezra, was in considerable part supported by his wife's family's money.

The Culvers' concern must have increased in the spring of 1931 when they learned that Marian was expecting a child. She had a difficult pregnancy because she and Basil could not afford the special pre-natal care that she required. Despite a gift of three hundred dollars from Ezra and Dorothy Pound, Basil and Marian were virtually penniless as the pregnancy neared its conclusion. Just as they were setting off to the Protestant Hospital in Genoa where the baby was to be born Basil learned that Poetry of Chicago had awarded him a fifty-dollar prize for his 'Villon'. The money paid for Marian's admittance to the hospital.

In November they became the parents of a baby girl whom they named Bourtai after the nine-year-old wife of Genghis Khan the Mongol conqueror who was a subject of the poem 'Vestiges' on which Basil was then working. The baby proved to be oversize and to have a tendency to diabetes. Such complications meant that Marian had to remain in the hospital until the end of the first week in January 1932. Every morning Basil took the train from Rapallo to Genoa to see her. Marian became angry when Monotti's wealthy friend, Miss North, told her that Basil, despite his much proclaimed lack of money, always travelled first class on the train. Presumably he obtained the money for his fares from his mother who was equally extravagant.

When Marian finally left hospital with Bourtai, Basil took them to his mother's flat in the centre of Rapallo rather than to their own more remote house. Basil's mother took good care of them but she was extremely houseproud. She would not permit them to do any cooking for fear they would dirty her kitchen. When, towards the spring of 1932, they did return to their mountainside home, Mrs Bunting immediately had her flat redecorated and the furniture re-covered.

Back in their own home Basil and Marian now entered into a happier phase of their lives. After the birth of Bourtai they received congratulatory gifts of money from numerous relatives and friends and no longer felt poverty-stricken. Basil even bought himself a boat and enjoyed daylong sailing. He continued to enjoy the company and stimulus of Ezra Pound whose parents, like Mrs Bunting, had moved to Italy to be near their son. As a poet and as a theorist and impresario of poetry Pound was as active and energetic as ever. In the year Basil and Marian arrived in Rapallo he was involving himself in yet one more of that succession of 'isms' which denoted new phases and emphases within the larger development of modernism as a whole in poetry in English. Pound, who had been at the centre of imagism and then of vorticism, now helped to promote objectivism. This literary initiative began in February 1931 as an issue of *Poetry* which was edited by Pound's friend and associate Louis Zukofsky. Pound bombarded him with advice.

In his introduction to the selection Zukofsky insisted on 'the clarity of image and word-tone' and also on the 'resolving of words and ideation into structure'. In its concern to represent objects and things rather than dreams and fantasies the new 'ism' was a marked contrast to the surrealism that had dominated literary life in Paris for the last ten years or so and that would soon take hold in London. Zukofsky chose a poem by Basil for inclusion in the volume, the one which in the *Collected Poems* opens with the lines, 'Nothing/substance utters or time/stills and restrains/joins design'. Its last stanza, which Basil subsequently published as an independent poem, begins 'Molten pool, incandescent spilth of/deep cauldrons'.

In the following year, 1932, Zukofsky, still encouraged by Pound, went on to publish a book entitled *An 'Objectivists' Anthology*. It was dedicated to Pound who 'is still for the poets of our time the most important'. The volume contained work by poets as different in character and ability as William Carlos Williams, Charles Reznikoff, Kenneth Rexroth, Carl Rakosi, Robert McAlmon, Louis Zukofsky, T. S. Eliot, Mary Butts and Ezra Pound. Basil's contribution was the third section of 'Attis: Or, Something Missing'.

This substantial poem, a hundred and seventy-nine lines long, which Basil datelined 1931, was in later collected editions of his work printed immediately after 'Villon', thus figuring as the second of his long poems or 'sonatas'. The epigraph to the poem is taken from Carmen LXIII of Catullus which tells how Attis, a young man of Phrygia in Asia Minor sails to the coast near Dindyma, the mountain that is sacred to Cybele, the goddess of nature. Here Attis and his followers are taken over by a religious frenzy and finally castrate themselves. When normal consciousness returns Attis both grieves and rages about his act of self-mutilation. He would like to sail back home but Cybele sends one of her lions to force him back on the mountain where he is condemned to remain as her eunuch. Basil's poem employs the binary form of the sonata to offer, in modern terms, a treatment of this contrast between the natural order on the one hand and unnatural and denatured man on the other.

The first image in the first movement is of a figure resembling T. S. Eliot's J. Alfred Prufrock, though more advanced in age, one who is 'slavishly circumspect at sixty' and with a 'warm obese frame limp with satiety'. This flaccidity is contrasted by the last twenty-three lines of the first movement which constitute the second term in the 'sonata'. These lines evoke the natural world; they recall the landscape of the Simonsides in Northumberland where Basil had lived a few years earlier and where he could see 'in the distance Cheviot's/heatherbrown flanks and white cap'. The lines are full of sound, the melodious echoing of the hunting horn, for instance, and they conclude with a song of praise to nature who is mother to both gods and eunuchs.

The second movement further develops the musical analogy with its heading, 'Variations on a theme by Milton'. The reference is to the sonnet 'Methought I saw my late espousèd Saint'. But the 'I' in Basil's poem is incapable of his predecessor's response. Not for him a love that can reach beyond death. 'I was not pleased, it is shocking to meet a ghost, so I cut her . . .' The response is made to seem all the more inadequate since it occurs in the beautiful and remote little Tyneside village of Bywell, an important location in the spiritual history of Northumberland, in that it has not just one but two, and adjacent, medieval churches. 'Gods awake and fierce' pulse in this second movement but modern men do not see or hear them. There is abroad a cowardice and fear that Basil associates with that experienced by Dante in the eighth Canto of the *Inferno* when the three Furies suddenly appear and threaten him with the words, 'Send for Medusa: we'll enamel him.' Such fear and disloyalty to the visionary are accompanied by a debasement of the art of poetry. Polymnia [*sic*], the muse of sacred poetry, is reduced to keeping a café in Reno, Nevada, well known in the 1930s as a town for fast divorces.

The third and final movement of the poem is titled 'Pastorale arioso for a falsetto, or eunuch'. The arioso, a melodious recitative, is another insistence on the musical element in the work. Neither statement nor full-throated song, the arioso in this last movement is mostly a dramatic monologue by the emasculated Attis figure who was finally, according to legend, transformed into a pine tree. The contrast between what he once was, a fine young man, and what he is now is sometimes just a comic indignity.

I also won the 14 carat halfhunter goldwatch
at the annual sports and flowershow.
The young girls simpered when I passed.
Now I am out of a job. I would like to be a lady's maid to Dindyma.

At other times it is a matter of miserable and uncomfortable resignation.

Pines, my sisters, I, your sister,
parch in calm weather, swelter in Scirocco, sway in northwind,
I am passive to the heave of spring.

74

The lament concludes with an appeal to Cybele who dismisses it in short, curt, scornful lines.

'Attis' is an ambitious work but not an entirely successful one. For a poem that seeks to allude to the presence of the divine in human experience there is no very compelling evocation of the gods. Scorn of eunuchs is there right enough; the mockery is trenchantly expressed, though sometimes the modern colloquialisms such as 'Oh Sis! I've been 'ad' introduce too broad and coarse a humour into this highly sophisticated poem. 'Attis' is a very clever work with all the limitations that adjective implies. The poem is full of literary allusions, including parodies of Lucretius and Cino da Pistoia, and manages intricate parallels between classical myth, Dante and the contemporary world. Prosodically there is great skill and delicacy. But for all its subtle musicalizing of language the poem leaves the impression of 'something missing'. The reader admires the very high degree of craft but is aware that the subject proposed requires more than just an indictment, however finely modulated, of the modern world.

In 1931 in Rapallo Basil also completed his two-part poem 'Vestiges' which owes something to Pound's enthusiastic research into the history and culture of China for his own Chinese *Cantos*. Basil's poem concludes with an exchange of letters between Jenghiz (Genghis) Khan and the Chinese sage Chang Chun. Tacitly it is a quiet and relaxed celebration of a good relationship between a man of action and a man of thought, reminiscent of that between one of Pound's heroes in the *Cantos*, Sigismundo Malatesta, and the *savants* and artists who surrounded him. In the same year Basil completed 'Aus Dem Zweiten Reich' by adding a finale satirizing the self-regarding but vacuous Gerhart Hauptmann, the German, Nobel prize-winning dramatist who like Yeats wintered at Rapallo at this time. In the following year, 1932, Basil finished his adaptation from the Japanese, 'Chomei at Toyama', and added three lyrics to his *oeuvre*: 'Mesh cast for mackerel', a poem with delicate perceptions about fishing and the sea; the satirical 'The Passport Officer' and 'Two Photographs', a poem about time and change in a woman's life written with fine compassion and psychological insight.

1932 was a comparatively happy and highly productive year for Basil. Shortly after Christmas he reviewed his situation in a letter to one of his correspondents and concluded that, in the terminology of one of his favourite poets, Lucretius, in his life at Rapallo the 'fortuitous concourse of atoms is reasonably satisfactory'.[3] An old peasant had presented him with a mongrel dog and a kennel. So with a cat and a baby as well the household was complete. If he just had enough money to keep them all fed properly, to have his boat painted, to buy a few books and to pay off his worst debts, then he would be perfectly comfortable. He loved the mountains around Rapallo even in the rain.

Basil was producing prose as well as poetry at this time. He contributed articles on Pound and on T. S. Eliot to the *New English Weekly*, recently founded by A. R. Orage who had first printed Basil's work in *The New Age* some dozen years before. He collaborated with Michael Roberts to help produce an 'English Number' of *Poetry* of Chicago and contributed an essay entitled 'English Poetry Today'. He managed to place occasional articles with the *Paris Tribune* and the *New York Sun*. Basil also wrote an essay on Pound for inclusion in a collection put together by Ford Madox Ford to help promote Pound's *Cantos*. Published in New York by Farrar and Rinehart at the same time as they brought out *A Draft of XXX Cantos*, the collection is entitled *The Cantos of Ezra Pound: Some Testimonies*. Basil's fellow contributors included Ernest Hemingway, Archibald MacLeish, James Joyce, William Carlos Williams, 'HD', Allen Tate, Edmund Wilson and T. S. Eliot.

At Pound's suggestion, Basil submitted a collection of his poems to T. S. Eliot who now had considerable influence in the publishing house of Faber & Faber. The submission began an awkwardness that continued in Basil's long literary relationship with T. S. Eliot. For Eliot rejected his manuscript out of hand declaring it to be just 'a rather fuzzy imitation of the cantos [*sic*]'. Pound saw the injustice of this and wrote to Eliot maintaining that Basil's poetry was 'not a simple steal from my language and metric/at least a subject matter is dealt with'.[4]

Basil was still working hard on his special subject, Firdusi's *Shah na Meh* and towards the end of 1932 he applied unsuccessfully for a Guggenheim award to finance a full translation. But other projects were underway. In the autumn Ezra Pound persuaded the editor of the Rapallo newspaper *Il Mare* to launch a literary supplement. On the masthead of the *Supplemento Letterario* were listed the four contributors who were responsible for foreign literatures or 'Affari Esteri'. The names given were, in order, Ezra Pound, Basil Bunting, J. R. Masoliver and Eugen Haas, a German musicologist who assisted Pound and Olga Rudge with the concerts they organised at Rapallo. The Rome correspondent was billed as Francesco Monotti who was one of the staff who translated Basil's articles into Italian. In September 1932 Monotti also translated a section of Basil's 'Villon' which appeared on the front page of the supplement. Basil contributed articles regularly. He also did a Latin version of a short lyric by Louis Zukofsky on the subject of the generosity of Ezra Pound. The poems were printed side by side in *Il Mare* as 'Verse and Version'. Basil wrote at considerable length to Louis about the problems he had encountered in making the Latin translation.[5] The letter is strong, even touching evidence of the professional and personal solicitude the group of poets at Rapallo felt for each other.

Basil concedes that Ezra 'knows more Latin than I do'; nevertheless during these years Basil persevered with versions from the Latin. The earliest to survive in the *Collected Poems* is a translation of the opening lines of *De Rerum Naturum* by the poet and philosopher Basil so much admired, Lucretius. The lines are an invocation to the goddess Venus. Datelined 1927 Basil's English lines, each one usually of twelve syllables, are vital, driving, forceful:

> In the first days of spring
> when the untrammelled allrenewing southwind blows
> the birds exult in you and herald your coming.
> Then the shy cattle leap and swim the brooks for love.
> Everywhere, through all seas mountains and waterfalls,
> love caresses all hearts and kindles all creatures
> to overmastering lust and ordained renewals.

In Rapallo Basil also translated one of the *Carmina* (LXIV) of Catullus to whose poetry he would, as a translator, return some thirty years later. And some months before he did 'Verse and Version' for Louis Zukofsky he did versions of two of Horace's Odes. One starts with lines that are startlingly colloquial and certainly not 'translatorese': 'Please stop gushing about his pink/neck smooth arms and so forth, Dulcie; it makes me sick.' In later years in his preface to his *Collected Poems* Basil would list Horace among the ten poets from the past who had helped him learn 'the trick of it'. He also told Louis Zukofsky that:

Horace works wonders with a word order which was crabbed even to his contemporaries, as one may see by reading Lucretius and Ovid on either side of him in time. It is not right to banish such effects, which have their place, one I think too much neglected now, even though we and especially I follow Yeats's example of plain diction and plain syntax.[6]

The crabbedness and intricacy of diction to which Basil refers here shows in his own work in later years. It is there in the long poems and in short lyrics such as 'At Briggflatts Meetinghouse' of 1975 which begins with lines that insist on a second reading: 'Boasts time mocks cumber Rome. Wren/set up his own monument.'

Yet in the early thirties it was the musicality of poetry that Basil chiefly emphasized. He took a keen interest in the high level of musical culture that Pound endeavoured to sustain at Rapallo. When Pound's friend, the pianist Gerhart Münch, gave a concert of works by Scriabin, Basil wrote an essay introducing the Russian composer to the readers of *Il Mare*. He then wrote a review of the concert in a subsequent issue of the paper. It was highly admiring as was his account, on another occasion, of the violin playing of Pound's lover, Olga Rudge.

In August 1933 the Rapallo group was augmented when Louis Zukofsky arrived on a visit from New York. Basil, wearing a stylish red jacket, went to Genoa to meet him when he disembarked and to escort him to the apartment of Homer and Isobel Pound, Ezra's parents, where the visitor was to live for the duration of his stay in Rapallo. Louis found Homer a very devoted parent. Ezra himself spent a lot of time just floating out at sea and meditating. When Homer, a kindly old man, escorted Louis out of the apartment and into Rapallo, he would stop, point out to sea and say proudly, 'See that over there floating? That's my boy.'

Louis ate most of his meals with the Buntings though Ezra Pound insisted on helping to pay for them. The three poets had numerous and intense discussions about their art. One very interested listener was the young James Laughlin, the future founder of New Directions publishing company, who had come to Rapallo to study at what he called the 'Ezuversity'. The group's activities, however, were by no means exclusively cultural and literary. There was much fun and partying which sometimes got out of hand, as, for instance, on the occasion the poets decided to celebrate Burns Night. They bought a large number of bottles of Scotch and imported a haggis from Scotland. The party had not been going long before the guests started throwing food at each other. Then they stumbled off to the harbour where they took boats, including Basil's, and sailed off wildly and erratically around the bay to the shock and consternation of the Italians.

Basil himself went in for experiences that Ezra and Dorothy Pound could not condone. After the Feast of the Madonna, when the image of the Virgin Mary was brought down into Rapallo from Montallegro, there followed a festival or, as Basil called it years later, an orgy on the summit of the mountain. The occasion had been celebrated in this way for centuries. There were giant sausages, barrels of wine and heaps of fruit. Everyone toasted everyone else; men and women, especially, drank to each other. Nearby were gorse thickets into which couples who had just met could conveniently vanish. When the Pounds learned that Basil had taken a girl into the gorse they were greatly put out. Basil noted that Ezra and Dorothy were frightened of Bacchus as a living force; they only liked him in books.[7]

As the autumn of 1933 approached, Basil was again troubled by a lack of money. The cost of living in Italy was rising markedly. He made enquiries about other places with warm climates where one might live more cheaply. And then suddenly he announced to Marian that they were leaving straightaway. Now expecting her second child, she was most reluctant to go. But Basil's impetuosity was not to be resisted. He now made the kind of snap decision that he was capable of making all through his life. Marian begged him to wait a couple of days until his mother returned to Rapallo from a holiday in England, but he would not delay.

Marian later suggested that political worries might have been responsible for Basil's decision. This was the year in which Hitler came to power in Germany. Basil, she remembered, had been greatly impressed by an article on Germany and its Führer published in a circulated newsletter edited by Claud Cockburn (later to be associated with the satirical magazine *Private Eye*). In the article Cockburn maintained that the War Office in London had drawn up plans for an attack on Germany the moment she left the League of Nations.[8] Marian sensed that Basil was frightened to think that he might find himself embroiled in another war and perhaps again imprisoned. He made up his mind to get as far away as possible from what Cockburn predicted would soon become a war zone. He had heard that the Canary Islands, a Spanish possession some sixty miles off the coast of north-west Africa, had a low cost of living as well as a warm climate, so that is where he finally decided to go. He and his pregnant wife and infant daughter arrived there in October 1933.

EIGHT
The Canaries and Hampstead
1933–1937

Marian later remembered their arrival on Tenerife, the largest of the Canary Islands, as an appalling experience. The hotel they could afford was filthy. Broken window panes in their room had been pasted over with newspaper; 'the toilet had to be approached through a mush of urine, soaked paper and debris'. Two-year-old Bourtai became ill. Marian was frantic with misery. But the horror was raised to a still higher level as they lay on their dirty bed that first night and heard a murder being committed immediately below their window.

From this moment on Basil developed an intense hatred for the Canary Islands that his wife, for all her own unhappiness there, regarded as irrational. The following morning they tramped the hot streets of Santa Cruz desperately seeking alternative accommodation. They were dismayed to find that there was a housing shortage on the island and that landlords demanded larger deposits and higher rents than the Buntings could afford. Their only income was the occasional remittance from Margaret de Silver and the small but regular allowance from Marian's family. They had to continue for some time in their squalid quarters before they managed to find modest but clean accommodation in the Hotel La Oratava on the north side of the island. A little later they rented a small house at Salto del Barraneo among the banana plantations near the little town of Puerto Cruz. The town was a resort and had a number of English and German residents. Marian was relieved and happy to live here but Basil still seethed with contempt for the place, calling it a hell hole. The only mitigation was that it was a free port and his favourite cigarettes, Gold Flake, were duty-free and cheap. Otherwise he railed at the Canaries and their Spanish-speaking population. He absolutely refused to learn any Spanish. In letters to Ezra Pound he sneered at the barbarity and lawlessness in this place which he had thought would be his safe and happy refuge. He reported that the local people murdered each other constantly and many of them lived on handfuls of semi-ground wheat dampened with a little water or spittle. One local lady had shot a man who braggingly claimed to have slept with her more times than he

Basil aged one with his mother Annie.

Scotswood, Northumberland, where Basil was born. The steep streets run down to the River Tyne.

Basil as a young man.

The Literary and Philosophical Society of Newcastle-upon-Tyne, built in 1822–1825. Basil's parents were members of the Society and here, as a boy, he was introduced to the lively intellectual life of the north-east.

38 Moorside, South Fenham, Newcastle-upon-Tyne, the house to which the Bunting family moved when Basil was in his early teens.

Ackworth School in Yorkshire, where Basil boarded from 1912–1916.

Leighton Park, the expensive Quaker school to which Basil transferred in 1916 in the hopes of winning a scholarship to Oxford or Cambridge.

(left) Basil in 1923, the year in which he went to live in Paris.

(below) Ezra Pound.

W. B. Yeats in the 1930s with Edmund Dulac and Edith Shackleton Heald.

Margaret de Silver, Basil's patroness, photographed in 1940.

Marian Gray Culver, Basil's first wife, at the time he met her.

Basil with his wife Marian and his mother Annie, Rapallo 1932.

The house where Basil and Marian lived on Montallegro overlooking Rapallo.

(left) Basil in Rapallo in the early 1930s.

(below) Louis Zukofsky in the early 1930s, when Basil met him.

Marian with Bourtai and Roudaba on Tenerife in 1934.

Basil in RAF uniform during World War II.

Basil's first three children in Wisconsin in 1942. From left to right: Bourtai, Roudaba and Rustam, the son Basil never saw.

actually had. After the murder she was seen kicking the corpse. When she was brought to trial she was found not guilty amid scenes of great enthusiasm; the honour of Canary womanhood was vindicated. Basil concluded that he was living among a population of uncivil lunatics, 'unclean moreover'.[1]

The islanders reciprocated his dislike and sneers. Marian was embarrassed and uncomfortable when the local men showed their hostility by pointing the finger of shame at her pregnancy. Husband and wife were both in a state of unhappiness when their second daughter was born on 4 February 1934 at Santa Cruz. Basil, still involved in the study of the *Shah na Meh*, named her Roudaba after the mother of Rustam in the Persian epic.

It is ironic that in the same month as he exiled himself to the Canaries, Basil's career and reputation as a poet were greatly advanced in London. A large number of his poems were included by Ezra Pound in his *Active Anthology* which he prevailed upon his friend T. S. Eliot at Faber & Faber to publish. Pound dedicated this collection of contemporary poetry, by writers he considered to be still evolving, to Bunting and Zukofsky, 'two strugglers in the desert'. Encouraged, Basil in his early days on Tenerife began putting together a book-length collection of his poems under the title *Caveat Emptor*. He submitted it to various publishers; but their responses proved as disappointing as the Buntings' new home.

Basil continually looked for ways to escape from Tenerife. In June Margaret de Silver sent him some extra money and he used it to go and investigate another sunny place where living was supposed to be cheap, the Algarve, the most southerly province of Portugal. In his absence Marian and the two babies moved into a boarding-house. Their old home among the acres of banana plants was taken over by two Americans with whom the Buntings had become friendly, Carlos Drerup, who was a painter, and his wife Gertrude. Well over thirty years later, in a letter to the Bunting scholar Roger Guedalla, Carlos Drerup recalled his times with Basil in the Canaries. The two men became very close. They saw each other daily over long periods of time. One important bond between them was their passionate hatred, and also fear, of fascism. Carlos saw Basil as a loner, one who did not make friends easily. Contemptuous of the islanders, Basil was also ill at ease with what Carlos described as 'the somewhat colonial type of English people, whom we met in Puerto de la Cruz'. Withdrawing from the other social groups on the Canaries Basil and Carlos spent hours together discussing politics and literature. Basil talked a great deal about James Joyce. *Ulysses* he regarded as a great comic masterpiece. He also spoke at length to Carlos about the classics.

Basil's disaffection with the English expressed itself in literary terms. While on the Canaries he completed a lengthy critical essay entitled 'The Lion and the Lizard'. In it he stresses the limitations which he sees in the English poetic tradition. He writes that 'English poets are too often on their dignity, they strive too constantly to be sublime and end by becoming monotonous and empty of lifegiving details like hymn tunes. They have often been slaves rather than the masters of their metres. This is partly because they have neglected the music of Byrd and Dowland so much more supple rhythmically than English poetry.' A little later he continues: 'Their movement, their vowel successions, their alliterations, have been too commonly splendiferous, until verbal splendour had lost its virtue in English . . . they frequently fail because they will not devote sufficient care and labour to anything much below the sublime . . .' Basil, who was still continuing his work on Firdusi and also on the larger Iranian literary tradition, draws a contrast between Omar Khayyam and his Victorian translator, Edward FitzGerald. Basil maintains that the rhythm in Omar's poetry is

> broken and colloquial or it dances or chatters as FitzGerald's never does. Omar is not upon his dignity. He is more concerned with the impression made by objects he has made than with that made by his own voice and figure; and those objects are such as the world is full of, not, for the most part, very august, though not necessarily therefore awkward.[2]

The view that poetry should attend to objects not 'very august' is an early announcement of some of the important yet humble items in Basil's last two long poems, for example a pot of tea brewing in *The Spoils*, an icicle melting in *Briggflatts*.

Doubtless these were some of the issues that Basil talked about in his long conversations with the respectful and attentive Carlos Drerup. Basil also sent a copy of 'The Lion and the Lizard' to Louis Zukofsky in New York City. Perhaps Basil hoped that his friend might help him to get it published there. But if Basil had any such hope, he was disappointed. He never saw this, one of his major pieces of literary criticism, in print.

*

The *pension* where Marian stayed when Basil was away in Portugal was run by prominent members of the German community on Tenerife, Baron von Loen and his wife. She had been the widow of the Kaiser's youngest son, a mentally retarded young man who had committed suicide when his wife ran away with the baron. Marian's landlords and their numerous German friends talked endlessly about the dramatic political developments in Germany and the policies of the new Chancellor, Adolf Hitler. On 30 June the violent crisis within the Nazi Party culminated in the Night of the Long Knives in which Ernst Roehm, General Schleicher and other prominent Nazis were, on Hitler's orders, dragged from their beds and massacred. Marian long remembered the shock and outrage of the English community in Tenerife. The Germans too were stunned. The following evening they all gathered together around a short-wave radio in a beach house to listen to the speech in which Hitler set out to justify what had happened. The Germans returned to their homes late that night insisting that the Führer had convinced them that he had done only what was necessary. The English were sceptical.

Some days later Marian received a letter from Basil from southern Portugal. He loved the white beaches of the Algarve and had found a place where he believed the four of them could live cheaply and comfortably. It was extremely remote, some fifty miles from the nearest town. All through his long life Basil would be attracted to such isolated places; but Marian found the proposal unrealistic and unacceptable. She was afraid to take her two somewhat sickly children so far away from a doctor. She was also daunted by the itinerary Basil sketched out for her. This entailed a trip from Tenerife to the Spanish port of Cadiz in what was little more than a cattle boat and then a fourteen-hour bus journey across Spain and into Portugal. It was midsummer and very hot. Marian would have to travel with a six-month-old baby and a two-year-old and just about no money. She refused to join her husband. She urged him to go to England, find work and find a home for them to go to there.

But Basil would not do this. Instead he returned to Tenerife angry and resentful at his wife. This, she later observed, 'was a low point in our marriage from which it never recovered'. They had managed to find a beautiful house in Santa Cruz, the Casa Fortuna, but they were not happy there. There was much quarrelling and blaming. Basil got into the habit of referring to his wife as 'mean and mingy Marian'. One way in which Basil hurt and embarrassed her was to flirt outrageously with Juana, the

Spanish nursemaid who for a pittance helped Marian with the children. Dark and shapely Juana was an extremely attractive twelve-year-old. All his life Basil would be drawn to pubescent or just post-pubescent girls. Every day when Juana left the Buntings to go home Basil would present her with a red rose. He caressed and fondled her. Marian was sure that the young girl was made ill at ease by these attentions. Juana tried to avoid Basil but to no avail. Her elder brother, a macho figure, finally gave her a terrible beating for, as he said, allowing herself to be compromised and cheapened in this way.

Interest in young women is a subject of a fine poem which Basil wrote during his time on Tenerife, 'The Orotava Road'. Forty-five lines of dexterously managed free verse and a vivid evocation of the place, the poem divides clearly into four parts. The first fourteen lines describe a passing fruit waggon drawn along the road by four white heifers under the goad of a driver who remains politely distanced and indifferent to the poet who so keenly studies him, even assessing the man's body under his shirt. Next down the road come camels with drivers who maintain a still firmer aloofness. But then in the third section come the milkmaids, 'friendly girls between fourteen and twenty'. They are responsive and smile and speak to him. And he in turn becomes greatly intrigued by them. This sudden personal involvement makes the poem more than an item of scene painting or travelogue. There is more mental undressing as the poet scrutinizes and ponders the milkmaids.

> You can guess their balanced nakedness
> under the cotton gown and thin shift.
> They sing and laugh.
> They say 'Adios!' shyly but look back
> more than once, knowing our thoughts
> and sharing our
> desires and lack of faith in desire.

The most ambitious poem produced by Basil during his Tenerife period is a much more sombre work than this piece of wry, wistful and amusing observation. Over six pages long, 'The Well of Lycopolis' was written, he remembered, when he 'got very gloomy in the Canaries'. It was, he judged, 'about as gloomy a poem as anyone would want'. Like 'Attis', the poem is in the tradition of *The Waste Land* and mocks and laments the vulgarization of life, particularly of love and poetry in modern times. But Bunting's poem is more thoroughgoingly concerned with the deterioration of sexual culture than Eliot's; there is also a recurrent ribaldry that is not to be found in *The Waste Land*. The poet-lover who is the protagonist and speaker of the poem admits that he is no singing bard; he can only

> tra-la-la
> a widowed tune in poor circumstances –
> tweet, tweet, twaddle
> tweet, tweet, twat.

Nor is he a robust lover; he endures 'detail by detail the cunnilingual law'. And sometimes even this relationship with the Venus figure in the poem is vicarious as he watches

> Aeolus' hand under her frock
> this morning. This afternoon
> Ocean licking her privities.

The title of the poem establishes the theme of sexual degeneration by recalling Gibbon's allusion in *The Decline and Fall of the Roman Empire* to a malign spring in Egypt. Bunting's epigraph supplies a further clause, explaining the spring 'with a draught of which the signs of virginity are town away'. This is the brutalizing water now used in London, says the protagonist, singling out Bloomsbury for special mention.

> We have laid on Lycopolis water.
> The nights are not fresh
> between High Holborn and the Euston Road,
> nor the days bright even in summer
> nor the grass of the squares green.

The poem often mentions nasty drinks and hangovers. When the here ageing goddess Venus (speaking rather stagey Cockney) and Polymnia [*sic*], the muse of sublime hymns and sacred songs, reproach the protagonist for his failures in love and art he responds with a powerfully unpleasant wish ending in some ugly monosyllables.

> May my libation of beer stood overnight
> sour on your stomach, my devoutly worshipped ladies,
> may you retch cold bile.

Nevertheless he has to admit that neither he nor his society in the years following the First World War have properly served the goddess or the muse. The poem dwells on the war and its horrific trench warfare, its Lycopolitan debauchery of the innocent, its patriotic claptrap phrases, its spreading of venereal disease. This is a period that has produced only 'Infamous poetry, abject love'. Yet the poem is not as unremittingly negative as 'Attis'. The fourth and final section, in part made up of a version of lines from Canto 7 of Dante's *Inferno*, concludes with a suggestion of a dawning compassion for modern people struggling with hellish waters now identified as the Styx. As he surveys the infernal river and those submerged in it, the protagonist ends with an image of beauty and possibility.

> The surface sparkles and dances with their sighs
> as though Styx were silvered by a wind from Heaven.

There is in 'The Well of Lycopolis' a larger, more encompassing vision than in the two previous sonatas. And this, despite the insistent echoes of *The Waste Land*, make it Basil Bunting's most successful work to date. Very much a 1930s poem with its pervasive gloom and disenchantment, it lacks the mature humaneness of the two greatest poems of the decade, *Burnt Norton* and *In Parenthesis*, both produced by poets of an older literary generation. But in its verbal richness and intricacy and its prosodic skill it compares favourably with anything produced by Bunting's contemporaries in this decade, that is to say by Auden and his circle.

The gloom which informs 'The Well of Lycopolis' was largely autobiographical. Basil felt both imprisoned and alienated on Tenerife; he was demoralized by his continuing lack of money and by his now unhappy marriage. The disillusion and disgust with sexuality that permeates the poem are deeply felt emotions. The swiftly deteriorating political situation in Spain and the Canaries was also making him ever more anxious. In both places Fascism was on the rise. The republic which had been proclaimed in Madrid in 1931 as a replacement for the centuries-old monarchy was extremely shaky. In 1936 the Popular Front, an alliance of centre and left-wing parties took office, determined to preserve the republic, but the reforms the Popular Front initiated provoked the Fascists in Spain to speak of rebellion. It was well known on Tenerife that Basil and Marian were strong supporters of the Popular Front. In 1935 Basil told Louis Zukofsky: 'I am not a Communist, nor have much sympathy with the communist dogmas: but the revolution I desire has several things in common with the Communist revolution . . . I desire Communism to be powerful.'[3]

Despite his well-known political attitudes Basil seems to have had social contacts with some of the Fascists on the Islands. Years later, reminiscing to Jonathan Williams, who reported the stories in *Rawthey's Madrigal*[4], Basil spoke of playing chess with the Fascist Governor of the Canaries, General Francisco Franco, who would later lead the revolution against the democratically elected government of Spain and go on to become the country's Fascist leader or El Caudillo. Although, when she came to annotate *Rawthey's Madrigal*, Basil's wife denied the story Basil maintained that he came to know the General through 'a man from St Helena who'd made friends with Franco, and, occasionally, there were all three of us at the table with a drink and the chess board'. It may have been at such meetings that Basil learned of the political developments both in the Islands and in Spain which so worried him. Basil sensed that the Fascists would soon attempt a take-over on the Canary Islands and was again in a state of panic about what might happen to him and his family.[5] A point came when he was convinced that he was in immediate personal danger. He abruptly fled from the island and made his way to England. From London he sent money (supplied presumably by his mother, who had recently returned to Britain) for Marian to bring herself and the children to join him there. They arrived in the third week of July 1936, the day after the Fascists rose against the government and the Spanish Civil War broke out.

A few days later Basil published in the *Spectator* an article entitled 'The Roots of the Spanish Revolt'. This marked one of the rare occasions when Basil's work appeared alongside that of his more renowned contemporaries. The contents page of the *Spectator* for 24 July 1936 announced that the film critic was Graham Greene and that the book reviewers included the poets Louis MacNeice and William Plomer and the novelists Richard Hughes and V. S. Pritchett. Ballet was covered by Adrian Stokes, author of *The Stones of Rimini*, a work inspired by Ruskin but even more by the 'Malatesta' cantos of Ezra Pound with whom, like Basil, Stokes had spent time in Italy. In that week's edition of the *Spectator* the art critic was Anthony Blunt, later Keeper of the Queen's Pictures and already a Communist sympathizer working as a secret agent for the Soviet Union.[6]

At this highly politicized moment Basil's own political beliefs appear to have become less intense. His article on the coming of the Spanish Civil War suggests a certain scepticism on his part concerning Socialism and the Left in general. This is not to say that the passionate supporter of the miners in Britain in 1926 had entirely abandoned his former political position. He writes: 'In my opinion, the Left has the better chance in the long run, for it has, in Spain, the better cause.'[7] But like George Orwell, soon to set off to Spain and to write *Homage to Catalonia*, Basil now had no time for the Communists. His article begins with an account of the ballot rigging by the Communist postmaster of Orotava. He goes on to regret that in Spain ideology, the party line, is more important than practicalities. 'Spanish socialism', he observes bitingly, 'is independent of economics.' He is, however, more sympathetic to the Socialists than to the Communists but deplores their part in failing to grapple with the real problems of the country. 'The problem of government in Spain is to feed the people. The peasants are half-starved and half-clothed, yet it has always been impossible to get a quorum in the Cortes for any economic debate.' The article ends with a scornful paragraph maintaining that neither of the leaders in the developing civil war had a policy to deal with Spain's material deprivation and suffering. 'Could Franco, could Largo Caballero, give the Canary peones, the Andalusian cowboys, enough to eat and a few coppers for the cinema? There is no reason to suppose that either of them has the slightest idea how to set about it.'

His tone could grow far more harsh and critical in some of the pieces he wrote in the later months of 1936, as he struggled to re-establish himself as a freelance journalist in London. One of these was his review of a book on the Victorian satirical novelist Samuel Butler by Malcolm Muggeridge. Basil tore into the Butler biography; he saw in it 'bluster', 'verbose repetition' and 'lack of humour'. Basil declared himself an admirer of Butler, regarding the opening chapters of *Erewhon* as 'better narrative prose than any other in English except Swift's and Borrow's'. Muggeridge's criticism of Butler does not show 'anything more elaborate than irritation'. Basil has nothing but contempt for the book. And

Muggeridge himself he places with Lytton Strachey and other Bloomsbury critics of the Victorian period, 'the hard-boiled but half-baked race
of perfunctory debunkers'.[8]

Bunting's bibliographer notes that his extremely hostile review 'was
said to have deeply harmed Bunting's prospects in the literary world
of London where Muggeridge had some influence'.[9] Marian begged
her husband to tone down the article. She too saw it damaging his
career. She also saw that its vehemence derived in part from the anger
and upset caused by their now very miserable marriage and their lack of
money.

In April 1936, a few months before Basil's review of Muggeridge
appeared in the *New English Weekly*, T. S. Eliot published in his
prestigious and influential periodical the *Criterion* a substantial work of
poetry by Basil. This was 'From *Faridun's Sons*', a seventy-four line version
of a passage from the *Sha na Meh* of Firdusi. It is a fine evocation of an
ancient civilization, geographically close to the one Eliot himself had
treated in his translation of *Anabase* by St John Perse. Basil's narrative
fragment tells of elemental experiences and emotions. In a manner that is
strikingly economical with words, the lines convey intense horror, shock
and grief, vengefulness and then more grief. The poem is a powerful
piece of dramatic narrative.

The people of Iran and Faridun expectantly await the return of his
son, the young king Iraj, from a military campaign. In great anticipation
they prepare his welcome.

> wine, music and dancers.
> They had fetched the drums and led the elephants
> out of the stable.

But then a messenger appears moving fast on camelback and bearing a
gold box. The poem becomes horrific as it tells vividly of the opening of
the box and the sight of Iraj's brutally severed head inside. After a
succession of images of numbing shock the poem tells of how Faridun
performed the desolating rituals of grief for his son, setting the pleasure
house alight, then burning the cypresses. After the old man's pleas to
God to live long enough to see Justice done, he and the people abandon
themselves to bereavement and mourning. The last section conveys most
strongly the mood of a people

> with tears in their eyes
> in black, past consolation,
> many a day, as though all life were death.

The writing in this fragment, which in subject matter clearly looks forward to Basil's next major poem *The Spoils*, is such as to make readers regret that he did not proceed further with his version of the *Shah na Meh*. And we can see why T. S. Eliot, usually the harshest critic of Basil's poetry, should have been ready to publish this. It is one of the major achievements from Basil's time on Tenerife.

After their return from the Canaries Basil and his family went to live in a flat at 6 South Hill Mansions in South Hill Park in Hampstead. It was a Victorian property in a fashionable suburb with a view over the Heath. Basil and his mother signed the lease. Marian refused to make such a commitment. The flat was rather cramped accommodation for the five of them and clearly tensions between Basil and Marian worsened. But the couple did their best by their children. Bourtai remembers Basil reading to her from Kipling's *Just So Stories* and Roudaba remembers being taken with her sister to see a Punch and Judy show. Granny Bunting used to intrigue the little girls by inviting them to reach into the deep cleavage of her ample bosom to find biscuits and sweets. The sisters were taken to the zoo in Regent's Park and to the old-fashioned music halls which Basil so enjoyed. There seems to have been a great number of outings. Perhaps they were a way of calming animosities that built up in the flat. Undoubtedly this home was a place of great unhappiness for Marian.

Here, little more than a month after arriving from Tenerife, she found herself pregnant for the third time. And here, some four months before her baby son was born, Marian decided that she could tolerate her husband's verbal and physical abuse no longer. Many years later Marian would tell her daughters of the cruelty to which she remembered being subjected, especially during her time in Hampstead. Roudaba remembers her mother speaking of a large blackthorn stick that Basil kept by the bedside with which to menace and control her. Marian also related how on one occasion in Hampstead when she was pregnant Basil had angrily pulled a dining-chair from under her so that she fell painfully to the floor.

Finally she determined to leave him and to take the children with her. Granny Bunting, seeing no future for the marriage, assisted her financially. In January 1937 Marian moved into a hotel with Bourtai and Roudaba. She retained a solicitor and obtained legal custody of the children. The three of them travelled on the liner *Queen Mary* to New York. They then took the train to Eau Claire, Wisconsin where Marian and her little girls were received back into her family.

For all his many rows with Marian, Basil was unhappy when she was gone; he was especially upset by the loss of his two children. For a while he remained with his mother in Hampstead, and in the spring of 1937 an old friend from Tenerife, the painter Carlos Drerup, came to visit them. Shortly afterwards Basil received the news that Marian had given birth to a boy in Eau Claire. Like his sisters the baby was named after a figure in the *Shah na Meh*; he was called Rustam. Perhaps Marian, in continuing the tradition begun with Basil of choosing names from the Persian epic, had not entirely rejected her husband. Indeed years later she contemplated being reunited with him. But Basil was never to see his son. That spring Basil left London. He was now in his late thirties. For almost three years he lived a lonely, rootless life as a solitary wanderer.

NINE
The Years at Sea
1937–1942

Basil went first to Essex. There in one of the coastal towns he saw a boat that he liked and that was for sale at a very good price. Presumably with some assistance from his mother he bought her for a hundred pounds. *Thistle* was her name and she was a six tonner. To live alone on a boat was, he thought, 'the best way to face up to the difficulty of life'. Expressing some of the frustration and Swiftian bitterness of that time he added: 'At least you were away from the mass of apes that call themselves mankind.'[1] Swift was one of the writers Basil most admired. Basil considered him one of the two or three best prose writers in English. And there can be no doubt that Swift's profound capacity for distaste and disgust with life was something that was also a part of Basil's character, and never more so than in the months and years after Marian left him.

For a time Basil sailed the many inlets on the Essex coast. Then he sailed south and through the Straits of Dover. He thought he might go over to France but discovered that the log of the *Thistle* needed complicated updating before she could legally enter a foreign port. So Basil sailed further west and decided to winter off the south coast of Devonshire. Sometimes he would sail up the River Dart and go ashore at the little town of Dittisham. Here there was an attractive waterside pub, the Ferry Inn, which became a great favourite with him.

To make a little money he would go to sea with the local herring fishermen or assist with the repairing of the seine-nets, but for the most part he lived a solitary and inexpensive life on the *Thistle* devoting himself to reading and writing. This was the year he wrote the sonnet beginning 'Let them remember Samangan . . .' a poem about grievous loss. Ostensibly about the Iranian city in which Rustam begot Sohrab, the poem also reads in its first five lines like a recollection of Venice and of his happiness there with Marian.

While still on the boat Basil also reviewed a volume of lyric poems translated from Chinese. The book had been sent to him by T. S. Eliot who published the review in the *Criterion* of April 1938. Around this time Basil received an offer for the *Thistle*. The buyer would pay almost twice the sum that the boat had cost Basil. He felt he had no choice but to accept. With the profit he made he determined to invest in some nautical education for himself, for he had decided that he would pursue a career in sailing. Accordingly he went back to Newcastle-upon-Tyne where he enrolled in the Nellist Nautical Academy, a cramming school for people seeking certification as mates or masters. The school was in an old house at 10 Summerhill Terrace, Rye Hill, in the same district of Newcastle where Basil had attended Miss Bell's dame school over thirty years before. The proprietor, old Mr Nellist, was a figure from Victorian times. He had a strong Geordie accent and sat smoking his pipe in such a thick cloud of smoke that Basil could not see across the room. From Mr Nellist he learned the theory of navigation, how to use the nautical tables and how to correct the error of the sextant. Mr Nellist and his associates took a special interest in Basil because he wanted to learn about sailing rather than steamship skills.

When he had acquired his qualifications Basil decided to try to market them in America rather than in Britain where unemployment was still acute. In the spring of 1938 he disembarked in New York bearing his sextant. He went to see his friend Louis Zukofsky who was much impressed by the 'yeoman muscles' Basil had developed during the year he had sailed and maintained the *Thistle* singlehandedly. Basil also visited Margaret de Silver. Perhaps he hoped that she might resume her financial support, but she appears to have shown no interest in renewing her role as his patroness.

However, he long remembered a musical evening in one of Margaret's luxurious homes with its numerous works of art when Margaret's twenty-year-old daughter Anne sang Handel's 'Largo'. Many years later Basil still recalled how Anne's singing 'in a light sweet insufficient voice', 'moved me as a clear block of marble must move a sculptor'. The following day in response to this performance of the aria he wrote the beautiful, if mysterious, two-part lyric beginning 'Not to thank dogwood nor/the wind that sifts' which he dedicated to Anne. The mention of bitterness in the poem may imply difficulties between Basil and the two de Silver ladies; it also contrasts with, and thus throws into relief, the writer's enduring susceptibility to what in a published note to the poem he called Anne's 'pure uncomprehending rendering of Handel's best known aria'.[2]

In New York Basil found it difficult to find work. But Louis Zukofsky thought there might be a possibility in Wisconsin. Louis's sometime lover was the fine lyric poet Lorine Niedecker of whom Basil once observed, 'No one is so subtle with so few words.'[3] Lorine lived in Wisconsin along with her father who owned the rights to fish carp over an extensive area of lake and river water. There was discussion about Basil going out to Wisconsin to assist the older man (now in his sixtieth year) and perhaps to become his partner. But Lorine's father finally decided against this idea. He felt that as a result of the Depression the market for carp had fallen too low to support the two of them.

Wisconsin was, of course, the state in which Basil's wife Marian and their three children were living, supported by her parents. When Bourtai and Roudaba learned that their father was in the United States they had high hopes that he would come and see them. He never did and they were hurt and disappointed. When, many years later, they asked him why he had not visited them during his 1938–9 stay in America he said that Marian's brothers resented him and that he feared they would beat him up. This fear may or may not have been justified. But it is understandable that Basil, without a job and without money, would feel reluctant to go and stay with his in-laws who doubtless criticized and resented him for his failure to sustain his marriage and his family.

During his time of unemployment in New York Basil spent time with old friends such as the painter Carlos Drerup, the scholar René Taupin and the poet William Carlos Williams. He also met another poet, Charles Reznikoff. Whilst looking for work he lived for a while with the Drerups in their home in Rockville Center, Long Island. He continued to spend time with Louis Zukofsky and was shocked and angered one day when Louis showed him a letter he had received from Ezra Pound in Rapallo. Pound's hostility to the Jews had been intensifying in recent years and the letter was full of what Basil called 'anti-semite bile'. In great indignation he wrote to Pound harshly criticizing him for the hurt done to Louis. Very much an anti-Fascist, Basil denounced all forms of racism and said it made him sick to see Pound cover himself with such filth. To write to Louis in that way, he went on, was very close to what could only be called the behaviour of the skunk. He deplored the 'rot' of Pound's mind and heart.[4] It was a critical moment in the history of his friendship with Ezra Pound, the most important and determining one in Basil's life. The relationship, which was from now on exclusively a matter of exchanging letters, did survive but was less easy than before. In the coming years Basil would often prefer to correspond with Dorothy Pound, clearly assuming that she would pass on his news and thoughts to her husband.

The process by which Basil distanced himself from Ezra Pound and, on certain issues of literary, cultural and intellectual importance, came to oppose him, had been underway for some time before this angry letter was written. The process is clearly visible in the annotations which Basil took the trouble to make to two of Pound's prose works. Pound had published his *ABC of Economics* in 1933; he wrote it in about ten days and most readers find it somewhat confused and slapdash. Basil's marginalia in his copy of the book make no allowances; his comments reveal his sometimes radical disagreements with its author. When Pound states that economics is a science and that its scope as a science must be defined, Basil responds by noting that economics is not a science but rather a department of law and justice. Pound's claim that no one in any society has the right to blame his troubles on any one else elicits from Basil a scribbled 'This is sheer nonsense.' Lower down in the margin he criticizes Pound's logic, observing that Pound's statement is also directly contrary to the assumption on which the book is based, collective responsibility for economic conditions. Sometimes Basil becomes exasperated by his former mentor. When Pound writes that in the early nineteenth century very few men thought about government, Basil responds with a three-word sentence: 'This is balls.'

In 1938 Ezra Pound published a much longer prose work, his *Guide To Kulchur*. Basil's numerous and often lengthy marginalia in this book constitute a spirited debate, a confrontation even, with the man with whom he had first studied the art of poetry. They disagree about the nature of language. When Pound insists on the need for clear definition, Basil responds by writing that 'Only a lack of understanding of what language is can make any[one] but [a] saboteur demand "definition".' Basil clearly still retains the notion of language which he had expressed in his poem 'Villon'. At the foot of the page on which Pound speaks of the importance of medieval scholasticism for every man who wants to set his ideas in order Basil writes: 'A man who wants to set his ideas in order wants to kill them: and that is what he will achieve via this misconception of scholasticism. He will substitute relations of language for relations of time, space, emotion etc. He will become rigid: blind to what seems, because of mere grammar to gainsay him.' A thinker much admired by Pound is Leibnitz, but Basil rejects the German philosopher declaring him to be 'another word-deceived and word deceiver'. And when Pound stresses the importance of ideas 'greek ideas, roman ideas, medieval, [*sic*] ideas', Basil retorts: 'Balls. The best thinking isn't ideas.' Their disagreements are often over very erudite matters. Basil's annotations challenge Pound's statements about Aristotle, Alexander the Great, Confucius, the history of money, Roman law, David Hume. When Pound's anti-semitism shows itself in some sentences about the issue of *neschek* or corrosive usury where he suggests that 'the forbidden fruit of hebrew story is a usury parable', Basil writes that 'This reads like a silly paragraph.' The poet who in *The Spoils* and *Briggflatts* will take up the issue of the nature and meaning of history here refutes Pound's view of the subject. By Pound's one-sentence paragraph that asserts 'You can write history by tracing ideas, exposing the growth of a concept', Basil has written 'You falsify it so.'

The differences in thinking and sensibility between the younger and older man are not invariably on a high intellectual level. At one point it is a matter of gastronomy. Pound praises French restaurants and cuisine as a high form of civilization superior to anything available in Italy. This clearly irritates Basil who writes in the margin: 'The guy has no palate. Food is better in Italy than France, except in expensive joints.' Such minor disagreements mount up and join the major ones to create an attitude of deep disenchantment. At the end of Part I of the *Guide To Kulchur* Basil's summary of his views on Pound's notions of civilization is both negative and dismissive; 'seems a thin kind of civilisation that appeals to E. P. One with anemia; or chlorosis. An adolescent's rather priggish, very egocentric dream.'

Until late in life and even afterwards Basil was regarded in some quarters as a follower and disciple of Ezra Pound. The annotations to Pound's *Guide To Kulchur* show that by the late 1930s Basil held literary and philosophical views that were markedly different from those of his sometime teacher.

In the summer of 1938 Basil managed to get a short-term job captaining a schooner owned by a very wealthy man who wished to sail to various points on the eastern seaboard. Basil was especially impressed by the quiet beauty of Chesapeake Bay. After his contract expired Basil decided to try his luck in Los Angeles. During the first part of 1939 he was hired by several shipowners and he came to like southern California. In later years he would remember with pleasure the character and atmosphere of Los Angeles before the freeways were built. He also grew very fond of Californian wines.

But living was precarious. None of his jobs offered permanence. Then in the first week of September 1939 came the news that Britain had gone to war with Nazi Germany. In his *Autobiography* William Carlos Williams writes, 'Basil had been a conscientious objector in England during the First World War and they had given him some rough treatment. It is worth noting, however, that for the Second World War he rushed across the United States from California to go to England, as fast as he could, to enlist.'[5] The suggestion here that Basil's hasty return home was prompted by political or ideological reasons may in part be true. He was profoundly hostile to Fascism. But it is also the case that Basil saw in the coming of the war new possibilities for employment. Certainly he volunteered for military service right away. But he was disappointed. The forces were not eager to recruit a man now in his fortieth year. In August 1940, almost a year after the war had begun, he wrote despondently to Louis Zukofsky that he remained idle. He had got himself on waiting lists for the army and the RAF but that was all. Since his return from California his only income had derived from six lectures he had given for the Workers' Educational Association on history from Alexander the Great to the Middle Ages. Otherwise he had to live off his mother. Annie Bunting had by now left London and bought herself a house in Throckley where she had grown up and where she still had relatives. Close to destitution Basil had no choice but to go and live with her there. To make matters worse, in 1940 Basil heard that his wife had divorced him. Marian, who was contemplating remarriage to a neighbour in Eau Claire, had finally been granted her decree absolute by the Wisconsin court. Basil was close to despairing about his future.

Yet in the end he managed to get himself accepted into the RAF. He feared that at the medical examination his poor eyesight might cause him difficulties; but the doctor in charge turned out to be an old friend of his father's and allowed him to memorize the letters on the eyechart before taking the test. In this way Basil scraped through and, in his forty-first year, became Aircraftsman Bunting, serial number 1119305. He was then sent to RAF Padgate to do basic training before being assigned to a squad in Hull that was being taught to man balloons. In the Second World War large balloons were used both as anti-aircraft devices and as reconnaissance tools. Basil's squad of trainee balloonists at Hull was made up almost entirely of Welshmen some of whom could not speak English.

Always interested in languages Basil now learned Welsh and felt rewarded by being able to read the great poetry in that language in the original.

After he had finished his balloon training Basil was posted to Leven on Largo Bay on the eastern coast of Scotland. Here he served on the *Golden Hind*, one of several luxury yachts commandeered by the government from millionaires and converted for use in the balloon service. The yachts had been fitted with powerful diesel engines and their masts had been removed to make way for the balloon ropes. The accommodation on the *Golden Hind* was superb and the food excellent. The authorities classed service on the balloon ships as 'dangerous and difficult work at sea'; but conditions on the *Golden Hind* were so comfortable that it was difficult to get the crew, partly RAF, partly Navy, partly civilian fishermen, to go ashore when they had a day in harbour.

The balloon ships were extremely vulnerable to enemy attack; the crew had only their personal weapons. Louis Zukofsky was taken aback to read in a letter that Basil had a machine gun and asked his Quaker friend how he felt about using such a weapon. Characteristically Basil replied in a way that related the practical and the aesthetic.

> What do 'I feel with a machine-gun?' Well it depends on the gun.
> I criticise a machine by nearly the same criteria as I do a work of art. A Lee-Enfield rifle, a Hotchkiss machine gun, have nothing superfluous nor fussy about them. They are utterly simple – having reached that simplicity via complication and sophistication galore. The kind of people who, if they had literary minds at all, would like euphemism or trickiness, prefer Lewis guns or Remington or Ross rifles. My machine-gun is a Hotchkiss and I feel toward it something similar in kind to what I feel for Egyptian sculpture . . . I think Holbein or Bach or Praxiteles, as well as Alexander, would have appreciated a Hotchkiss gun.[6]

There is no evidence that Basil ever had to use his machine gun in combat but he and his colleagues in the balloon ships had to undertake some dangerous missions. In June 1941 Nazi Germany attacked the Soviet Union and shortly afterwards Britain's programme of aid to her new ally began. The balloon ships had to escort the convoys that carried supplies up the North Sea, through the icy waters of the Arctic and into the Russian port of Murmansk. Some of the convoys were marshalled in Largo Bay close to where Basil and the *Golden Hind* were based.

Sometimes Basil would climb Largo Law, the hill above the town of Leven, to watch. The sight supplied a striking concluding image for his poem that deals with the war, *The Spoils*.

During his time in Leven Basil made friends with Violet, a young local girl who worked as a secretary. According to Rick Caddel and Anthony Flowers Violet typed up Basil's poems for him;[7] and she is the dedicatee of the only poem that Basil datelined from the war years. Attributed to the year 1941 it reads as if Basil could imagine that his career as a poet might not continue. Addressed 'To Violet, with prewar poems', it begins, 'These tracings from a world that's dead/take for my dust-smothered pyramid'.

Before the end of 1941 an altogether new balloon technology was developed and Basil suddenly found that his expertise was no longer required. He was sent ashore. He had been promoted to the rank of leading aircraftsman, but his future assignment was uncertain. At first he was ordered to an RAF base in Scotland for a course in driving heavy trucks. One day when it was his turn to practice leading a convoy of lorries, he noticed a sign to George Younger's Brewery, so he led the convoy there and entered the yard. His superior officer and instructor remonstrated angrily with him but Basil's independence of mind was rewarded. As a friendly, supportive gesture the brewers gave every airman a free drink.

The question of what would happen to him next in the RAF greatly worried Basil. He decided to try a long shot. He wrote a letter to the Air Ministry in London describing his knowledge of the Persian language and asking if the Ministry could make use of it. After some time he received orders to present himself for an interview in Whitehall. Upon his return to duty in Scotland he heard nothing from London and feared that his initiative had come to nought. But to his great surprise, relief and excitement he finally received a reply that he was to be posted to Iran as an interpreter.

The journey was long, roundabout and uncomfortable. With German and Italian armies in the Mediterranean theatre he could not travel the most direct route. He sailed first to Sierra Leone where the grandeur of the mountain ranges made a lasting impression upon him. He then crossed Africa by road and train to Kenya and then to Natal where he embarked on a troopship bound for India. Here he had a case of scurvy and lost several teeth. From Bombay he made his way westwards to Iran.

His arrival there began a great upswing in his fortunes and an exciting decade in his life. A literary initiative undertaken casually with Ezra and Dorothy Pound some ten years before now had the effect of transforming his career. Iran brought him fascinating new experiences of life, love and art. It made him a different man and a different poet.

TEN
A Very Good War and a Lively Peace
1942–1950

When Basil arrived in Teheran in the spring of 1942 the nominal ruler of Persia was the young inexperienced Shah, highly uncertain about the extent of his powers. He had only recently replaced his father on the 'Peacock Throne' and found himself head of a state divided into two zones of influence dominated by foreign powers. His northern border had been infiltrated by military and political personnel from the neighbouring Soviet Union, and as Hitler's armies pushed deeper into southern Russia, the Soviets prepared a stubborn defence of Iran and its invaluable oilfields. The southern part of the Shah's dominions was, as it had been since Victorian times, a British zone of influence, an outlying element of the strategy for the defence of India. In 1912 British investors created the Anglo-Persian Oil Company which developed a vast oil refinery at Abadan near the head of the Persian Gulf. Just before the outbreak of the First World War the British government purchased a controlling interest in the Company which, as the age of the internal combustion engine progressed, became an indispensable part of Britain's economy and defence. To protect this vital interest London sent out a large number of technicians, diplomats and soldiers. They constituted what was virtually a colonial administration. Despite the protest of nationalists such as the eloquent young lawyer Mohammed Mossadeq in Persia's second city Tabriz, the country was in many respects a protectorate. Like his father before him, the new Shah could do little without British approval.

His political problems were not, however, all the creation of foreign powers. He found it difficult to control and reconcile the several racial and religious groups that made up the population of his ancient and dramatically beautiful country. Among the most colourful of these peoples were the Bakhtiari tribesmen of south-west Iran. For generations they and a related tribe, the Lurs, had not feared to defy the government in Teheran when they considered their interests threatened. A nomadic, Islamic people then numbering some 600,000 and made up of related patriarchal lines each headed by a chieftain or 'khan', the Bakhtiari engaged in spectacular mass migrations twice a year. In late April they would fold their tents and set off in search of new grassland for their sheep, cattle and horses. After a long perilous climb through the snow-capped Zagros mountains the Bakhtiari would descend to the sub-tropical lowlands and ford wide, fast-flowing rivers to reach their summer pastures. Here they would remain until September when they recrossed the mountains to return whence they had come.

An American film-maker who had spent time with the Bakhtiari some seventeen years before Basil's arrival had been greatly impressed by their costume of 'black coat, white sash, black full skirt-like trousers, soft white shoes and the jaunty little round black hat'.[1] His visual imagination was captivated by the landscape through which the tribesmen journeyed: 'Shining gold and red in the west. Snow-mountains dyed golden. Green valleys, black tents, rock-covered hills – all this tinted and radiant with glowing gold.'[2] And the epic character of their journey excited him:

> Yes, hundreds of thousands of tribesmen and vast herds, unac-countable, will be astir. On horseback, afoot, women carrying cradles on their backs and driving beasts loaded with all their possessions, men, children, animals, will struggle onward.
>
> Up over hill and mountain, on through desert and forest, beaten by storm and rain, sweating under a burning sun, shivering in glacial snows – over thousands of miles of wilderness the migratory tribes of Persia will be on the move.[3]

The southern part of the tribal area lay close to the vast British oil refinery at Abadan near the head of the Persian Gulf. Some of the Bakhtiari worked for the British and most Bakhtiari were keen to buy rifles from them. The tribesmen were passionately interested in shooting, but there were others beside the British who in 1942 could supply rifles to these brilliant, horseborne marksmen. The Bakhtiari country and Abadan were right on Iran's border with Iraq where, a year before, there had been a pro-Nazi Prime Minister, Rashid Ali, and where German agents and their employees were still at work. Fascist agents also operated from the nearby French colonies of Syria and Lebanon which remained loyal to the German-controlled Vichy government established in France after that country's capitulation to Hitler. As the German armies threat-ened Iran and its oil by their advances into southern Russia, German espionage sought to create a political power base inside Iran by winning, or purchasing, the goodwill of the independent-minded Bakhtiari people. British Intelligence worked strenuously, desperately, to prevent this. The loss of Persia and the oilfields would have a drastic effect upon global strategy.

Espionage activity was rife on both sides. In August 1943 the British Ambassador to Iran, Reader Bullard, warned the Foreign Office, 'Reported continual arrival of German agents by air has greatly aggravated an already dangerous situation.'[4] A few days later he reported 'early this morning our people captured two Germans in this country. One has been living in hiding . . . The other, a recent arrival, was taken with a secret wireless transmitter.' A cause of special concern to the British was the Persian General Zahidi, the military governor of Isfahan and a strong German sympathizer. Fearing that Zahidi might instigate a pro-German rising among the Bakhtiari, the British brought in one of their most daring agents, Fitzroy Maclean. In his autobiography Maclean later described how he kidnapped the general at gunpoint from among his heavily armed bodyguards and whisked him away to a British airfield from where he was flown to detention in Palestine.[5]

If Basil was not, at the outset, instructed to participate in the complex struggle going on between the pro-German and the pro-British families within the Bakhtiari, he very soon found himself involved. For though the antique Persian he had taught himself was not very effective in communicating with the people of Teheran, it was readily intelligible to the members of this ancient tribe. His formal position was that of interpreter to an RAF squadron based in the country of the Bakhtiari. He had to travel around the 75,000 square kilometres of wild terrain that made up this region, assisting with the construction of various installations which Bakhtiari workmen were helping to build for the British. After the war he made large claims for his achievement as a British agent. In 1951, when he was again in Iran working in British Intelligence, he told a visitor that 'He had quelled a German-aided revolt of the Bakhtiari tribesmen almost single-handed, and to that extent he may have altered the course of the war, for the Germans were within an ace of succeeding in creating a foothold in Persia.'[6] The justification for such boasts can only be assessed at some time in the future when Basil's MI6 file is available for public inspection and no longer protected by the Official Secrets Act.

Basil came to feel intense admiration for the proud, courageous Bakhtiari. He loved them, he told Louis Zukofsky, as he did the peasants of southern Italy, 'as burningly as ever I loved'.[7] And they clearly took to him. He was often invited to enjoy their lavish hospitality. On one occasion he drove up into one of their mountain strongholds where the feast began about noon. For some nine hours hosts and guest alternated tea and whisky all the time eating little sweet cakes. About nine o'clock in the evening each diner was served a large plate of porridge. Then each was brought half a turkey smothered in rice. The final course was a leg of mutton for each person. After all this food Basil felt terrible. It was a relief when the time came to go and lie down in the tent the Bakhtiari had prepared for him.[8] On other occasions the tribesmen entertained him 'as Bakhtiari should, with pipes and drums, dancers and singers, sweet-meats and rice and strong drink and a man to fan me all the evening – very welcome in the terrific heat of Khuzistan'.[9]

Basil's first stay in Iran was brought to an end by distant events that were changing the course of the war. By the beginning of 1943 in the great battle for Stalingrad the Russians had managed to halt the German advance. The Red Army then began to drive Hitler's forces westwards; the military threat to Iran and her oilfields was at an end. With the Germans in retreat the British decided that the weapons and ammunition they had stockpiled in Iran would be more use to the Eighth Army in the campaign against the Germans and Italians in the desert of north Africa. The supplies in Iran were loaded into a vast number of trucks and the convoy was ordered to transport them to Tripoli, near El Alamein, site of a recent British victory, for further consignment. Basil was directed to help organize and lead the convoy and to drive one of the trucks. It was a long and memorable journey. They set off from the head of the Persian Gulf near Basra; they drove across the deserts of southern Iraq and Saudi Arabia; they crossed the Red Sea; they continued on through Egypt, into Libya, and came at last to their destination at Tripoli. The journey had been one of more than fifteen hundred miles. Some members of Basil's squadron experienced discomfort and difficulties; the trucks often broke down in the hot desert sun. Some of the Arab drivers were none too expert; they would have been happier on camels. But at last the long trek was completed. They had done it in a month which, Basil thought, was 'almost a miracle'.

The desert battlefield near to Tripoli where the British had recently pushed back Rommel's army made a strong visual impression on Basil. Littered about were the broken pieces of aeroplane fuselage and tanks with their turrets and guns twisted crazily about. There were smashed and abandoned cars and shelled trucks with German beer still in their cabs. Hundreds of Axis prisoners of war marched eastwards, unguarded. Six years later when Basil wrote *The Spoils*, his fine, long poem about the

Second World War (it is also a poem about all war), he used these images remaining from the victory in the western desert to create an especially vivid passage.

But at the time of his actual arrival in Tripoli Basil was evidently in a mood for more light-hearted pursuits. The line in *The Spoils* about Arab 'girls hawked by their mothers/from tent to tent' suggests one likely indulgence. He did also remember taking part in a coarse practical joke. Shown a castor tree by a local guide Basil and some of his companions from the squadron collected a bagful of the nuts and took them back to the mess. They told the cooks that the oil from the nuts was a delicate local flavouring. The chefs sprinkled the oil very liberally over the food they were preparing. The following day members of the squadron spent a good deal of time running to queue agonizingly at the latrines. Basil and his fellow conspirators were greatly amused by the sight, but their laughter ended when they were summoned to a disciplinary hearing and, Basil reported, reduced to the ranks. In his case this meant losing the corporal's stripes he had gained some time earlier and becoming again a mere aircraftsman.[10]

This humiliation did not last long. Clearly British Intelligence still had need of Basil and, to give him the necessary standing and authority, arranged for him to be commissioned as an RAF officer. He was raised to the rank of Pilot Officer. His new standing was to assist him in his assignments with the Eighth Army and its allies as they invaded and captured the island of Sicily and then landed in Italy and slowly fought their way northward. As it became liberated, Italy posed difficult diplomatic, political and intelligence problems for the Allies. Churchill and the British supported the claim to power of King Victor Emmanuel despite his twenty years of countenancing the Fascist government of Mussolini. The Americans, uncomfortable with the idea of a monarchy, despised the king and preferred to work with the liberal opposition parties whose leaders now returned from exile. The Americans were also made uneasy by the vast number of Italians hastening to join the Communist Party. Much of the military activity by the Italian partisans north of the German lines was directed by the Communists. What would happen when the Germans were finally driven out? Certainly there was a good deal on which Basil, as a speaker of Italian and a former resident of Italy and student of her politics and culture, could advise.

Basil broke his journey from north Africa to Sicily with a brief stay on the island of Malta which the Luftwaffe were still attempting to obliterate. This experience would also figure in *The Spoils*. When he arrived in Sicily in July 1943 he helped to set up General Eisenhower's war-room and used his new rank to deal with a succession of problems. He took charge of the telephone network co-ordinating the Allied landings on the island. In the city of Catania, where there was famine as the Germans retreated, Basil swiftly organized a peasants' market, and also created a missing persons' bureau to cope with the massing of uprooted families. But for about a year his main task was to serve as a de-briefing officer. It was strenuous work but, he later concluded, it made him much shrewder in his estimation of men and helped him in surpassing other political intelligence officers when, after the war, he worked for MI6. His job was to plan the missions for a fighter squadron. In so doing he used not just official information but also his own personal knowledge of the temperament and capacity of each of his pilots. He would 'brief' them by giving them their exact orders, including their route, flight plan and an estimate of the amount of enemy 'flak' which they would encounter. When the sortie was over and the fighters returned he would de-brief each pilot, compiling a careful and thorough report of all that had happened. Basil found these procedures 'good mental training'[11] but also demanding and exhausting. The squadron was frequently in action and there was always a flood of information to assess and assimilate; there was little time to sleep or even to eat properly. Basil continued the same work as a de-briefing officer when the campaign moved on into Italy. He was nearly killed as he drove north out of Naples when a German delayed-action bomb suddenly exploded and destroyed the Post Office.

It also seems likely that British Intelligence employed Basil's knowledge, gained as a deckhand many years before, of the rocky, intricate coastline of the Italian Riviera south of Genoa. Writing to Dorothy Pound after the war Basil recalled how he had been the officer in Catania who had briefed the American Mitchell bombers that were ordered to fly north to bomb the Zoagli viaduct in the mountains south of Rapallo. Weather conditions prevented the pilots from completing their mission; they dropped their bombs on Rapallo instead. Around this time Ezra and Dorothy had been forced to go and live with Ezra's mistress, Olga Rudge, in her small apartment in the mountainside village of Sant' Ambrogio just above Rapallo. The Italian authorities had compelled the Pounds to leave their seaside apartment for reasons of military security. Olga was the only person who could receive them. Living at close quarters with his

106

wife and mistress, who hated each other, began that hell which continued until May 1945 when Pound, the Mussolini sympathizer, was arrested by Italian partisans and handed over to the Americans. After a spell in the military prison at Pisa which nearly broke his mental and physical health the now sixty-year-old Pound was flown to Washington DC to stand trial for treason. The pro-Mussolini broadcasts which he had made over Rome Radio directed at Allied military personnel in the Mediterranean theatre had led, in his absence, to his indictment by a Grand Jury in Washington DC, back in July 1943, on the very day Mussolini's government fell.

In the middle of 1944 Basil found himself in a peculiar situation. At Naples he was but a few hundred kilometres away from his old friend and sponsor at Sant' Ambrogio. But it was impossible for him to seek Pound out. They found themselves on different sides in a war. The political divisions between them that had exploded in the 1930s had put them in opposing camps. The distance between Sant' Ambrogio and Naples was in the war torn Italy of 1944 an uncrossable gulf.

Later on in the year Basil's fighter squadron was transferred from Italy to Normandy to supply extra air support to the Allied armies in the aftermath of the D Day invasion. But Basil did not stay in France for very long; he was ordered back to London. With the war now clearly approaching its end, Basil looked foward to demobilization and to the gratuity that demobilized members of the armed forces were to be given. His plan was to use the money to buy a boat again, live cheaply at sea, and write. But this was not to be. The Foreign Office at the instigation of MI6 offered him a job so well paid that he could not refuse it. They proposed that he take up the position of British vice-consul at Isfahan, the beautiful, historic city on the eastern edge of the country of the Bakhtiari.

Basil became fascinated and entranced by the city. From it he developed a deeper understanding of, and an appreciation for, Islamic architecture. For a poet who would become known as very much a poet of place Isfahan become one of his very special places; in *The Spoils* it figures as an image of what is good in life. For Basil Bunting the city came to have the same sort of importance that Byzantium had for Yeats. In Basil's letters there pulses the same passion for Isfahan that fired the writing of George Nathaniel Curzon, *The Times* correspondent in Iran in Victorian times. This is how the future Viceroy of India depicts Isfahan at its peak in the seventeenth century when it was made capital of the entire Persian empire by the renowned Shah Abbas.

This great monarch would ill have sustained his own conception of royalty had he not provided for himself, and adorned with all the magnificence that an enlightened taste could suggest, a new seat of residence and power . . . Of the new empire which he had won, and which stretched from Georgia to Afghanistan, Isfahan was the natural geographical centre. The instincts of a prudent centralisation commanded him to fix his capital at a spot where he would be within equal distance of all corners of his huge dominion, and where, in reasonable proximity to the Persian Gulf, he could at once overawe the maritime provinces, control the foreign trade, and enter into easy diplomatic relations with the potentates of Europe. This decision arrived at, he sketched the outlines of a colossal plan. A new city, approached by superb bridges and stately avenues, furnished with public buildings, as beautiful as they were large, and embellished by terraced gardens, and palaces, and pavilions, sprang into existence. The embassies of mighty sovereigns flocked to the new capital from the uttermost parts of Europe, and were received with all the splendour of a court immensely rich and versed in a fanciful and fastidious etiquette. The factors of great trading corporations occupied a position little short of the accredited representatives of royalty; and a life of gorgeous ceremonial, mingled with holiday festivity, rendered Isfahan the most famous and romantic of the cities of the east.

In the time of Abbas II the king possessed, in addition to his own numerous residences, 137 royal palaces (probably in many cases only private mansions) in different parts of the city, acquired either by inheritance, purchase, or seizure, and devoted to the entertainment of foreign envoys and strangers of consideration. When the former were received in public audience in the Chehel Situn, or Forty Pillars, all business was suspended for the day; a magnificent but tedious ceremonial preceded and delayed the approach of the ambassador to the foot-stool of royalty; gorgeous banquets, culminating in general intoxication, followed; while in the Great Square the populace were regaled with the exibitions of wrestlers, fencers, jugglers, and acrobats, with polo-matches and puppet-shows; and with combats of animals, bulls, rams, buffaloes, wolves, and, on great occasions, lions and panthers. When night fell fantastic fireworks illumined and prolonged the festive scene.[12]

Basil delighted in the magical city and its history and elegant buildings just as much as Curzon had done. And it was a pleasure for him to be working with the Bakhtiari again. Basil later told Louis Zukofsky that leaders of the tribesmen had sent a formal note to the British government requesting his return to them. But British Intelligence also had their own reasons for sending him; they needed an experienced agent in the area. For though the covert political struggle against German influence was at an end, another struggle had begun. The British had agreed to reduce and then abolish their military presence in Iran after the war. But the Soviets had not. The Russians also began to put pressure on the Shah to accept members of the communist Tudeh party into the cabinet in Teheran. The most determined resistance to Tudeh participation in the government came from tribesmen such as the Bakhtiari and the Luri. Basil's tasks in Isfahan included briefing the Bakhtiari about the larger political context and reporting back to London.

Basil, the once impoverished Bohemian, now lived in style. In January 1945 he had been promoted to the rank of Squadron Leader in the RAF, the equivalent of a Major in the Army. This was a rank which he would retain in war and peace until his career in Intelligence came to an end some nine years later. In Isfahan he had a fine house and garden and was looked after by four servants. He was also provided with a horse and a groom. In a letter to Zukofsky he commented 'you wouldn't recognise the old bum in his present surroundings'.[13] Another old friend in new York with whom Basil still occasionally corresponded was Carlos Drerup who later remarked that Basil's 'happiness in Iran was like a dream come true and reflected in his letters'.[14]

Basil had regular dealings in Isfahan with the American organization later known as the CIA and also with those working for the Soviets. When the Russians alerted him to the activities of a young American woman from Chicago he witnessed the silly, and in her case miserable, side of intelligence work. Formerly the mistress of a British official in South Africa from whom she passed information to the Japanese, she subsequently became the mistress of a British agent in southern Iran. An introduction to the British embassy in Teheran and an affair with one of its members brought her intelligence of possible interest to the Soviets. When she arrived in Isfahan, Basil, tipped off by the Russians, observed her and finally handed her over to the Americans. He thought that such a guileless, amateur spy would simply be told off and sent home to

Chicago. He was horrified to learn, three days later, that the American office of Strategic Services, the forerunner of the CIA, had shot her.

In June 1946 after some eighteen months of service in Isfahan Basil was recalled to England. He was sad to go. During a stopover in Cairo on his way home he wrote to Louis Zukofsky saying how he was going to miss the pleasant journeys 'amongst mountain tribes, long trips on horseback, mouflon (or wild sheep) hunts, banquets with provincial governors and cocktail parties with diplomats'.[15]

Basil went to live with his mother in her house at Throckley, the rather drab mining town a few miles east of Newcastle. And here one day in November a friendly letter arrived from Dorothy Pound who was then living in a small apartment in Washington DC close to St Elizabeth's mental hospital in which Ezra was being detained. So pleasant contact with the Pounds was resumed after the angry political quarrel of the late 1930s and after total silence for the duration of the war. In St Elizabeth's Ezra was completing his *Pisan Cantos* in which there are several kindly reminisces of Basil. Ezra remembered, for instance, how Basil had written the word Firdusi in Iranian script on the door of his house in Rapallo. He asked Basil to send him a copy of the script to include in the fourth of the *Pisan Cantos*. Basil spent a whole day working on a reproduction of the complex design for him. The inscription duly appeared towards the end of Canto LXXVII.

Ezra, ever the promoter and booster, also urged Basil to found a literary magazine as a platform for the poetry and poetics they believed in. But Basil felt that he had neither the energy nor the commitment to do so. He was somewhat ill at ease with the course of the modernist movement. He felt that Yeats, Ezra himself, Carlos Williams, T. S. Eliot and Marianne Moore were all stages on a road to a degree of subjectivity that precludes a readership. He thought that the road had finally reached this point in the poetry of Louis Zukofsky; he maintained that 'nobody *can* read Zukofsky'. Reading this statement in St Elizabeth's Ezra wrote over it an emphatic 'NO'.

Looking out on the dark colliery landscape around Throckley Basil contemplated buying a boat again and living at sea, but he found that boats were now very expensive. He also longed to return to Iran. He wrote enthusiastically to the Pounds about Isfahan and its beautiful architecture. He contemplated writing a book about the city. He urged the Pounds to get hold of the volumes on Iranian art and architecture by the American scholar Arthur Upham Pope. Meanwhile Basil wrangled with the Foreign Office about diplomatic appointments and salaries but gradually began to despair of obtaining anything. Life in the Throckley house was marked by the austerity of that time. The early months of 1947 were brutally cold in England and there was a great deal of snow. Basil and his mother, though living in a mining community, could not obtain sufficient coal to keep the house warm. Their ration was not enough. Gas for cooking was also inadequate, the pressure so low that often they could not boil a kettle on the stove. Basil's attitude to the miners among whom he had grown up and whom his father had tended was changing. The industry had recently been nationalized by Clement Attlee's Labour government, and conditions had greatly improved. But Basil was irritated by their high wages and extra rations. He thought the miners' continuing demands unreasonable, particularly their insistence that a very big share of beer, in this society of shortages, should be earmarked for them. In this second year of a Labour government bent on creating a welfare state, Basil in his letters is no longer as sympathetic to the miners or the working class generally as he had been two decades before.

Food was tightly rationed in post-war Britain and this created a problem for Basil when he finally managed to buy his boat. How to provision her? Ration books operated on a weekly basis but Basil intended to be at sea for a far longer period. How could he assemble enough food? He finally hit on the solution of getting Dorothy Pound to send him some large 'unsolicited' food parcels from America. He would pay for them by putting money into the sterling account which she still maintained in the bank close to her old home in Kensington.

But before this manoeuvre could be started Basil had unexpected and wonderfully welcome news which made the parcels unnecessary. What he referred to as 'a Government department' offered him a job in Iran with an excellent salary, and he accepted with alacrity. He was asked to resume his combined activities in diplomacy and espionage. He was also given a higher diplomatic rank and more responsibility. In the spring of 1947, after kitting himself out with new clothes and a rifle, he returned to Iran. This time he was based in the embassy in Teheran. His position was that of Chief of Political Intelligence. He wrote to Louis Zukofsky in the first week of May 1947 that the job demanded 'all the astuteness and tact' that he could summon.[16] But he enjoyed his work. In that same year he told Dorothy Pound in a letter that he thought he would want to be 'at grips with people and outwitting them until I die'.

He was given good accommodation in Teheran, a fine, large house with a pillared terrace in an attractive suburban village, and he was supplied with an ex-army station wagon to use until his new car could be delivered. He found that he liked the ambassador, Sir John Le Rougetel, whose daughter Bridget was the same age as Basil's elder daughter Bourtai. Bridget keenly supported Basil's idea of inviting Bourtai to come over from Wisconsin for a while. Initially Marian agreed to the proposal and arrangements were made. Ezra Pound's son Omar, a young man whom Basil very much liked and admired and who was studying Islamic literature in Iran, agreed to escort Bourtai to Teheran. But at the last moment Marian decided against the idea. Basil was angry and disappointed.

He travelled a great deal throughout Iran renewing and developing his contacts. His journeys were often dangerous, on narrow, ill-maintained roads over high snow-capped mountains and into valleys where bears and wolves prowled. Though often tired out by the long hours of driving he found time and energy to continue studying the literature of Iran. He was very contented with the lifestyle of the country which he found free of the western cult of efficiency. He shared the Iranians' pleasure in their teas and tea ceremonies. He took to their favourite alcohol which was vodka. He fell in with their habit of opium smoking. He reported one specially memorable evening spent smoking opium in a remote province, with a colonel of police and an ex-governor general of the province. They produced the most sumptuous opium outfit that Basil had ever seen. The pipe was of the finest porcelain and ebony in a soft leather case embroidered with silver thread; the charcoal was burned in a chased silver brazier that stood on a specially made carpet. Basil smoked two pipes with his hosts but claimed that the experience meant little to him. He neither liked nor disliked it. To a friend he recalled the story of the three Iranians who had been indulging their vices in a suburban garden and late at night found the gate into the city locked. The drunkard urged that they batter down the gate. The hashish man disagreed; he suggested that they crawl through the keyhole. But their friend the opium smoker couldn't see what all the bother was about; he thought they should just lie down and sleep until the gate was opened in the morning.

In his first years in Teheran Basil developed a close friendship with another intelligence officer, Ronald Oakshot, who brought to espionage the skills of one who had worked both in banking and the Criminal Investigation Department at Scotland Yard. Basil once described his fifty-eight-year-old friend as, a 'hard-drinking ex-British officer "gone native" '. Oakshot was married to a very attractive Iranian woman in her mid-thirties; he was also infatuated with her younger sister who had her fourteenth birthday in 1948. He insisted that the girl live with him and his wife even when he was sent on a mission into remote Kurdestan. Oakshot enjoyed the Persian way of life; he especially liked his spectacularly beautiful sister-in-law to wear elegant clothes as she served as his winepourer or *sakki*. When Basil was introduced to her at the Oakshot home he fell immediately in love with her.

Her name was Sima Alladallian and she was half Armenian, half Kurd. She had finely formed features, luxuriant hair and long lithe limbs. She was also a tomboy who loved physical activities such as climbing trees, swimming and tennis. When her mother sent her to a boarding-school, she escaped repeatedly to the Oakshots and her mother finally gave up the idea of school. Her family belonged to the pro-British section of Iranian society. Her father had worked for the Anglo-Iranian Oil Company. He had died in 1946 when Sima was twelve and left his widow and daughter comfortably off. Sima was very much the baby of the family but her mother and sister were keen to see her married.

Sima was three years younger than Basil's older daugher Bourtai, now aged seventeen, and just about the same age as his second daughter Roudaba. Nevertheless Basil made up his mind to propose to her. He was fully aware that there would be those who would object to the idea of marriage between a fourteen-year-old girl and a forty-eight-year-old man. Under English law of the time Sima was not marriageable, had not even reached the age of consent. Such a marriage might, and indeed did, affect his position at the embassy and his standing with the Foreign Office. But such prudent considerations had no effect. Basil was utterly compelled by Sima's beauty. Supported and encouraged by her mother and sister he asked her to marry him.

Not altogether confident of her decision she accepted his proposal.

They went on a trip together to see the ancient monuments at Persepolis. They never forgot the great columns which were the remnants of the palace built by Darius, the King of Kings, extended by Xerxes and finally despoiled by Alexander the Great and his Greek soldiers when they conquered Iran in the fourth century BC. Basil and Sima marvelled at the large, dramatically carved animals, some of them mythical, that adorned the columns around which wolves wandered in the daytime. At night the engaged couple were entranced by the sight of the massive carvings standing out in bright moonlight against the dark blue Persian sky.

Then Sima had her doubts about the engagement and finally said that she did not want to marry Basil. He was utterly devasted. He told Dorothy Pound that when the lady who worked as his secretary saw the look on his face after he learned of his rejection, she locked up all the small arms and took away the key. Writing miserably to Margaret de Silver at the end of August 1948 he said that he felt like someone who had won the lottery and then learned that a mistake had been made. He acknowledged the problem of the thirty-four-year difference in age. He also recognized, he told his former patroness, that as the years went on Sima would be bound to tire of him. But he had hoped that this 'very young, beautiful, barbarous' girl 'without any of the usual assumptions and inhibitions' might be his for at least a few years.

He got his wish. Sima changed her mind and the marriage was on again. When in the spring of 1996 I talked to Sima about this decision she said that she had no regrets whatsoever and that if the marriage looked improbable from the outside, that was because everyone underestimated Basil's charm. The wedding took place on 2 December 1948 at the Teheran Club, the social headquarters of the large British colony in Teheran. Sima's mother and sister were present together with a number of schoolgirls who were Sima's friends and many of Basil's friends and colleagues from the embassy. By now it had been made clear to Basil that once he had married such a young bride, he could no longer retain his position at the embassy. He would need a new cover for his intelligence work. Nevertheless, despite this dismissal, the ambassador gave the couple a handsome wedding present, a set of liqueur glasses which Sima long treasured. The wedding reception was extremely lively but Sima did not remember how it ended. She had, she told me, far too much to drink to be able to do that.

On the day he gained his new wife Basil also wrote a letter to Zukofsky in which he spoke of a new literary love he had discovered in

Iran. This was the poet Rudaki whose 'Lament in Old Age' Basil had recently translated with the title 'Abu'abdulla Ja'far bin Mahmud Rudaki of Samarkand says'; Rudaki, Basil told his American friend, belonged in 'the list of the world's very great poets, even though the remains are so few and fragmentary'.[17] Certainly Basil's version of the 'Lament' is a fine addition to translated poetry in English. Over sixty lines in length it encompasses a succession of attitudes to the shock and demoralization of ageing. It begins with a long line, a 'fourteener' bursting out with dismay at the simple fact that 'All the teeth ever I had are worn down and fallen out.' The poet then ponders whether the loss of his once beautiful teeth was 'ill-luck' but concludes 'it was God's decree'. The wry humour is replaced by philosophic resignation as the poet goes on to consider the mutability of things. He remembers his more robust days as a lover and as a poet rejoicing in the acclaim and the money he received. But now come debility and poverty which are accepted with stoical calm. One section of the poem has an especial relevance to the situation of the translator at the time, that of an older man contemplating his teenage bride:

> What can you know, my blackhaired beauty,
> what I was like in the old days?
> You tickle your lover with your curls
> but never knew the time when he had curls.
> The days are past when his face was good to look on,
> the days are past when his hair was jet black.

A few weeks after their wedding, in January 1949, Basil and Sima set off for their honeymoon in England. Flying on a propeller-driven aircraft of the British Overseas Airways Corporation they had to have three stopovers. They landed first at Nicosia in Cyprus where Sima saw the sea for the first time in her life. They hired a taxi to take them to see some of the ancient Greek ruins. Then they flew on to Rome where Sima delighted in the opportunities for ballroom dancing. Then they were off, over the Alps, to Paris where Basil showed Sima the sights and some of his haunts of nearly a quarter of a century before. Finally they arrived in London and settled into luxurious quarters at the Savoy Hotel in the Strand.

Immediately there was a problem. Teenage Sima had a very hearty appetite but in England there was still stringent food rationing and the offerings in the restaurants were meagre. Basil's solution was to take his young wife to a succession of restaurants in Soho giving her one meal after another. Sima was amazed by the English food. Steaks were made of substitutes such as snook and whale not beef. The townscape of London was also a shock; everywhere including the West End there were still gaping bomb-sites. But she enjoyed spending money on clothes at the large department stores.

The newly weds then took the train north to Throckley, the first time Sima had been on a train, and Basil presented his young bride to his mother. Annie Bunting still lived in the red-brick Edwardian house she had bought for herself. She was now seventy-four-years old and looked, Basil thought, very old and unwell. Annie had stinted herself over the last few weeks in order to save up enough coupons in her ration book to buy a small roast with which to welcome her visitors. Sima was touched and there now began a strong and enduring affection between Annie and her daughter-in-law.

In London Basil had obtained a job with *The Times* as correspondent in Teheran. He was to be paid at the rate of £350 per year but the appointment was to be reconsidered after six months. He took up his duties when he and Sima returned to Iran in March. Though formally a journalist Basil also seems to have continued his intelligence activities. When he wrote from the Hotel Russell in London in January to Ralph Deakin, the Foreign Editor of *The Times*, concerning the job, he noted that he had reason to suppose that the appointment would not be unwelcome to the British embassy in Teheran and that he could hope for their assistance 'in appropriate matters'.[18]

The house where Basil and Sima lived when they returned to Iran had a sophisticated security system which included some half dozen highly trained guard dogs. The leader and most ferocious of these was Fortnum. Once when Basil and Sima were out, another agent arrived at the house and was shown by the servant into a sitting-room. The visitor placed his briefcase on the floor; Fortnum immediately sat beside the case as though claiming it. After some time the agent decided he could wait no longer and made to pick up his case. But Fortnum would not permit this. He forced the visitor to drop the case and proceeded, snarlingly, to keep watch over him for the several hours that passed before Basil and Sima, much embarrassed, returned home and reassured Fortnum. Some time later the dog's mouth was badly ripped when he fought an intruder trying to break into the saferoom where Basil kept his papers.

Basil wrote to Margaret de Silver in September 1949 describing how hectically busy his various jobs kept him. Having to drive about all day he had become as handy in the Teheran traffic with a big car as any of the taxi drivers. He had also travelled outside the capital. He had spent four days on a bad bus on bad roads travelling to one of the shrine cities, sacred to Islam, Meshed, a place of spectacular mosques. He spent two days there disguised, wearing the robes of an Islamic priest, a mullah, his camera concealed under the robes. Some time later he drove Sima and her cousin down to her native city, Isfahan. On the way they ate excellent kebab at Nejafabad and bought cotton sandals. A little later by the slow moving river Zayandehedrud came a sight that charmed Basil greatly: the shapely limbed Sima and her cousin trying to catch fish in the river by hand and tumbling in.

Despite these excursions Basil found himself confined to Teheran for most of the time. He complained to Margaret that he had no opportunity to read seriously; he had time and energy merely for detective stories. He added that he was not getting any writing done. However, his poem 'On The Fly-Leaf of Pound's *Cantos*' is datelined this year, 1949, in *The First Book of Odes*. It is a generous homage to his mentor, now at the nadir of his fortunes and reputation, still detained in St Elizabeth's mental hospital in Washington DC as psychologically unfit to face his trial for treason.

And despite his protestations that his job left him no time for literary pursuits, Basil was studying closely the work of another Iranian poet for whom he had developed an intense admiration. This was Manuchehri, a younger contemporary of Firdusi. A letter to Louis Zukofsky in July 1949 conveys the degree of Basil's enthusiasm. The comparisons that he adduces by way of 'placing' this new admiration are also interesting as indications of others who were important to him as a poet.

If one puts Homer and Firdosi [*sic*] carefully in one place and then looks for the three or four greatest poets remaining I don't see how anyone who has the luck to read him can omit Manuchehri. His variety is enormous and everything he did he did better than anyone else. You want the directness of some Catullus? Go to Manuchehri. You want the swiftness of Anacreon? Manuchehri. The elaborate music of Spenser? Go to Manuchehri. The formal, full dress ode with every circumstance of solemnity and splendor? Not Pindar, Manuchehri. Satire direct and overwhelming, Manuchehri all alone – no competitor.[19]

117

In the course of 1949 Basil did translations of poems by Manuchehri but he deemed only one of them good enough for inclusion in his *Collected Poems*.[20]. This is 'Shall I sulk because my love has a double heart?' which is rendered as a sonnet. It is a pleasing piece but scarcely illustrates the great and many qualities claimed for Manuchehri by Basil. Perhaps his sense of failing here as a translator is what led him to exclude other translations from his formal oeuvre.

During January 1950 Basil worked on one of his longest articles for *The Times*. Published on the 30th of that month, it was entitled 'Persia as a Modern State – Obstacles to Agricultural and Industrial Progress'.[21] This substantial piece depicted a society struggling unsuccessfully to modernize itself. Basil describes in detail the political deadlock, aggravated by corruption and electoral malpractice, that impedes action. He reports the difficulties caused by recent droughts, by unemployment and by an inadequate infrastructure, particularly in the country's ports which are in a state of rapid decay. But for all the parlous conditions prevailing in Iran Basil is impressed by a special quality in the people, their national pride. Colleagues in the newspaper business would later admire Basil's prescience as a political analyst and in this article he shows himself sensitive to the popular feeling that a year or so later would entirely destroy British influence in Iran. Basil warns his English readers that it is 'a strong emotion which ought to be respected'. It is founded 'on a half-conscious recollection of Persian history, its compact civilization, its individuality' all of which have been imperilled by the infiltration of the West and of Russia.

Basil, who was coming more and more to admire the Iranians and their way of life, could readily understand their growing nationalism. He could sympathize, as most of his compatriots could not, with Iranian resentment that Abadan, their second largest industrial city, was built in a foreign style, was filled with foreign institutions, was for the most part an English-speaking city and was wholly dependent on a single industry, namely oil, controlled, and at the upper echelons mainly staffed, by the English and other foreigners.

Four months after Basil and his wife arrived n Teheran Sima, now fifteen, found herself pregnant. The baby, 'the Northumbrian Kurd' as Basil called her, was born in January 1950. Basil told a correspondent that Sima insisted on the child being called Maria. So he decided to add Sima in front 'to distinguish her from ten million other Marias'. Sima Maria and her mother brought Basil great happiness; 'glad am I to have them about' he wrote. But the prospect of unemployment detracted from his sense of well-being. *The Times* or MI6 or both indicated that they would not renew his contract. Basil looked for other jobs but unsuccessfully. He approached the Anglo-Iranian Oil Company but was told that at fifty he was too old. He wrote to Margaret de Silver hinting and hoping that she might help him. Listing to her his work experience and qualifications he described himself as 'a man who was a writer, with a little political experience in extreme youth, very varied journalistic experience (but none in the office), a successful military career, some years of diplomacy and the prestige of *The Times* job here'. He said he could claim to be an 'expert' on 'the Middle East, on literature and on counterespionage'. He thought he could be 'a good policeman or professor or leader writer or reviewer'.

But none of these, or indeed any other jobs, was forthcoming and in April 1950 Basil had no choice but to leave Teheran and return with his wife and three-month-old child to his mother's house in Throckley. Here, he told Dorothy Pound, he spent a good deal of his time washing baby-clothes and when his mother had a couple of bad falls he had to do the housework too. But he found time to re-read all of Ibsen and admired the last plays greatly. He placed *Little Eyolf, John Gabriel Borkman* and *The Master Builder* on the same level as Beethoven's final quartets about which he had written with such enthusiasm during his time as a music critic. When the Pounds, remembering his strong, forthright opinions, suggested he become a critic and establish himself as a latterday Dr Johnson, Basil demurred. He said he certainly had the indispensable indolence but every year felt less and less able to pontificate.

During the summer months Basil often left his family in Northumberland whilst he had extended stays in London negotiating for work as a journalist. On one of these trips he had a meeting with Olga Rudge who, he reported briefly and tactfully to the Pounds, had told him things about the past he had not known before. He also stayed with Omar Pound, who was just then beginning to share Basil's interest in Persian and in Arabic poetry. Basil worried that the twenty-five-year-old Omar idealized him. Basil regarded himself at this time as a very poor role model and mentor for the young. He told Dorothy that at the age of fifty he had to own to a monstrous personality; he had failed to live the life he intended, he was not greatly satisfied with what he had written, and he recognized that he was considered immoral even by those who claimed to be 'advanced' in their thinking. The immorality was presumably chiefly a matter of his marriage to Sima. He also saw himself as irresponsible. He confessed that he was content to be 'amused' by all that had happened to him, even by the endless interviews in London which still continued to lead to no employment.

In fact, however, on his visits to London Basil worked hard to advance himself and especially to reinvigorate and promote his literary career. This had received a considerable and unexpected boost when, early that year, at the urging of Ezra Pound from his ward in the mental hospital a right-wing publisher in Texas brought out a volume of Basil's poems.

The imprint was the Cleaners' Press of Galveston which was operated by Dallam Flynn who also used the name Dallam Simpson. In 1948 he had created the journal *Four Pages* for the purpose of disseminating Pound's political, economic and financial ideas. Flynn put the collection of Basil's poems together whilst the author was still in Iran. Basil had no opportunity to do any proof-reading and the book has numerous small errors. It was entitled *Poems 1950* and had a print run of about one thousand copies. Flynn supplied a preface, clearly inspired by Pound, in which recent British poetry was disparaged, T. S. Eliot referred to with less than total respect and Basil praised as a long neglected and unappreciated talent. The publication of the book helped restore Basil's sense of himself as a poet. He sent a copy to Marian and his family in Wisconsin. Rustam, the thirteen-year-old son Basil had never seen, promptly signed his name in the front.

In London Basil showed copies to publishers, hoping to see the book brought out in Britain. One whose help and advice he sought was Peter Russell, then very active in poetry circles and editor of the literary periodical *Nine* in which Basil published translations from the Persian, including several versions from Manuchehri which he later decided not to include in *Collected Poems*. Pound's old friend T. S. Eliot agreed to dine with Basil and expressed his readiness to look at *Poems 1950* with a view to publication by Faber & Faber. But before he received any decisions on his book Basil managed to find himself employment. The position again combined his skills as journalist and intelligence officer, but not in Iran. This time the work took him to his second area of espionage expertise, the then new and extremely unstable Republic of Italy.

ELEVEN
Italy and *The Spoils*
1950–1951

Basil's 'cover' as a British agent was his job as a newspaper correspondent working for the Westminster Press and for an English provincial paper, the *Northern Echo*. But undoubtedly MI6, which was very active in Italy, was his chief source of income. At that time there was great concern in London and Washington that Italy might become communist and, to a greater or lesser extent, assimilated into Soviet-dominated eastern Europe. In 1948 Italy had held its first national elections since the Fascist period. A pro-western Christian Democrat government had gained power, but the communists and socialists were extremely strong and capable of destablizing the country with strikes and demonstrations. Both the Soviet block and the western countries had numerous agents in Italy closely studying and seeking to influence the course of events.

In October 1950 Basil, Sima and Sima Maria settled into a pleasant marble-floored apartment in Lido di Camaiore, an attractive little resort on the Mediterranean coast some miles south of Rapallo and just three or four miles west of the historic city of Lucca. They were some distance from the sea but had a good view of the Apuan Alps. The winter was very rainy and in order to meet his contacts Basil had to drive around Italy in often hazardous road conditions. He drove to Milan, to Parma, to Siena and to Rome. But in his free time on the Lido di Camaiore, Basil made a strong effort to resume his literary career. He tried to persuade the Loeb publishing company to introduce some oriental texts into its well-known list of translations from the classics. Basil proposed to supply prefaces and advice. The venture did not succeed but he was not dispirited. Indeed in November he committed himself to a major literary enterprise, the writing of *The Spoils*, the long poem which is now generally regarded as second only to *Briggflatts* among his sonatas. *The Spoils* and Eliot's *Little Gidding* are the two finest long poems that derive from the British experience of the Second World War.

The Spoils is divided into three parts. In the third and final part Basil recalls and seeks conclusions concerning his personal experiences in the war which, as he told Dorothy Pound, brought out 'things in me that could hardly have been suspected before, at least by me . . . It is not merely that I have had more experience but the experience has been different in kind.'[1] In the poem war experience is usually related to intensely visual scenes. For instance the coastal desert after the battle of El Alamein is remembered and evoked with detainingly rich particularity of vocabulary. The abandoned German tanks are 'leaguered in line'; the British note 'a new-painted recognisance/on a fragment of fuselage'. Throughout the passage the image of the western desert in the aftermath of Rommel's defeat is created in such highly crafted phrasing.

> Broken booty but usable
> along the littoral, frittering into the south.
> We marvelled, careful of crates and minefields,
> noting a new-painted recognisance
> on a fragment of fuselage, sand drifting into dumps,
> a tank's turret twisted skyward,
> here and there a lorry unharmed
> out of fuel or the crew scattered;
> leaguered in lines numbered for enemy units,
> gulped beer of their brewing,
> mocked them marching unguarded to our rear;
> discerned nothing indigenous, never a dwelling,
> but on the shore sponges stranded beyond the reef
> unstayed masts staggering in the swell,
> till we reached readymade villages clamped on cornland,
> empty, Arabs feeding vines to goats;
> at last orchards aligned, girls hawked by their mothers
> from tent to tent, Tripoli dark
> under a cone of tracers.
> Old in that war after raising many crosses
> rapped on a tomb at Leptis; no one opened.

The last line sounds like a disappointed echoing of the Christian assurance 'Knock and it shall be opened unto you' (the choice of the word 'rapped' rather than 'knocked' conveys the urgency and insistence of the poet's effort to make his experiences intelligible). But Leptis, once an important Carthaginian port and later a Roman city adorned by its conquerors with much imposing architecture, has no message for any of the victorious

British in the Libya of 1942. Beautiful Isfahan not Leptis will prove to be the instructive city. The fabulous Iranian city to which the poem moves in the second section will supply a more illuminating perspective on history.

The desert campaign in north Africa is but one of the war experiences considered in *The Spoils*. Here is an image of war in the North Sea as Basil would have known it prior to his departure for Iran. (Staithes is a fishing village on the Yorkshire coast.)

> old men who toil in the bilge to open a link,
> bruised by the fling of the ship and sodden
> sleep at the handpump. Staithes, filthy harbour water,
> a drowned Finn, a drowned Chinee;
> hard-lying money wrung from protesting paymasters.

And from Largo Law, the Scottish harbour in Fife, the poet urges on his reader the bleakly ethereal prospect of the Arctic convoys setting out across the North Sea to the Soviet ports of Archangel and Murmansk.

> From Largo Law look down,
> moon and dry weather, look down
> on convoy marshalled, filing between mines.
> Cold northern clear sea-gardens
> between Lofoten and Spitzbergen.

The Spoils moves through great expanses of time. It also moves through great distances. The poem that begins under the high sun of Babylon and remembers the terraces of modern Teheran ends with the chill of the North Sea succinctly imaged in the five words 'Cold northern clear sea-gardens'. It is a journey to and from the ends of the earth such as many of the combatants in the Second World War were compelled to make.

As the poet remembers his own wartime journeyings he also, in the first two parts of the poem, remembers stages in mankind's journey through history. His attitude to history inheres in certain recurrent motifs and emphases. These serve to unite the three sections which upon a first reading may seem discontinuous and highly differentiated. There is, for instance, throughout the work, a continued returning to historical periods that show weariness, demoralization and disgust. The mood of the Jews exiled to Babylon is one of misery and exhaustion.

By the dategroves of Babylon
there we sat down and sulked
while they were seeking to hire us
to a repugnant trade.
Are there no plows in Judah, seed or a sickle,
no ewe to the pail, press to the vineyard?
Sickly our Hebrew voices far from the Hebrew hills!

At the same time there is a feeling of contempt for the dominant and
venal civilization of the Babylonians, a feeling that is reinforced by the
recalling of the heroic achievements of David during the great age of
Israel's history. His 'dancing before the Ark' and his renewal by Abishag
who 'lent her warmth to dying David' contrast with the energylessness of
the sexual culture of the generation of the captivity.

This and other allusions to an impoverished sexuality underline one of
the deeper concerns of the poem. For the force of history that is shown
operating in all three parts of the poem is characterized by the use of a
metaphor which simultaneously suggests sexuality and the profound
energies of the planet itself.

Shot silk and damask white
spray spread from
artesian gush of our past.

Many of the civilizations alluded to in *The Spoils* fail to be at one with
this elemental force. And the poet, for all that he was on the winning
side in one of the greatest military actions in history, faces a similar
alienation. The opening lines of the third section describe his futile
efforts to live a life in close accord with the forces and processes of nature.
The earthy monosyllables and the wearily perfunctory tone and pace of
these ten lines indicate a realization of the quaintness of the enterprise.
Alienation is, after all, here to stay.

A fancy took me to dig,
plant, prune, graft;
milk, skim, churn;
flay and tan.
A side of salt beef
for a knife chased and inscribed.

> A cask of pressed grapes
> for a seine-net.
> for peace until harvest
> a jig and a hymn.

But whilst tacitly, in his prosody, conceding the unworkability of such aspirations to the simple life, he nevertheless proceeds in the following lines to denounce the causes that make such an option unassailable. He begins with an historical question:

> How shall wheat sprout
> through a shingle of Lydian pebbles
> that turn the harrow's points?

The phrase 'Lydian pebbles' that is insistently repeated in the passage alludes to an important moment in the history of the ancient world. The Lydians, whose king was Croesus, were, according to Herodotus in his account of what was for him a world war, the first people to introduce gold and silver coins and the first to sell goods by retail.[2] Money consciousness, so the poem implies, frustrates natural impulse and process. It detracts from a right sexuality and is also at variance with another important part of our humanity, the heroic impulse. As in all extended poems about war the nature of the heroic is a recurring theme. Within the sonata-like structure of *The Spoils* it sounds out against all that is negative in the poet's experience and in human history.

A hero figure in *The Spoils* is an American flier who 'for fun of fighting and pride' volunteers to help in the defence of Malta during the heavy, relentless air attacks upon the island in 1942. Given the water motif in the poem and the notion of the 'artesian gush of our past' it is felicitous for the poet that this modern hero's home town should be Grand Rapids.

> Flight-lieutenant Idema, half course run
> that started from Grand Rapids, Michigan.
> wouldn't fight for Roosevelt,
> 'That bastard Roosevelt', pale
> at Malta's ruins, enduring
> a jeep guarded like a tyrant.
> In British uniform and pay
> for fun of fighting and pride,

> for Churchill on foot alone,
> clowning with a cigar, was lost
> in best blues and his third plane that day.

This hero does not fight in order to obtain the best pay, nor does he fight for his country. For all Basil's determination to enlist in 1939, his poem *The Spoils* is not an expression of patriotic feeling. The war raises other and deeper concerns than a celebration of cause and country. 'O public spirit!', exclaims the poet in the second section as he contemplates the decline of the Seljuk empire in Iran. And his tone is a compound of exasperation and amusement.

In the three elegantly worded and phrased tercets that follow he remarks the ultimate futility of seeking to explain and overcome certain problematical features of the human condition through political forms or social organization. First, there is the misplaced yearning to dragoon human multiplicity.

> Prayers to band cities and brigade men
> lest there be more wills than one:
> but God is the dividing sword.

Then there is the creating of public forms as diverse as monuments and legislation as a means of contending with another fact of the process of life, death.

> A hard pyramid or lasting law
> against fear of death and
> murder more durable than mortar.

Then, finally, there is the resort to power and technology to programme the troublesomely unpredictable in life, sexual choices, for instance:

> Domination and engineers
> to fudge a motive you can lay your hands on
> lest a girl choose or refuse waywardly.

There are other passages in the poem which show sexual feeling and heroic feeling to be at variance with the destructive rigidities of financial and political systems. The long historical purview of the poem shows

126

that the conflict is by no means confined to the present time. But the poet has a special disdain for the current social order in which the 'artesian gush of our past' is no longer experienced. To seek the full force of the past is to be subversive. Orthodoxy is to accept (and again water is the metaphor) the stagnant and the polluted.

> Let no one drink unchlorinated
> living water but taxed tap, sterile,
> or seek his contraband mouthful
> in bog, under thicket, by crag, a trickle,
> or from embroidered pools
> with newts and dytiscus beetles.

This dwelling on sterility recalls the mood of Eliot's *The Waste Land* and Bunting's own earlier sonatas. But overall in *The Spoils* Bunting's feelings about the Second World War differ entirely from Eliot's feelings about the First World War. And to describe this difference is a way of saying what constitutes the particular distinction of Bunting's handling of language, of his method as a poet.

Unlike T. S. Eliot's *déracinés* in *The Waste Land*, Bunting's exiles in *The Spoils* feel more than they consciously realize. Throughout the poem there is a tension between discursive language and imagistic language. In the opening quartet which, Basil told Zukofsky, presents the outlook of 'the Semitic peoples'[3] an early speech is spoken by Lud who is farmer and husbandman. His experience of the exile, he declares in his concluding lines, is one of depression, a depression that is spiritual, emotional and economic.

> There is no clamour
> in our market, no eagerness for gain;
> even whores surly, God frugal,
> keeping tale of prayers

Yet this statement is at odds with what had been expressed just a few lines earlier. There Lud had described the River Tigris in flood. And the flood (taking a further significance from its position in the pattern of water imagery in the poem) is an occasion of beauty, fascination and wonder.

When Tigris floods snakes swarm in the city,
coral, jade, jet, between jet and jade, yellow,
enamelled toys. Toads
crouch in doorsteps. Jerboas
weary, unwary, may be taught to feed
from a fingertip.

There is within Lud's speech a contrast between what the speaker discursively thinks he feels and what he actually feels. Through differing verbal textures a major theme of the poem emerges: the contrast between thoughts and opinions about existence, on the one hand, and the actual instant by instant experience of the processes of consciousness, life and history, on the other.

There is another example of this contrast in the second part of the poem. Here Persia and its Islamic, especially its Seljuk, history and the mosque architecture in Isfahan are discoursed upon by a voice that is distinctively English. It is a voice that suggests someone, like Basil himself at one time, from the Foreign Office. It is urbane and faintly condescending. There is an Augustan confidence in the antitheses of some of the well-managed sentences in which Iranian civilization is reviewed.

But their determination to banish fools foundered
ultimately in the installation of absolute idiots.
Fear of being imputed
naive impeded thought.

But this rather world-weary view of history is suddenly terminated as the speaker goes on to consider the deeper impulses informing history, impulses which, he suggests, can only be grasped and rendered by art. He now completely abandons the public persona voiced in the British English of the first fifty lines of the second section and gives himself up to an enthralled, sometimes rapturous, evocation of Persian music, drawing and story-telling. The language is sinuous, subtle, delicately musical; the Persian names now sound not as exotica but as mysterious resonances. Again *The Spoils* has switched from the language of opinion to the language of emotional involvement, from the language of the distanced observer to that of the entranced participant. If the Second World War is regarded elsewhere in the poem as an unintelligible

128

dislocation in world history, here, in Iran, are certain underlying permanences, the perennial flowing, the 'artesian gush of our past' of which the present can be felt to be a part. Of a singer of classical Persian odes Basil writes:

> Nothing that was is,
> but Moluk-e-Zarrabi
> draws her voice from a well
> deeper than history.

Such an ancient and continuing process is evoked imagistically in the following slowly moving passage in which soft sounds gradually give way to a beautifully realized stillness and calm.

> A fowler spreading his net
> over the barley, calls,
> calls on a rubber reed.
> Grain nods in reply.
> Poppies blue upon white
> wake to the sun's frown.
> Scut of gazelle dances and bounces
> out of the afternoon.
> Owl and wolf to the night.
> On a terrace over a pool
> vafur, vodka, tea,
> resonant verse spilled
> from Onsori, Sa'di,
> till the girls' mutter is lost
> in whisper of stream and leaf,
> a final nightingale
> under a fading sky
> azan on their quiet.

In a note on the word 'azan' Basil remarks: 'The azan is the mo'ezzin's call to prayer. You hardly hear its delicate, wavering airs at other times, but an hour before sunrise it has such magic as no other music, unless perhaps the nightingale in lands where nightingales are rare.' Another helpful gloss tells us that 'vafur' 'signifies the apparatus of opium smoking'. But the explanations are not essential to our grasp of the sound and the semantics of sound in the passage. These, together with the images, are what direct the lines rather than syntax and statement.

It is true that the language of discourse returns. In sonata-fashion the bluff, wordly-wise English voice enters again to make an ironic statement about the Persian people.

> They despise police work,
> are not masters of filing:
> always a task for foreigners
> to make them unhappy
> unproductive and rich.

The statement contains some sympathy. Nevertheless the moments of intense empathy with an ancient culture are over. The public voice has taken control over the private awareness. But it is the previous eighteen lines, the evocation of stillness, which are the most memorable in this second part of the poem. This is what enables the poet, as he goes on to evoke the destructions, menace and terror in life, to deny the radical question finally and logically arrived at by the discursive language of thought 'were we not better dead?'

The same dialectic of language contributes to the process of the third and final section in which the poet turns his attention to his own exile, his own war, his own alienation. The first three passages are, as I have suggested, a criticism of the poet's own society; they culminate in the fourth passage in which the parlous conditions of the great modernist poets are described.

> One cribbed in a madhouse
> set about with diagnoses;
> one unvisited; one uninvited;
> one visited and invited too much;
> one impotent, suffocated by adulation;
> one unfed: flares on a foundering barque,
> stars spattering still sea under iceblink.

The first poet is clearly Ezra Pound; the fourth, or perhaps the fifth, is T. S. Eliot. But such identifications are not the main point of the passage. Its chief significance is as an indictment of a western world that does not know how to respond properly to what its true artists have to offer. There is here a contrast with the second section of the poem. For in contemporary Iran art and artists are shown to have a central and creative role in the life of the society.

However, the pessimism is soon mitigated by the images associated with Flight-lieutenant Idema and his heroism. Yet the poet's own war experiences as he evokes them culminate with a sense of the unintelligibility of the war. But to discover the meaning of the war in terms of simple causes and effects is not the concern of *The Spoils*. That sort of endeavour Basil leaves to a poet such as Blind Bashshar bin Burd and his like who

> doubted, glanced back,
> guessed whence, speculated whither.
> Panegyrists, blinder and deaf,
> prophets, exegesists, counsellors of patience
> lie in wait for blood,
> every man with a net

But the meaning, *The Spoils* insists, is not to be netted. It is for ever elusive. What this poem offers instead is a verbally realized state of mind in which the life process can be felt and commended along with, and in spite of, its unintelligibility. It is a form of the old virtue of hope. And it is not confined to the poet's Iranian experiences. At the end of the poem, in a cold northern climate, it is present in two such very homely images as 'tea's drawing, breeze backing and freshening'. It is a hope that had no special end in view but that can trust and delight in life despite danger, demoralization and pain.

During the first six months of 1951 as he worked to complete the poem Basil sent drafts of various passages to Louis Zukofsky and corresponded with him about them. Basil originally wrote a poem that had four, rather than the present three, movements. But Zukofsky, whose judgement Basil always respected, thought that parts three and four were rather thin, so Basil conflated them into the present third movement. He feared this made the poem a little lopsided, there was not enough about western experience to balance the first two sections on the Middle East. He also thought he had made the final section obscure. But his hand was forced. His espionage activities in Italy were becoming so demanding that he had no time to continue work on the poem. As he told a friend twenty years later, there were 'pretty strenuous doings in Italy which obliged me to hurry the last two movements far too much'.[4]

Basil's intelligence work in Italy ended abruptly. One evening he returned home and told Sima that they must leave straightaway. He was very agitated. When she asked the reason, he replied that he was 'being followed'. When Sima enquired further, Basil was unforthcoming. In her forthright, no nonsense fashion she insisted on knowing but the only extra information he gave her was that it was the Russians who were after him. He insisted that they pack up immediately and leave Italy the following day. This they did. By the end of June and in a state of shock they found themselves back in Throckley.

Twelve
Paradise Regained and Lost
1951–1952

For several months life in Northumberland was difficult for Basil and Sima. They had little income and were dependent on Basil's mother. As on the previous occasion when he had suddenly become unemployed Basil travelled frequently to London seeking to resume his career as a journalist, 'diplomat' and poet. It was the year of the Festival of Britain centred on the south bank of the Thames. The Festival was intended to compensate for, perhaps to mark the end of, the drab years of austerity in post-war Britain. But for Basil the poet, keen to see himself published, 1951 brought nothing to celebrate. He was disappointed to learn that Peter Russell had decided not to publish a British edition of *Poems 1950*. Russell thought that Flynn's preface was lacking in dignity. But, a stickler to principle, Basil would not abandon the preface. To do so would mean disloyalty to the American publisher who had believed in him.

There came another literary disappointment when he learned that T. S. Eliot, then at the height of his fame and influence as a poet, playwright, critic and publisher, had finally decided not to accept Basil's poems for publication by Faber. Eliot, Garth Clucas has noted, found them 'too Poundian'.[1] Basil's sole achievement as a poet that year was in November when *The Spoils* had its first publication in *Poetry* of Chicago. But he would have to wait another fourteen years, until 1965, before seeing this major work published in England.

A month before the Chicago publication, however, Basil managed to find a job as a journalist. *The Times*, in association with the *News Chronicle*, employed him again, offering him a year's contract as their correspondent in Teheran. The prospect of going back to the country which he so loved and admired gave him immense pleasure. Sima too was overjoyed to be returning home. By now, however, the political situation in Iran had become highly explosive. In May 1951 the Shah had found himself compelled to appoint the nationalist leader Mossadeq Prime Minister. As he had long promised, Mossadeq immediately nationalized Iran's greatest resource, the Anglo-Iranian Oil Company. The non-Iranian management personnel eventually fled and by July all oil exports ceased. The Labour government in Britain led by Clement Attlee was uncertain what to do, but in October, the month Basil arrived back in Teheran, it was defeated in the General Election and replaced by a Conservative government, headed by Winston Churchill who sneered at his Labour predecessors 'who had scuttled and run from Abadan when a splutter of musketry would have ended the matter'.[2] But in this world energy crisis the Americans were reluctant to support such a high-handed approach to Mossadeq who impressed them with his wide popular support and anti-Communist stand. They urged the British to negotiate with him. The Americans also sent trouble-shooters to help calm the situation and enlisted the assistance of the World Bank.

Basil's reports from Teheran were not just of complex political negotiations behind the scenes but also of dramatic and often violent activity on the streets. For as Mossadeq gradually began to lose the confidence of members of the Iranian parliament (the Majlis), he turned more and more to the Teheran crowd. Speaking in parks and public places he excited his large and responsive audiences by delivering a succession of increasingly inflammatory anti-British speeches. Riots followed, in one of which a Greek newspaperman was killed. Most western journalists left, but Basil, always a courageous man, refused to be intimidated and stayed in Teheran even though he received a succession of death threats. Years later he relished telling the story of the occasion on which the mob demanded his death. He was in the Ritz Hotel with the Reuters correspondent when he heard outside the increasingly loud chant, 'Death to Mr Bunting'. To his colleague's dismay Basil decided after a while to go and have a look at the crowd; he was confident he wouldn't be recognized. Once outside the hotel he joined in the chant 'Death to Mr Bunting' with everyone else.

Politics aside, Basil and his family enjoyed a pleasant, gracious style of life in Iran just as they had on their previous stay. One witness to this was Robert Payne who later published a book on Iran full of rich insights in the tradition of the poetic travel writing of Ruskin and Adrian Stokes. In his introduction he speaks of his 'special debt to Mr and Mrs Basil Bunting of the London *Times* who allowed me to keep them awake at Teheran over their own Scotch whisky on too many nights.'[3] Payne was a member of a research expedition brought to Iran by the distinguished scholar Arthur Upham Pope, the Director of the American Institute of Persian Art and Archeology, whom presumably Basil also met. Payne was greatly impressed by Basil's knowledge of Iranian artefacts. Payne had bought a small bronze statue of a girl which he called 'the winged goddess' but which he could himself neither date nor ascribe to any artist or workship. Basil unassumingly revealed a wide knowledge of the interrelations between Iranian and European art: 'One day in Teheran my friend Basil Bunting solved the mystery. He explained that she must have been made in Isfahan by Italian workmen at the court of Shah Abbas to grace a salt-cellar or a bronze chafing dish.'[4]

Robert Payne enjoyed bathing in the waterfall that splashed into the red-tiled swimming-pool in Basil's garden. The garden, warm and full of roses, was beside the road which led in the far distance into the snows of the Elbruz mountains. Payne thought that Basil 'looked like an intelligent monkey and there was something in the quick, sharp voice that reminded you of Socrates'.[5] He enjoyed life, delighting in 'his exquisitely handsome Armenian wife, his books and his pipes', and was 'credited with possessing the best cook and the best collection of whisky in Teheran'.[6] To Dorothy Pound Basil confirmed his delight in Persian food. A particular gastronomical pleasure for him was rice with duck stewed in pomegranate juice and strewn with almonds.

But the days of contentment were numbered. Mossadeq's anti-British feeling continued to intensify and Basil became one of the special targets of his anger. The Prime Minister disliked the reports which Basil sent to *The Times*, declaring them to be prejudiced and dishonest.

Certainly Basil made no attempt to conceal the brutality with which the police and army dealt with all the many protesters against the Mossadeq regime. On 7 December, for instance, Basil cabled to *The Times* an article which appeared under the headline 'Fixed Bayonets in Teheran – Boy Demonstrators Dispersed'. Describing a day of rioting the article supplies some horrific details about the way student protestors were treated. Basil writes, 'Your Correspondent saw more than 20 policemen beating a boy of 14 with rubber truncheons in a main street . . .' Another correspondent, he reported, saw police stamping on a schoolboy's head. Then some fifteen hundred soldiers in trucks arrived to reinforce the police; they drove the trucks into the mass of students and schoolchildren many of whom were badly hurt. Later thugs with clubs turned up looking for any remaining demonstrators they might attack.

Basil's colleague, Michael Clark of the *New York Times*, wrote that the atmosphere of incipient terrorism was Dr Mossadeq's best ally. For this, Basil reported, the American journalist was denounced as an agent of the former oil company and given just forty-eight hours to remove himself from Iran. Exactly a week later on 13 December Basil cabled another article in which he reported the expulsion of Reuters correspondent Leopold Herman who had been in Iran for ten years and was well known as a careful and accurate reporter. The expulsion took place against a succession of demonstrations and counter-demonstrations in Teheran.

Three days before Christmas an article by Basil transferred attention from the violence on the streets to the Shah's palace. *The Times* reported what were headlined as 'Dr Mossadek's [*sic*] Manoeuvres' to embarrass the Shah whose family had once exiled him and who was himself no friend. Mossadeq demanded no less than that the Queen Mother, who he knew supported the opposition, be sent into exile. Should the Shah refuse, Mossadeq would resign. In a private letter to his boss, the Foreign Editor Ralph Deakin, from his home at Khiaban Amol 35 in Teheran, Basil supplied a shrewed assessment of Mossadeq's skill in presenting this ultimatum to the Shah. If the Shah refused the demand he would face the possibly violent hostility of Mossadeq's numerous supporters. 'If the Queen Mother leaves Teheran, Mossadeq has won. The opposition will be disheartened and he can go ahead and establish the virtual dictatorship at which he is aiming.'[7] Mossadeq did force the Queen Mother into exile but this action did not help him as much as Basil expected.

Just over two months later, in early March 1952, Basil reported another initiative against those who opposed Mossadeq. One of their leaders was arrested and imprisoned on an accusation of fraud. He joined several others who remained in jail without formal charges being brought against them. Towards the end of the month one of the opposition groups, the Communist-inspired Democratic Youth Movement, took to the streets and battled with the police. On the last day of March an article in *The Times* reported that Dr Mossadeq had declared martial law. This step, Basil suggested, gave Mossadeq powers that the electorate would not have given him. Basil concluded that 'the pretence that the Government represents an overwhelming majority of the nation is growing thin'.

This was to be Basil's last article from Teheran. Over a month earlier Basil had warned Ralph Deakin 'that there is a considerable probability of my being heaved out of Persia within the next week or thereabouts'. And indeed he soon met the same fate as that of other foreign correspondents about whom he had reported. In the second week of April 1952 Basil was formally expelled from Iran. It was a blow to him, and also to

Sima. Basil wrote to Deakin: 'My poor wife is stricken at leaving her country, family and friends.'[8] *The Times* defended its correspondent; an editorial of 14 April 1952 spoke of the way Basil had 'devoted his life' to Iran and its culture and insisted that his despatches had 'always been scrupulously fair and honest'.

Undoubtedly Dr Mossadeq and his advisers did not take this view. But Basil's activities as a journalist were not the formal reason given for his expulsion. This was rather that he was not a true journalist but a diplomat and, the implication was, a spy. His time as vice-consul at Isfahan was cited as proof that he was not a genuine newspaper man. He had obtained his current visa, the authorities maintained, by failing to disclose important information about himself.

The Associated Press Correspondent in Iran, admittedly no great friend of Basil's, declared subsequently that Basil's expulsion had nothing to do with his journalism. And one wonders if it had anything to do with the major intrigue then underway in Teheran. For the British had finally managed to persuade the Americans that Mossadeq was unreliable and dangerous, and the two powers were now co-operating on a covert plot to overthrow him. The Americans referred to it as Operation Ajax; the British called it Operation Boot. MI6 sent out a special agent from London to direct the enterprise. This was C. M. (Monty) Woodhouse who has described the complex history of Operation Boot in his autobiography.[9] His American counterpart was Kermit Roosevelt, grandson of President Theodore Roosevelt, and at the time head of CIA operations in the Middle East. To what extend Dr Mossadeq was aware of what was being planned against him is not clear; but it was against this background of a highly funded and ultimately successful clandestine operation to destabilize the Iranian government that Basil was told to leave the country.

Basil tried hard to get the decision reversed, but in vain. He and his wife were given just fifteen days to pack up their home and remove themselves from the country they loved so much. They would never return. His expulsion began one of the most painful phases of Basil's life.

THIRTEEN
Flight into Poverty
1952–1957

Many other foreigners had been given an early deadline by which to be out of Iran. When Basil went to buy the air tickets he discovered that all the flights were fully booked and that there was a long waiting list for cancellations. He decided that there was no other choice than to return to England overland in the car which *The Times* had provided for him. It was a large American car, a Ford Mercury. He proceeded to rig it up for the long and dangerous journey. The rear seat was replaced with a mattress on which Sima, now pregnant again, and two-year-old Maria could sleep. At the expense of much of the luggage space the boot was packed with large canisters full of petrol. Two whole sheepskins were filled with water and strapped to the sides of the car. Well over forty-five years later, in a long conversation I had with her, Sima still remembered how wonderfully cold the water remained in this simple cooling system.

Their first destination was Baghdad. In the seemingly endless desert Sima was astonished by the mirages that she experienced. Then when a sudden violent sandstorm slowed, almost stopped the car, she was afraid they could be buried alive. But Basil grimly persevered with his driving, keeping his eye on the oil drums that marked the road where the sand was firm. To miss the way could mean fatal disaster. The car might become immovable, sink into the sand and its occupants die in the intense heat.

Sima developed a passion for bacon and eggs as they approached the Iraqi capital. Basil promised that she could have them but, she remembered, never kept his promise. In the meantime the iron rations that Basil had decided on were dates stuffed with almonds. Sima came to detest them and refused to eat until they arrived in Baghdad. Here they waited for a day or two while Basil urgently telegraphed various places for money with which to replenish their supplies. Then they were off to Syria and Damascus. On the way they ran into a plague of locusts. All the car windows were entirely and thickly covered and inside it was dark. Basil had to get out and use a shovel to clear them off. This was one of the infrequent occasions on which he stopped the car. He preferred to keep driving, fast, through the desert, without ever sleeping. Even when camel-drivers waved to him in a friendly way, inviting him to stop and talk, he drove on. He would take no risks.

In Damascus they stayed in a pleasant hotel while the car was extensively serviced. When they were on their way again they were greatly dismayed to find that their battery had been replaced with an old one that was almost dead. But there could be no turning back; again Basil drove on, on into the hills of eastern Turkey where armed bandits looked down upon them from the hills. They arrived in Istanbul and again stayed in a hotel while they waited for more money to be sent. The hotel had a grand major domo, a large black man in a splendid Ruritanian uniform. He was extremely kind to the tired travellers but little Maria was terrified of him.

They crossed into Europe, travelling some way into Greece then north into Bulgaria. In this communist country the large American car provoked anger among the peasant people. As Basil slowed down to go through the villages, the inhabitants would run after the car and stone it. He and Sima were much relieved to cross into Yugoslavia. Here they were struck by the destruction that had occurred during President Tito's bitter guerilla war against the Germans. Seven years after the war had ended the roads were still pitted with deep craters; churches, houses and schools stood in ruins by the wayside. On several occasions as Basil sped down a bumpy main road towards a bridge over a river, he was disconcerted to find the bridge blown up. He would have to turn round and try to find detours. Sima was impressed by his abilities, particularly his improvisational skills, as a navigator. Never did she feel that they were lost. From the British embassy library in Teheran he had taken excellent maps of the several stages of their journey. In Zagreb, in the northern part of what was then Yugoslavia, they again rested for a couple of days and Basil became involved in complex arrangements to restock the car with petrol which was a very scarce commodity.

When they crossed into Austria the driving became easier. They went to Vienna to await more funds. By past and future standards the old Hapsburg capital was a little drab, having the appearance evoked in the film *The Third Man* which was being shot around this time. But they had a good time there before driving south-west over the Alps into Italy. Forty years before, Ezra Pound had made a literary pilgrimage to Sirmione where the poet Catullus had lived on Lake Garda. Pound had been overwhelmed by the beauty of the place and had spoken of it often. So now Basil had the opportunity to visit the little town associated with the poet who had a special importance in his own literary development and whose work he had translated, years before, into English. Basil and his family spent more than a week at the Albergo Catullo in Sirmione on its little peninsula at the southern end of Lake Garda. It was very warm and the lake glittered brilliantly in the bright spring sunlight.

Then they drove north again, into France and ever colder weather. At Calais they put the car on the ferry to Dover. After a few days in London where Basil had unsatisfactory talks about his future with the people at *The Times* and the Foreign Office, they set off up the old Great North Road which in those days could be rather narrow for such a large American car. Their journey came to an end at last when they parked outside Mrs Bunting's house on hilly Leyburn Road in Throckley. The exotic, travel-stained car with its dents and peculiar fittings must have been an object of fascination for the Throckley miners and their children.

British Customs and Excise were unsure about the status of the car; Basil had lengthy and wearying negotiation with them. But the Iranian customs were in no doubt about what they would do about the heavy baggage which Basil had been forced to leave behind in Teheran. They simply refused to release it for forwarding to Britain. Basil faced the prospect of losing practically all his possessions including his 'largely irreplaceable library of Persian books'.[1] In this same letter which he sent to Ralph Deakin from Throckley after his contract with *The Times* had ended, he also referred, a little reproachfully, to another likely consequence of his expulsion. Possible employers, he wrote, seemed to think that this must have been due to some lack of discretion on his part, 'otherwise *The Times* would not have dispensed with my services and the Government would have made more fuss than it did'. Basil found it difficult to combat this idea effectively and to reassure those whom he approached for employment.

The return to his mother's house in the shabby, small colliery town marked a painful come-down in Basil's life which he had to endure for close to fourteen years. As he approached his fifty-second birthday he was shocked to discover that he simply could not find work in England. Neither the Foreign Office nor *The Times* could be persuaded to reconsider their dismissal of him. No one in London took any interest in him and no one was prepared to employ him locally at his old trade as a journalist. For a brief time he managed to obtain occasional work for the

Manchester Guardian, but otherwise the best he could find were menial proof-reading jobs. From time to time he would work on bus and train timetables and electoral lists for the Newcastle printing firm of Thomas Reed and Son. The National Coal Board published a magazine called *Mining* and sometimes engaged him as a proof-reader. But he found the work both demeaning and physically painful. He had to work in the same room as the cacophonous printing machines; the job was a torment to his ears as well as to his increasingly weak eyes.

But except for such poorly paid jobs Basil could see no future for himself during the first weeks and months back in Throckley after the eventful, adventurous journey from Iran. He was unemployed and apparently unemployable. On 1 October 1952 he wrote to Margaret de Silver complaining bitterly about his situation. He told her that the British embassy in Teheran and also *The Times* had encouraged him 'to take the boldest course' and had clearly indicated (without actually promising) that if he were expelled, they would ensure that his family would not suffer and that his income would not be affected. But after his expulsion no help had been given and his money was now running out. *The Times* was under contract to pay him for a few more weeks but had reduced his money by half on the grounds that he no longer needed a foreign allowance. Other British newspapers, knowing *The Times* had let him go, were extremely doubtful about employing him. In Teheran the Persian authorities had finally sequestrated all his belongings and valuables, including the library of Persian books which had taken him twenty years to build up.

Sima's pregnancy would soon be coming to term but, as recent arrivals in Britain, they could claim 'no rights in the Welfare State. No insurance or help of any kind.' To Margaret he lists his various skills. He leaves her in no doubt whatsoever about the extent of his misery and desperation as he asks her about job possibilities in the United States.[2]

But whilst he waited and hoped for suggestions from Margaret, there came a message from someone else in America which utterly devastated him. That same October Roudaba phoned her father to let him know that his fifteen-year-old son Rustam, whom Basil had never seen, had died at his boarding-school in New Hampshire. The death had come just hours after polio had been diagnosed. Basil's grief for the son who had been born after Marian left him to return to America was painful and intense. It finds expression in the elegy 'A Song for Rustam', a poem rooted in very raw, personal emotion. Basil showed the piece to close friends such as Louis Zukofsky but never permitted it to be published in collections of his work during his lifetime. The poem shows Basil's characteristic crafting of language but there is also in it a depth of private feeling, of his own personal suffering such as was not to be found in any of his poems up to that date. The elegy as a whole and particularly the three lines of, for Basil, inadequate 'Words slung to the gale' which 'stammer and fail' but which he gives as Rustam's epitaph exude the writer's agony.

> *Unseen is not unknown,*
> *unkissed is not unloved,*
> *unheard is not unsung.*

Less than two months after the news of Rustam's death, there occurred an event which must have been both an alleviation and a distraction for Basil in his misery. On a chilly December day in a poorly heated Northumberland nursing-home Sima gave birth to her second child, a boy. They called him Thomas Faramy. The latter name was that of a character in the *Shah na Meh*, the brother of Rustam.

When the baby was brought home that Christmas, the family could barely afford to eat. Except for his meagre earning as a proof-reader Basil was now without money. His mother had lost most of her assets because of the activities of a dishonest solicitor who had absconded. All she had left was her house. In 1953 he again told his troubles to Margaret de Silver, doubtless hoping to engage her sympathy and enlist her help. He told her that his mother had run through her overdraft to the limit the bank would allow. The security was her house and now the bank was pressing her to sell the property to pay back the £500 she presently owed. If the house had to be sold, then his mother would have to go and live with his sister Joyce. But the two could not get on; they quarrelled all the time. Annie was happy living with Sima. But Basil had to face the painful fact that if he could not find a job and a decent income Sima would have to return to Iran with the children to be housed with and supported by her mother. He exclaims, 'I think the break-up of my family would be the end of me.' His letter to Margaret ends, 'Yours rather desperately'.[3] When in the same year Ezra Pound wrote urging him to rescue his literary career, Basil burst out, 'oh Ez I am disheartened to such an extent I doubt if I can do anything at all.'[4] Two years later his depression was still there. To Pound's friend and sympathizer, the BBC producer D. G. Bridson, Basil wrote, 'I am perishing in the swamp still where Mossadeq threw me and *The Times* left me.'[5]

As one way of raising money Basil attempted to sell the now rusting Ford Mercury but Customs forbade him. All that was left was to go on welfare. The senior RAF officer and son of one of the once wealthiest women of Throckley had to go to the Labour Exchange in the little town and apply for National Assistance. With this small allowance, eked out by the occasional money from proof-reading, the family of five managed to scrape by into 1954. In the summer of that year Basil at long last managed to find regular employment. It was by no means a good job but Basil was so frightened by the prospects which his utter poverty presented that he felt compelled to take it. The job was on the *Newcastle Daily Journal*. The former *Times* correspondent now had to settle for the lowly position of a sub-editor on a provincial newspaper, working a night shift from five in the afternoon until two in the morning. To save money he travelled the several miles to and from work on his bicycle. Years later in an interview he gave to the BBC he remembered what was interesting about travelling home through the suburbs in the small hours as well as the sheer grind of the sub-editing at

> the bloody newspaper . . . In the middle of the night you saw all sorts of creatures on the road that you never see in daytime. Every kind of owl I got familiar with. Foxes carrying chickens in their mouths and things of that sort. It was very nice in some ways. Of course you were terribly tired. Tiring business being up all night working on the newspaper and then trying to sleep when everybody is up and about during the day.[6]

And Basil was not at all comfortable with his colleagues on the *Newcastle Daily Journal*.

> Provincial journalists are not capable of thought of any sort at all. No doubt he writes what he thinks is expected of him and his notions are framed on God only knows what. Certainly not on any experience of life . . . I have never at any time seen people so wholly without experience of life as journalists. They go to newspaper offices from the most ignorant parts of secondary-modern schools. That's where they're recruited. And they are never outside the newspaper office again for the rest of their days, except to do a little shorthand writing in the police court or something

like that. They see nothing and their notions of life are probably adopted from out-of-date novels.[7]

But for all his discontent with the newspaper Basil always strove to be honest, accurate and responsible as a journalist. Someone who worked with him at that time was the young Newcastle poet Barry MacSweeney. They worked just ten yards apart in the office and talked much about poetry. MacSweeney remembered Basil as 'a good bloke' even though, as he also recalled, 'Basil used to have to tell me off every time I made the tidetables incorrect, because he was the sub who dealt with that. I used to have to do the shipping forecasts, and he used to come up and scold me and say you've added this up all wrong.'[8]

Basil's discontent with his job, his irritation and his exhaustion cannot have helped his relationship with Sima. He was no longer the distinguished, romantic figure she had married. At the age of fifty-six Basil was a poorly paid, night-shift drudge on a provincial paper. As a result of the proof-reading his always poor eyesight had deteriorated badly and he had to wear glasses with very thick, unbecoming lenses. The standard of living in the three-bedroom house at Throckley was not high and Sima was worried about the health of Thomas Faramay. He was suffering badly from croup and the doctor advised that the child should spend some time in a place warmer than Northumberland. Grandly, unrealistically, Basil proposed Italy. But Sima knew that this was financially impossible. She made up her mind to take the children to her mother in Iran. In the autumn of 1956, just as the world was shaken by the Soviet invasion of Hungary and the British and French parachute landings by the Suez Canal, Sima, now in her twenty-second year, left England with Maria and Thomas. Given the hardships and difficulties in their relationship Basil must have wondered when, and indeed whether, she would return. Her departure with the children had painful similarities with that of Marian almost exactly twenty years before.

The year brought another sadness. In December came the news that Nina Hamnett, Basil's flamboyant friend and sponsor in Bloomsbury and Paris in the 1920s, had died in tragic circumstances. Distressed and drinking heavily, even by her own standards, she had fallen from the window of her flat in Little Venice in London and been impaled on the spiked railings below.

The weeks and months went by and Basil wrote to Sima regularly. At Christmas his loneliness was alleviated by an unknown and entirely

Three chieftains or 'khans' of the Bakhtiari tribe in Iran such as Basil had to negotiate with when he was working for British Intelligence.

The Zagros mountains of Iran with the Bakhtiari making their annual migration.

Basil in Iran at the time he was working for British Intelligence.

Tom Pickard at the time Basil first met him. On the left: 'Shaggers' Alley' and the Morden Tower Bookroom.

Sima with Basil in Iran.

Shadingfield, the substantial house in Elm Bank Road, Wylam, Northumberland, to which Basil and his family moved in 1957.

Basil in the rear garden of Shadingfield overlooking the River Tyne.

Sima with her mother, left, and her mother-in-law Annie Bunting in the 1960s.

(left) Basil reunited with his first wife Marian in Wisconsin in the summer of 1966.

(below) Basil with his daughter Roudaba and granddaughter Monica in Santa Barbara, California, in 1966.

(left) The Quaker meeting house at Briggflatts.

(below) Peggy Greenbank's house in Hope near Minsterley, Shropshire, where she and Basil were reunited at the time of the publication of Briggflatts.

A family gathering in 1979. To Basil's left in order are his sister Joyce, his daughter Roudaba, his granddaughter Monica and his wife Sima.

Basil's youngest daughter, Maria, with Roudaba.

Greystead, Basil's remote cottage near the North Tyne in Northumberland.

Basil with Bourtai at Orono, Maine, in 1980.

The Fox and Hounds pub in the remote hamlet of Whitley Chapel. Basil's cottage is the furthest building on the right.

Basil at Fox Cottage in the last year of his life.

Together with Michael Shayer, Basil makes his way from Fox Cottage to the Fox and Hounds. This photograph was taken in the week that he died.

unexpected visitor. One day there came a knock at the door and a young man in his late twenties enquired where Basil Bunting was now living. When Basil laughingly identified himself, the young man introduced himself as Gael Turnbull. He was a doctor who had worked as a general practitioner in London, California and norther Ontario. He had been born in the north of England and had lived for some years in Jarrow where he was now spending the Christmas holidays with friends. Gael Turnbull was also a poet and one attracted to the Poundian tradition rather than to the assertive parochialism which in the fifties dominated poetry in Britain. In an American poetry magazine he had come upon a list of subscribers which included Basil's name and address. When Gael visited Tyneside, he determined to seek Basil out.

The visitor's first impression was that Basil was 'my story-book image of a scout-master'. When told this, years later, Basil had laughed and said, 'Oh that was the Squadron Leader Bunting.' But Gael's second impression at that first meeting was entirely different; it was one 'of dignity and humour'. When Basil remarked of someone, 'There was no side to him', Gael decided that this was true of Basil also. The young poet and the older man who was twice his age quickly warmed to each other:

> We sat in the kitchen and talked. He spoke of his life and the writing of poetry. Of the war and of his travels. Of Persia and Ispahan [sic] of the wines of California, and of Los Angeles before the freeways came. Many places, many people.
>
> He showed me a Koran, and translations from the Arabic, ornate and sinuous verse. Reading to me with a slight Northumberland accent, a roughness to the consonants.[9]

One sign of Throckley's emergence from the unchanging drabness of the war and the immediate post-war years was the building of a new pub just across the street from Basil's home on land that had once been part of his aunt's farm. To commemorate Throckley's proximity to the Roman wall, the brewery had named the pub *The Centurion*. When opening time came Basil suggested that they go over and try the place. Gael found the pub 'uncomfortably new', but nevertheless he and Basil enjoyed themselves. Gael remembered, 'He drank double brandies, enjoying them easily, the good humour in his eyes deepening and becoming almost rakish.'

It was with a sense of a relationship forming that the two poets stood waiting for the bus to take Gael on the first stage of his return journey to Jarrow. This was the first of several occasions on which someone from a younger generation would come seeking Basil's acquaintance and, through it, living contact with the literary tradition he represented. Such visits from the young also made for a renewal of Basil himself as a poet. Gael Turnbull's coming to Throckley in December 1956 was the first sign of Basil's rescue from the neglect and misery he had endured in recent years.

A few months after Gael's visit, when Sima was still lingering in Iran, Basil had another, more material piece of good fortune. His father's sister, wealthy Aunt Hetty, who had brewing interests in Burton-on-Trent, died and left him a substantial sum of money in her will. Suddenly there were new possibilities in life. He and his mother decided to buy a larger, more spacious house to which Sima, whom they both sorely missed, might be persuaded to return. He chose one in the pleasant village of Wylam, a few miles to the west on the banks of the River Tyne. He wrote to Sima telling her what he had done and appealing to her, as he put it, to help put up the curtains in the big new house, called Shadingfield. In June 1957, after an absence of eight months, Sima, together with their two children, returned to him.

FOURTEEN
The Years of Obscurity
1957–1965

Basil often told interviewers that his early years in Wylam were a poverty-stricken time. But in fact he lived in a very attractive upper middle-class area and Shadingfield is a substantial twelve-bedroomed property in Elm Bank Road, a pleasant street with a sharp rise so that from Basil's garden there was a fine view over the River Tyne to the centre of the village. Wylam is very much a country place, quite plush and prosperous, and visually a great improvement on the decaying mining village of Throckley. The look of the new house and its setting suggests that the Bunting family had, in this move, very much gone up in the world.

At the foot of steep Elm Bank Road stands *The Boatman*, the pub which Basil frequented very regularly. A few yards further on towards the village beside the wide fast-flowing Tyne there is the little railway station from which Basil used to commute the ten miles into Newcastle. Sometimes, however, he did the journey on the Lambretta motor scooter which he had bought with some of the money remaining from his aunt's legacy.

Basil would also say that when he made the down payment on Shadingfield, he became a mortgage slave. But in May 1996 Sima told me that her mother sent the money to pay off the balance on the £700 which the house had cost. Sima and Annie had three servants; a woman to do the laundry, a cleaner and Maggie, Annie's personal maid who had served her for years and whom she brought with her from Throckley. Basil himself maintained the large garden. He worked hard at it and enjoyed doing so. Nevertheless, if Basil had a more prosperous middle-class life than he cared to admit and if his financial woes were not as great as he suggested, there can be no doubt that the late 1950s were a drab and unsatisfying time for him. The work he did to support his family gave him no pleasure. He had by now moved to the *Newcastle Evening Chronicle* where he had been put in charge of the financial page. This involved checking all the figures in the stock market report, a painful task for someone with such very weak eyesight. He regarded his job at the newspaper as mere drudgery. One of his few consolations was to spend some of his lunch hours in the Library of the Literary and Philosophical Society of Newcastle. In this imposing building to which he had been taken by his parents in his early years he had the opportunity to continue with some serious reading.

The newspaper work occupied many hours each day and Basil did not see enough of his two children, Maria and Tom, or the rest of the household which was becoming quite a large and complex ménage. His mother Annie Bunting had her own impeccably maintained room with her piano. Sima's mother came on frequent visits from Iran. She and Annie could not understand each other's language but they got on famously together. They played card games and Annie told fortunes. Edmund Kahn, known as Eddie, had also come to live at Shadingfield. A handsome young Iranian, just a little older than Sima who was now in her early twenties, he was reportedly a distant relative of hers. His formal role in the house was to serve as her tutor. He was extremely quiet and reserved. Eddie had trained as an architect and was adept in practical matters as Basil was not. Sima herself was developing an interest in household improvement and Eddie was able to assist her in the necessary skills. They spent a good deal of time together. Eddie also took Sima and the children on holiday in Switzerland. One visitor to Shadingfield could see that Basil, now approaching his sixtieth birthday, resented Eddie.

Basil became increasingly cut off from the literary world. One rare stimulating contact occurred when in 1957 Louis Zukofsky brought his wife Celia and son Paul to stay at Wylam for some weeks. Basil took off holiday time from work and he and Sima took their guests on numerous trips around Northumbria and the north-east. The hosts were somewhat troubled by Louis' insistence that Paul should remain behind at Shadingfield to do the practice necessary to achieve his ambition to become a professional violinist.

In the months and years after the Zukofskys' visit Basil was in contact with ever fewer literary people. Nor did he write or publish any poetry. As the 1960s began it looked as though his career as a poet was over. In 1962 he received the news that Margaret de Silver had died; an important link with the days of his literary ambition was lost to him.

But then in the following year, the year of Beatlemania and the assassination of President John F. Kennedy, there was a sudden, dramatic upturn in Basil's fortune as a writer. What happened had something of the miraculous about it.

One Sunday evening the telephone rang in Shadingfield and Basil heard a rather nervous young man announce that he was one of the editors of a magazine called *Eruption* which was about to begin publication in Newcastle; he was wondering whether Basil would care to contribute. Basil indicated his interest and invited the caller to come and see him in Wylam. In little over an hour there was a knock at the door. When Basil opened it he saw for the first time the young man who would be the main force in recreating his career, in connecting him with an admiring younger generation and in entirely changing his life.

The young visitor was Tom Pickard; he was then seventeen years old, of an age to have been Basil's grandson. He was shabbily dressed and had very long hair. In the two years since he had left his secondary modern school he had had temporary jobs on building sites and in warehousing but had spent most of his time unemployed. He and Connie, whom he referred to as his 'lady', had a baby boy.[1] Tom was very left-wing and belonged to a group of young Trotskyists, socialists and anarchists. He was active in the Campaign for Nuclear Disarmament and in its militant wing the Committee of One Hundred. He was one of the young radicals whose activities, in Britain and America alike, would form an important part of the character of the decade.

Tom was passionately interested in poetry and was himself an aspiring poet. However he did not care for the literary parochialism and conservatism of Philip Larkin and the Movement; he preferred the poetry of the Beat Generation in the United States. This interest had led him on to admire the work of other American poets such as e. e. cummings, Walt Whitman and Ezra Pound.

Tom and Connie were living with the baby in one small room in a flat shared by three others, but despite their poverty they decided they would like to open a poetry bookshop and reading room where poetry might also be performed. Morden Tower, one of the medieval fortifications on the city walls of Newcastle, had become vacant. Its most recent tenants, the Northumbrian Pipers Association had found it too damp. The Pipers may also have been put off by the human excrement in the narrow dark lane outside. It was much used by prostitutes, littered with used condoms and known in Newcastle as Shaggers' Alley. But Connie, undeterred, went ahead and took a lease on the place. Bringing poetry out into society as performance, in however modest and underfunded a way, was a characteristic of the energetic regeneration of the art in Britain in the 1960s.

In a 'little magazine' which a poet friend brought to his attention Tom saw an advertisement for Jonathan Williams's Jargon Press, based in North Carolina. Always interested to be in touch with current American poetry Tom wrote him a letter, mentioning his own several projects. He received a kindly reply. Jonathan Williams now supplied Basil's address to Tom. This is what led to the telephone call to Wylam.

When he arrived at Shadingfield Tom was taken into the kitchen of the large house overlooking the River Tyne. He was introduced to Basil's mother whom he found 'a proud old woman' and also to Sima's mother who spoke no English. She had brought supplies of caviar with her from Persia and Tom was given lavish amounts on bits of toast. Basil also served plenty of whisky to the visitor. They talked intensely and at length about poetry. Then, as they ate and drank, Basil read aloud his last major work *The Spoils*. Though Tom could not understand everything in the poem, he found the experience of hearing it overwhelming. Moved, excited and 'half drunk' he asked if he might take the poem away and publish it under the imprint of the Morden Tower Bookroom. Basil agreed. He also urged Tom to return to Wylam soon and to bring some of his own poems. It had grown late and Tom had to take the train back to Newcastle. As he made his way through the darkness to the little station by the river and waited on the platform, lines from *The Spoils* echoed through his head. A historic literary friendship had begun.

A few weeks later, early in 1964, Basil went to the shabby bookroom in the Morden Tower and read his poems to an audience of some seventy people, most of them young, 'students, grammar school kids, apprentices and the unemployed'. He read by gaslight since there was no electricity. The audience sat on the floor. Tom Pickard remembered that 'The young people loved him and were attentive.' They recognized and respected this 'sailor come home'. Two years later Basil told Jonathan Williams that 'Tom Pickard tapped an audience I didn't know existed.' The audience were the 'unabashed boys and girls' to whom in 1968 Basil would dedicate his *Collected Poems*. Undoubtedly this new sense of an admiring audience, together with the developing friendship with Tom, surely the most unabashed of the unabashed, helped create the spectacular regeneration of Basil's literary career that now occurred.

During 1964 Tom managed to obtain a grant from Newcastle

University to enable the Morden Tower Bookroom to publish *The Spoils*. The poem was set up in print by Richard Hamilton, subsequently to become known as one of Britain's leading 'pop' artists and at that time teaching art in the north-east. Distribution posed a problem for the novice publisher, but this was solved by Gael Turnbull who had recently returned from California to England and had renewed his friendship with Basil begun some years earlier. Living now in Worcestershire where he worked as an anaesthetist, Gael in association with two other poets in the Midlands, Roy Fisher and Michael Shayer, had founded Migrant Press for the publication of progressive new poetry. Migrant, which already had some experience in distribution, agreed to take on *The Spoils* which was finally published early in 1965. When the first printing was sent from Newcastle to the Midlands the bulky parcel was lost in the postal sorting office in Birmingham. But Basil's backers were not to be daunted and a second printing was quickly completed and sent to Migrant.

Around this time Basil, inspired by these new developments in his career took the decision to commit himself to the writing of a new long poem. An old friend whom he had come to know through Ezra Pound was the actor and poet Denis Goacher who performed regularly in BBC radio plays, often on the Third Programme, later renamed Radio Three. It was to Goacher that Basil wrote in mid-December 1964 explaining his attraction to the long poem which was 'much neglected' as a form. Basil conceded that it would be easier for him to try nothing longer than 'a dozen lines or so'. But like other major modernist poets, T. S. Eliot, Ezra Pound, Hugh MacDiarmid, Charles Olson, David Jones and William Carlos Williams, he found it impossible to resist the lure of larger poetic forms. He was, he said, 'impelled by love of a larger shape, more architectural'. So now he set to work on what would prove to be his masterpiece. In his sixty-fifth year with retirement from the newspaper imminent, he returned to the serious practice of his art. As he did not have much free time he worked on the poem on the commuter train that he took to and from Newcastle every day. He would show or read passages to Tom Pickard, now his close friend. When Tom expressed his admiration Basil was greatly pleased. On the few occasions that Tom confessed that he found certain lines weak or flat Basil would become 'grumpy'.[2] Basil also sent drafts of sections to Louis Zukofsky and to Gael Turnbull inviting their suggestions. In the spring of 1965 Basil told the Birmingham poet Roy Fisher that 'The music is complete; all I have to do is to make adjustments to the content.'[3] A note in Gael Turnbull's journal for 15 May mentions receipt of a letter from Basil in which he confirms that the poem is completed.[4] In June he sent it off to *Poetry* of Chicago where it was accepted. The poem bore the title *Briggflatts*. It is his greatest work and one of the masterpieces of English literature in this century.

The twenty-four-page poem is subtitled *An Autobiography* and indeed its five sections, or movements, do evoke successive phases of Basil's life and his different senses of himself. The first section deals with his youth and his times with Peggy Greenbank (the dedicatee of the poem) at the Quaker settlement that provides the title to the work. The second section remembers his days in London and in Italy. The third is set mostly in the Middle East and the fourth and fifth constitute a *nostos*, a homecoming in Northumbria. Given Bunting's intense admiration for Wordsworth and the numerous allusions to Wordsworth in the poem, we may incline to think of it as an account of 'the growth of a poet's mind'. But in one of his notes to the poem Basil qualifies the term 'autobiography'. It is not, he tells us, 'a record of fact . . . The truth is of another kind.' It is, I think one may say, not so much a narrative truth as a musicalized truth. Like other modernist poems *Briggflatts* is a succession of images and discourse that are tightly patterned and made to sound and resound.

The poem has a very evident relationship with *Four Quartets* despite Basil's reservations about T. S. Eliot's poem. In his *Note On Briggflatts* published after his death Basil, identifying the title as referring to 'a remote hamlet and a Quaker meeting house', remarks that 'Unfortunately T. S. Eliot's *Four Quartets* are also named after little hidden places.' He regrets the apparent connection, because Eliot's *Quartets* 'expound the mystical Christianity that nineteenth century theologians brewed from a mash squeezed ultimately, I think from Plotinus'. Basil adds emphatically: 'No scheme of things could be further from my own.'[5] However, one great work of art will often allude to, emulate or challenge comparison with another and Basil, though in temperament and sensibility a very different poet from Eliot, clearly had that earlier masterpiece in mind when writing his own long poem.[6] The title of each quartet is, like *Briggflatts*, the name of a place which, however remote and unfamiliar to its first readers, is of special importance in the author's development. *Briggflatts* also follows the five movement design within each of Eliot's quartets in musicalizing the most significant places and experiences in the poet's life.

Basil's opening movement is a virtuoso display of prosodic skill. It employs a very rare stanza form of thirteen lines with an intricate pattern of rhyme and sound. The twelve image-packed stanzas recall occasions in the poet's boyhood, the landscape of the fell country so close to Wordsworth's landscape and also a happy and tender adolescent love. But this movement, like the opening movement of *Burnt Norton* is more than an evocation of past happiness. Together with the remembered well-being there is the more difficult registering of the final abandonment and betrayal of the girl. From the outset a profound issue is raised which will recur, and painfully, throughout the poem: the question of man's propensity to do that which goes against his best interest and his happiness. This theme of human perversity, on occasion showing itself as perversion, culminates in the vividly rendered image of Pasiphae and the bull at the end of the second movement. We are

> reminded of sweltering Crete
> and Pasiphae's pungent sweat,
> who heard the god-bull's feet
> scattering sand,
> breathed byre stink, yet stood
> with expectant hand
> to guide his seed to its soil;
> nor did flesh flinch
> distended by the brute
> nor loaded spirit sink
> till it had gloried in unlike creation.

In the first movement there are other tensions in the emotionally volatile stanzas. Happy recollection is continually undercut by uneasiness, guilt and shame at the deserting of the girl. The joyous outcry of the first stanza, the excited pleasure in the natural world, the tenor bull, the slow worm and the sound of the River Rawthey are suddenly quietened by the sombre, countering, sobering mood of the second stanza. Here the poet becomes mindful of another part of the memory, the carving of a tombstone by the stonemason who was the girl's father. Looking back on his first love, fifty years on, the poet is aware, as a young man would not be, of death as one of the conditions of life and love. Certain moments with the girl he recalls in terms that simultaneously suggest post-coital play and the laying out of the dead.

Gentle generous voices weave
over bare night
words to confirm and delight
till bird dawn.
Rainwater from the butt
she fetches and flannel
to wash him inch by inch,
kissing the pebbles.
Shining slowworm part of the marvel.
The mason stirs:
Words!
Pens are too light.
Take a chisel to write.

Aware of the continuities between certain offices of love and certain offices of death the poet is also aware of another balance in perspective that has to be maintained if the office of the poet is to be properly discharged. The last four lines just quoted introduce this other tension which runs through the opening movement and indeed through the whole poem. The desire to remember, to articulate and commemorate valuable experience is constantly tested and menaced by the fear that shame, doubt or sheer lack of verbal and poetic competence might prevent the achieving of a true formulation. Again like *Four Quartets*, *Briggflatts* has as one of its concerns the struggle involved in the actual composition of the poem. 'Shame deflects the pen.'

Brief words are hard to find,
shapes to carve and discard:
Bloodaxe, king of York,
king of Dublin, king of Orkney.
Take no notice of tears;
letter the stone to stand
over love laid aside lest
insufferable happiness impede
flight to Stainmore.

The unexpected intrusion of the memory of Eric Bloodaxe into the above lines of meditation on the difficulties of proper commemoration is an early example of the more than immediately personal concerns of this autobiography. A somewhat shadowy figure in the Anglo-Saxon Chronicle and Icelandic Sagas, Eric, the last king of Basil's native Northumbria, was treacherously murdered in the year 954 whilst fleeing to Stainmore, driven, the poet will later suggest, by some unknown but perverse compulsion, thus making him an analogue for the poet himself. As autobiography *Briggflatts* speaks of a lost love; also as a long poem containing history it speaks of a lost king, a lost kingdom, a lost culture. The figure of the murdered king serves to translate into historical terms the poem's preoccupation with human error, perversity, loss and fate.

The second movement of the poem is the longest of the five. And, however unostentatiously, the geographical and emotional range of the poem is greatly enlarged. Passages of free verse alternate with different stanza forms and these contrasts underscore the poet's ambivalences and hesitations as he recollects certain phases of his exile, seen in Odyssean terms, that followed upon his leaving the girl and his native place. Ulysses' ship is there in the five-line image:

> Thole-pins shred where the oar leans,
> grommets renewed, tallowed;
> halliards frapped to the shrouds.
> Crew grunt and gasp. Nothing he sees
> they see, but hate and serve.

The first stage of the journey was London. (The sonata *Briggflatts*, like Eliot's quartets, is a version of pastoral in that it contains a contrasting of the rural and the metropolitan.) The writing here is less concentrated, more colloquial as he recalls the London he knew in the 1920s, the northern part of Soho, especially Charlotte Street and Kleinfeldt's Fitzroy Tavern where he met Nina Hamnett and her Bloomsbury friends. He remembers himself in those years as a spy, convict, Bohemian and, above all, apprentice poet:

> despised
> by toadies, confidence men, kept boys,
> shopped and jailed, cleaned out by whores,
> touching acquaintance for food and tobacco.
> Secret, solitary, a spy, he gauges
> lines of a Flemish horse
> hauling beer, the angle, obtuse,

> a slut's blouse draws on her chest,
> counts beat against beat, bus conductor
> against engine against wheels against
> the pedal, Tottenham Court Road, decodes
> thunder, scans
> porridge bubbling, pipes clanking, feels
> Buddha's basalt cheek
> but cannot name the ratio of its curves
> to the half-pint
> left breast of a girl who bared it in Kleinfeldt's.

The poem journeys on into Italy where the time the poet spent living by the Ligurian Sea is evoked by a three-line image of the nearby quarries at Carrara which supplied Michelangelo. In this way the art of the Northumbrian stonemason is related to that of the great Renaissance master of cut stone. That concern with the nature of heroic possibility continues through *Briggflatts*. On this same coast Shelley drowned and Byron attended his cremation. As Bunting ponders his own exile Byron's hero, that other poetic wanderer Childe Harold, is brought to mind as yet another figure for comparison. There are numerous similarities between the protagonist of *Briggflatts* and Childe Harold; the following four lines from the first canto of Byron's poem constitute a good précis of the subject of *Briggflatts*.

> for he through Sin's long labyrinth had run,
> Nor made atonement when he did amiss,
> Had sigh'd to many, though he loved but one,
> And that loved one, alas! could ne'er be his.

The autobiography now moves on beyond the lands and traditions of the west; the third movement remembers Asia, the Middle East, Iran. And here is introduced a new analogue in the figure of Alexander the Great, that journeying leader who led his armies far from their native Macedonia and who in Persia attempted to unite the traditions of what we are long in the habit of calling East and West. The poem is mindful of the Koran and of the Buddha as well as of the epics of ancient Greece and Rome and northern Europe.

In the following imagist lines from the second movement orient and occident are collocated in an arresting way.

Asian vultures riding on a spiral
column of dust
or swift desert ass startled by the
camels' dogged saunter
figures sudden flight of the descant
on a madrigal by Monteverdi.

The music of the great Italian Renaissance master is familiarly beautiful. But to it the poet relates what in the case of the ass might seem uncomely and, in the case of the vulture, distasteful. But such similes, such figures, we come to see, serve one of the main enterprises of the poem which is to achieve holism, to perceive and to accept the world, the geographical world and also the natural world, as a unity. Most difficult to assimilate are the enduring facts of human perversity and unnaturalness. Throughout the work the poet contends with the two problematical emotions of disgust at humanity and self-disgust. At one point, in lines that express simultaneously self-loathing and defiance, he declares his closeness to vermin.

Where rats go go I,
accustomed to penury,
filth, disgust and fury;
evasive to persist,
reject the bait
yet gnaw the best.
My bony feet
sully shelf and dresser.

The sonata-like conflict between on the one hand disgust and squalor and on the other hope, cleanliness and creative formulation supplies the design of the third movement of *Briggflatts*. Here the poet's journey becomes an inner journey. The first half is a description of a nightmarish hell; the second half is an account of release from it. The opening narrative, as Basil once explained, derives from a section of the Persian epic the *Shah Na Meh* in which Alexander the Great

wanders through country after country where the most horrible things are going on, and ultimately comes to the mountains of Gog and Magog on the edge of the world. And his troops refuse

157

to follow him, but all alone he climbs up to the top of the mountain and there he sees the Angel sitting exactly as in my poem, with the trumpet ready to his lips to blow, and looking anxiously to the east for the signal to blow the trumpet and put an end to the world. And that of course does Alexander's business *for* him: he falls off the mountain, comes to, and leads everybody home in peace to Macedonia.[7]

But there is much more to the central movement of the poem than is conveyed by this summary of Alexander's heroic perseverance and his moment of eschatological awareness. Here more than in the two preceding movements we are impressed by the many and deep layerings of Bunting's art. The new semantic richness that presents itself in the hell section is in part the complication of voice and tone. We are given dramatic monologue and then dramatic monologue within dramatic monologue. In the first half of the movement, for instance, the governing pronoun is 'we'. The lines, we presume, are spoken by one of Alexander's soldiers. There is also a brief interjection by the voice of Hastor who, the poet informs us in a note, was a Cockney hero. The joke is at the expense of Colonel John Astor who was the proprietor of *The Times* when Basil was that paper's correspondent in Iran. Hastor is a figure of fun because of the pomposity and self-righteousness with which he defends and justifies himself against charges of corruption. In the course of the surreal journey of Alexander's soldiery we have a glimpse of an autobiographical actuality. The meld of voices brings together images of corruption from both ancient and modern times.

After some seventy lines the Macedonian persona who speaks for 'we' seems to tire. His account of the long journey through human foulness, sickness and folly becomes disheartened. There comes a desire to give up, to turn back, to go home. Basil Bunting at the end of *Briggflatts* presents his own *nostos*, his return to Northumbria. But the language employed by Alexander's soldier in the third movement reminds us that 'going home' can be a sentimentality, an evasion, a self-indulgence.

> But we desired Macedonia,
> the rocky meadows, horses, barley pancakes,
> incest and familiar games,
> to end in our place by our own wars
> and deemed the peak unscaleable.

From now on the soldier no longer speaks about 'we' but rather about 'he', Alexander. And this is an important switch. The 'we' are those whose lives have normal limitations and are confined to the expectable. The 'he' is the hero who is capable of going further, of climbing the mountain, of speaking with the angel and thus confronting the supranatural. In this part of the third movement the dichotomy between the natural and the unnatural is being re-examined and redefined. What Alexander does may not be normal or natural but it is nevertheless a glorious and an heroic achievement which compels the admiration of the soldiers who look on intensely, fascinated. The highly particular vocabulary and the tentative, suspenseful lineation of the passage in which the soldier describes Alexander's superhuman climb establish compellingly the rapt attention of his followers as they watch him.

> but he
> reached to a crack in the rock
> with some scorn, resolute though in doubt,
> traversed limestone to gabbro,
> file sharp, skinning his fingers,
> and granite numb with ice, in air
> too thin to bear up a gnat,
> scrutinising holds while day lasted,
> groping for holds in the dark
> till the morning star reflected
> in the glazed crag
> and other light not of the sun
> dawning from above
> lit feathers sweeping snow
> and the limbs of Israfel.

The consequences of Alexander's daring are that he encounters the Angel Israfel and then, following his fall from the mountain top, is given a radically new understanding of the natural world. As Basil pointed out in his *A Note to Briggflatts*, 'What Alexander learns when he has thrust his way through the degraded world is that man is contemptibly nothing and yet may live content in humility.' The lesson is relayed to him in the song of the slow-worm. This song contained within the dramatic monologue spoken by the soldier is a crucial occasion in the autobiography. It is a measure of the ambitiousness of *Briggflatts* that the poet

159

should attempt the writing of such a song. Such revelatory songs sung to human beings by the creature kingdom are audible only to a heightened religious sensibility such as that of St Francis of Assisi or to an artist of the vision of a Richard Wagner. The slow-worm's song, in fact, recalls the song of the forest bird in Wagner's *Siegfried*, a song which the hero hears only when he has passed far beyond the known and the familiar. Basil Bunting may also have had in mind the song of the wood dove in Arnold Schoenberg's *Gurrelieder*, a work about which he had written admiringly as a young man.

The slow-worm's song is not the only song sung by the natural world in *Briggflatts*. In the second movement the sea wind composes a seductive, sirenic song encouraging resignation and an acceptance of inevitable oblivion.

> Who sang, sea takes,
> brawn brine, bone grit.
> Keener the kittiwake.
> Fells forget him.
> Fathoms dull the dale,
> gulfweed voices . . .

The slow-worm's song is, in contrast, a song of survival and inspiration. It is a song of the cleanliness of nature after a vision of infernal filth and pollution. It is a song of goodwill and hope after the experience of horror and demoralization. Once he has heard it the hero whom the poet ponders as an analogue may properly return home.

> So he rose and led home silently through clean woodland
> where every bough repeated the slowworm's song.

The fourth movement introduces a sharp contrast in sound, rhythm and pace. After the short jaunty lines of the song we now have very extended lines, on occasion containing as many as nineteen syllables. Such long, slow lines create an adagio mood of careful meditation. Heroism is still the principle concern but the setting is no longer Asia but the landscape of Bunting's boyhood in the north of England. The campaign is no longer that of Alexander the Great but that of the Welshmen who were defeated at the battle supposedly fought at Catterick in Yorkshire.

These were the soldiers lamented by the sixth-century Welsh poet Aneurin in *Y Gododdin* which David Jones, a writer much admired by Basil, categorized as an 'epical poem'.

On three occasions in this movement Basil expresses his sense of closeness to Aneurin, the poet of defeat and massacre. In the previous movement heroic action was commended with keen, delicate empathy. But now, with slow deliberation, the poet takes up a more problematic aspect of heroic action, the suffering, destruction and death which such action can entail.

The poet's attitude to such matters is forthright and illiberal. He recalls an experience, presumably in Iran, when he fired his rifle and knew

> tomcat stink of a leopard dying while I stood
> easing the bolt to dwell on a round's shining rim.
> I hear Aneurin number the dead and rejoice,
> being adult male of a merciless species.

Accepting neither concern 'for bodily welfare nor pauper theorems' these lines assert that what is unpalatable in man, his violence and destructiveness, has to be recognized and admitted. True vision is a matter of 'excepting nothing that is'. The first forty or so lines of the movement move from a mood of quiet meditation to a passionate assertion of heroic and bardic vision and a scornful depreciation of a more restricted calculating perception.

These lines also switch continuously from the present to the past and back again. The movement begins with a visual image of mutability.

> Grass caught in willow tells the flood's height that has subsided;
> overfalls sketch a ledge to be bared tomorrow.

These two lines, in themselves an imagist poem, establish a double perspective which will continue in the following lines. At one moment the poet is contemplating the northern landscape in the present and at another, still using the present tense, he is in the past.

> I see Aneurin's pectoral muscle swell under his shirt,
> pacing between the game Ida left to rat and raven.

The fourteen centuries that separate the poet from Aneurin and King Ida
(who, Bede suggests, was the founder of the kingdom of Bernicia north
of the Tyne) are here cancelled. Such simultaneity persists when, in the
second and gentler half of the movement, the poet remembers the love
which fifty years before he left behind in this same landscape. The
abandoned love is now perceived in the present tense. What was past
becomes actual.

> My love is young but wise. Oak, applewood,
> her fire is banked with ashes till day.
> The fells reek of her hearth's scent,
> her girdle is greased with lard;
> hunger is stayed on her settle, lust in her bed.
> Light as spider floss her hair on my cheek which a puff scatters,
> light as a moth her fingers on my thigh.

But then he remembers his leave-taking and at the end of the movement
the lines contract with a sudden outburst of self-reproach and self-
contempt.

> My bony feet
> sully shelf and dresser,
> keeping a beat in the dark,
> rap on lath
> till dogs bark
> and sleep, shed,
> slides from the bed.
> O valiant when hunters
> with stick and terrier bar escape
> or wavy ferret leaps,
> encroach and cede again,
> rat, roommate, unreconciled.

The movement of feeling here is complicated. The poet's distaste for
himself (which follows the lines in which he associates himself with the
rat) modulates into acceptance, a commendation even, of the rat. The fit
of disgust once spent, there develops a perverse pride in that ugly,
elemental intransigence and courage which enable the self, like the rat,
to endure. It is another difficult instance of 'excepting nothing that is'

and it constitutes an important stage in the making of self-composure which is a chief subject of the poem. If love is to be recalled and saluted, so also must that other element that is there in human life and confessedly in the poet himself, that which subverts and destroys. After the problematical ambivalence of the second salute, that to the rat, the fourth movement concludes with a new calm in which, through the use of the first person plural, we are all implicated.

The opening part of the final movement is a beautiful evocation of a silent coastal landscape in Northumbria in winter. It is prefaced by a statement about poetic procedure that explains how this pre-eminently musicalized finale operates.

> Slur, ratio, tone,
> chime dilute what's done
> as a flute clarifies song,
> trembling phrase fading to pause
> then glow.

Slur, ratio, tone and chime are heard throughout the movement, as indeed throughout the whole poem. The final 'glow' to which the poet refers begins some forty lines before the end. It is an extremely ambitious passage; it is an evocation of cosmic harmony.

One reason for the success of these last lines, dealing with such a large subject, is that they are preceded by and grounded in entirely convincing renderings of earthy, homely realities, people and things of this world, such as the shepherds and sheep-dogs of the Simonsides in Northumberland or the action of the sea upon the shore. Here are two lines that exemplify the closeness of attention, visual as well as auditory, in such writing.

> Silver blades of surf
> fall crisp on rustling grit.

Convinced by this kind of verbal representation of things of this earth we are carried along by the poet's rendering of an order that transcends them. As the stars begin to appear over the North Sea, the first to be seen is Aldebaran which, chiming with an important motif in the poem, is in the constellation of Taurus, the bull. The procession of stars has its accompanying music.

Young flutes, harps touched by a breeze,
drums and horns escort
Aldebaran, low in the clear east,
beckoning boats to the fishing.
Capella floats from the north
with shields hung on his gunwale.
That is no dinghy's lantern
occulted by the swell – Betelgeuse,
calling behind him to Rigel.
Starlight is almost flesh.
Great strings next the post of the harp
clang, the horn has majesty,
flutes flicker in the draft and flare,
Orion strides over Farne.

The poem ends with a sounding of wonder and calm. The autobiography does not arrive at any new self-knowledge but rather at a new state of consciousness and being. The seventeen-line coda that follows the fifth movement declares explicitly, even rhetorically, the impossibility of knowing about our deepest motivations and compulsions. Knowledge is denied us. What *Briggflatts* offers us at the last is, instead, an ontological experience.

In this it is very much a part of the modernist tradition. Its conclusion is of an order similar to that of Basil's older contemporary at the end of *Little Gidding* and to that of his younger contemporary and friend, Roy Fisher, at the end of his profoundly ambitious and wonderfully achieved long poem, *A Furnace*. Basil's long poem, like theirs, is a working through of a redemptive process which at the last conduces to a state of being in which a life with all its pains and guilt can be surveyed with composure and acceptance.

FIFTEEN
The Years of Eminence
1965–1979

The completing of *Briggflatts* was one of the several wonders of Basil's life during 1965. Another was the re-entry into his life, after half a century, of the lost love who was a subject and the inspiration of the poem, Peggy Greenbank.

Basil wished to dedicate the work to her but felt he could not do so without her permission. However, he did not know where she was or how he might get in touch with her. When he heard that his by now close friend Gael Turnbull was planning to drive up from Worcestershire to Scotland, Basil urged him to travel via Sedbergh and to go and see the Quaker settlement at nearby Briggflatts. Basil was so keen on his visiting the place and the local people that Gael sensed that Basil had some ulterior motive.

In the event Gael's visit to the remote hamlet in north-west Yorkshire brought about the reunion of Basil and Peggy. Arriving at the Quaker meeting house the doctor went inside and stood contemplating the simple wooden benches. Then the door opened and the custodian entered. Gael asked him questions including the whereabouts of the stonemason's yard. After searching his memory the custodian recalled that he had heard talk, many years before, of such a yard and the marble fragments it contained. He also told Gael that one of the mason's relatives was still living in a house nearby and he encouraged him to go and talk to her. Gael knocked on the door and the elderly lady who opened it identified herself as Cissie, Peggy's sister. She invited him inside and they had a long talk.

Peggy, he learned, was still alive; she was married and the mother of two daughters. Her husband was Edward Edwards who worked in management in the motor industry close to Wolverhampton in the West Midlands. Cissie gave Gael Peggy's address. He was taken aback to discover that she lived not many miles from his own home in Malvern. She and her husband had a cottage in the small village of Hope, just south of Minsterley in rural Shropshire. Edward had lodgings during the week close to Wolverhampton and returned to Hope for weekends and holidays. Peggy, who had become a teacher, had a post in the Hope village school.

Basil was excited to learn that, when he next visited Gael in Malvern, it would be easy for him to see Peggy again. He duly drove over to Hope and their reunion was joyous and tender. They grew close again, seeing a great deal of each other on days Edward was away at the factory. Basil was greatly moved by Peggy's beauty as an older woman. To his daughter Bourtai he later spoke at length about Peggy's silver grey curls. Basil sent Peggy gifts. Michael Shayer recalls Basil entrusting him with a beautiful but delicate Persian vase to take to Peggy.[1]

In May 1965 Basil tried to get Peggy to meet him in London. Denis Goacher had used his influence at the BBC to get Basil a job reading some of Pound's *Cantos* on the radio. For all his customary shortage of money Basil told Goacher that he would definitely not go to Broadcasting House to do the reading on the day Peggy came to London. All he would do on that day would be to sit and look at her. He added that there was half a century of looking to be caught up with.

When Edward found out about the new relationship between his wife and Basil he determined not to be jealous. He declared that they were all too old to think of breaking up marriages and families. But Basil confided to Gael Turnbull that he and Peggy were considering going off together. And in a note to Denis Goacher in May Basil spoke of Peggy making up her mind 'to what seems the inevitable break with her husband'. Edward and Peggy even went to stay at Wylam where presumably the possibilities and practicalities of such a splitting up were discussed. Sima, now in her early thirties, was not greatly perturbed. Indeed she was quite amused by the romance of two people in their sixties. However, Basil and Peggy did not elope together. When, in the summer of 1966, Basil accepted a teaching position at the University of California at Santa Barbara, he flew to America alone.

Basil wrote to Peggy a good deal but she finally decided to remain with her husband and came to be embarrassed by the urgency of Basil's attentions to her. During his time in America, or perhaps a little later, she took the decision that all contacts between them should be suspended.

The year that brought Peggy Greenbank back into his life and saw the successful completion of twelve months' work on *Briggflatts* also brought a great resurgence in Basil's acitivity as a writer of short lyric poems. It was yet another wonder. Basil's careful datelining of the items in his oeuvre shows that after 1949 fifteen years went by without a single poem being contributed. Then seven appear bearing the dateline 1965; they constitute well over half the collection entitled *Second Book of Odes*. These poems display a wide range of subject-matter and mood. There is mockery of the philistinism of provincial England in 'What the Chairman Told Tom', a poem based on Tom Pickard's experience in trying to obtain funding from local government in order to write his poetry. From the time of Basil's first visits to the Morden Tower Bookroom comes 'A thrush in the syringa sings', a twelve-line poem of great profundity, one of Basil's best shorter pieces. 'Birthday greeting' is a recollection of the Canary Islands; it is slight but charming. A version from Catullus skilfully captures the Sapphic elements of the original, and there is an amusing and optimistic poem about old age beginning 'You idiot! What makes you think decay will/never stink from your skin?'

Whilst Basil worked on these and other short lyrics, his long poem *Briggflatts* was enjoying an immediate success. It was enthusiastically received by the young people at the Morden Tower Bookroom and by the visiting American poet Allen Ginsberg. Basil described Ginsberg (who read his own poems in the bookroom for four hours in May) as looking 'like an owl in a bunch of ivy' and found him 'amusing and very likeable'. Basil also read *Briggflatts* to fellow poets, including some in London whom he had come to know through Gael Turnbull. On his visit to the capital he met William Cookson, the editor of *Agenda*, a magazine that sought to promote Poundian poetics and which in the coming years published a good deal of Basil's prose and poetry. A young Rhodesian, Stuart Montgomery, who together with his wife Deirdre had recently set up a poetry publishing house, asked if he might publish *Briggflatts* in book form. Basil signed a contract with him and the first edition of the work appeared in February 1966. Three months earlier, in the November of Basil's *annus mirabilis* 1965, Stuart Montgomery's Fulcrum Press also published a limited edition of Basil's *First Book of Odes*, the title page giving Fulcrum's address as Stuart's home, 16 Lawn Road in Hampstead. A month later Fulcrum Press, which had a major role in the revival of poetry in Britain in the sixties, brought out, in a much larger print run, *Loquitur*, a near eighty-page volume which contained the poems in the *First Book of Odes* together with 'Chomei at Toyama', eleven translations and adaptations which Basil called 'Overdrafts' and his four early sonatas: 'Villon', 'Attis', 'Aus Dem Zweiten Reich' and 'The Well of Lycopolis'.

Suddenly all his work was in print again. He attributed his good fortune entirely to *Briggflatts* and to the friendship of Tom Pickard who had provided the stimulus for the writing of that poem. At the end of September 1965, in a letter to Dorothy Pound, Basil spoke of *Briggflatts* as having an ongoing magic in his life. He told her that all his luck had changed since he had begun writing it. More importantly, he added it was the best thing he had ever written, by far.

His good fortune and new happiness brought about a change in his appearance. A photograph taken in 1966 just before his retirement shows him as a very middle-class figure. Taken for and by Thomson newspapers, his employers, the picture shows him as the alert journalist, pen and pad in hand, wearing a smart suit with a white shirt and a neatly knotted tie. His hair is cut short and his moustache is well trimmed. Photographs of him after his retirement and after he had become a part of the youthful set at the Morden Tower show how he had let his hair grow long and his moustache become bushy. The suit has now given way to the sort of clothes worn by the young men of Tom Pickard's generation: duffle coat, scarf and sweater. A wine or beer glass replaces the reporter's pen. On retirement Basil did not take on the appearance of a pensioner; very visibly, and also clearly very happily, he aligned himself with the young.

He was becoming happier too in his family life. His mother was now ninety-years-old and very deaf but still capable of insisting that she go alone into Newcastle to visit the shops. Basil's relationship with Sima still endured although he admitted to Dorothy Pound that they some-times quarrelled, but not for long. He said that there were traces in Sima's temper of the hard times they had recently gone through together. The couple took great pleasure in their two children. Maria in the year of *Briggflatts* was fifteen and showing talent as a painter. She was also becoming interested in poetry and was proud of her father. When Basil went down to London to read *Briggflatts* Maria accompanied him and impressed the people they met with her prettiness.[2] Tom Bunting, very Iranian in appearance, was now twelve years old and Basil began to talk about sending him to a public school as he himself had been. Sima was horrified; she could not understand or accept this English middle-class notion of schooling. She thought it cruel to send a child of Tom's years away from his home. Basil finally agreed that if Tom could pass the entrance examination for the Royal Grammar School in Newcastle, to which he could commute each day, then he could continue his education there. Sima brought all the force of her formidable personality to bear on her son to do his best. And Tom succeeded. He was one of the three candidates, out of more than three hundred, to pass the examination and enter the School. He was excellent at mathematics but his favourite subject was Latin, an interest that had been an important part of his father's literary and intellectual life. Tom's acceptance into the Royal Grammar School removed the problem of how a public-school education could be paid for. As usual Basil was in debt and short of money. His financial difficulties were however somewhat alleviated when Gael Turnbull on his own initiative approached the Northern Arts Council telling them of the achievement represented by *Briggflatts* and obtained a grant of three hundred pounds for Basil.

When it appeared in book form *Briggflatts* received excellent reviews including those from such long-established critics as Cyril Connolly and Herbert Read. On 2 June 1966 Basil took up an invitation to appear with the Northern Sinfonia Orchestra in the City Hall in Newcastle where he read his poetry to the music of Vivaldi, Corelli and Albinoni. He told an *Evening Chronicle* reporter that he was a little uneasy with such a star role, since he was not trained as an actor or an opera singer. But he devised a loudspeaker system which allowed him to project his voice in the large hall at different levels of volume.

Basil's reputation also soared in academic circles and in 1966 the great Pound scholar, Hugh Kenner, then Chairman of the English Department at the University of Santa Barbara in California invited him to teach there for a time. Basil accepted the offer. Neither he nor Sima appear to have minded the lengthy separation. Sima was by now involved in an extensive social life in and around Wylam and she was pleased to have the extra money that Basil was able to send from America.

Basil's career as a journalist in Newcastle formally ended on 30 August 1966 when he retired from his job on the *Evening Chronicle*. He decided that he would not fly directly to California but go via Madison, Wisconsin, where, after thirty years, he could meet his first wife Marian again and his elder daughter Bourtai and get to know her six sons who were his grandchildren. When he was a drifter in the United States in the late 1930s Basil had felt unable to go to Wisconsin. Now, with a great literary success behind him and a university salary before him, Basil set out to see his first family.

Understandably the reunion was not an easy one. A photograph of Basil and Marian taken that summer shows them looking constrained together. Though Roudaba has told me that Marian had hoped that she and Basil might resume their lives together, Bourtai felt uncomfortable with Basil's clearly expressed wish to renew his role as her father. Now in her thirty-fifth year and the mother of a large family Bourtai was one of the student activists of the 1960s on the University of Wisconsin campus. Jailed more than once for her involvement in demonstrations against the war in Vietnam and in favour of the Civil Rights movement, Bourtai was now studying to become a lawyer after working her way through university to obtain a degree in history. She still had her causes, a husband and six sons. She also felt let down by Basil in time past and found it difficult to be filial in the way he wished.

By September Basil had moved on to Santa Barbara where he took an apartment close to the Pacific ocean. The retired provincial journalist and old-age pensioner now embarked upon a brand new career in academe that would take him to posts in a succession of North American universities. In California, as on campuses elsewhere, he was a great success with the students even though, as he told Dorothy Pound, his first class considered lynching him when they saw the examination paper he had drawn up for them. There were many stories about him as a teacher. In one of his Santa Barbara classes he got the students to read aloud Wordsworth's 'Idiot Boy'. Gradually they came to find that tall tale funny and started to laugh. They had never before thought that Wordsworth might be entertaining. The laughter intensified and became thoroughly contagious. Hysteria seemed about to take over the young Californians. From the adjacent lecture rooms came bangings on the walls to get the young devotees of Wordsworth to shut up.

The high spirits of this time also showed in a letter to the young American poet Robert Creeley that year. Basil said that he was considering writing a poem about Salome. But not in the fashion of Wilde, Flaubert and Laforgue. Basil's Salome woud jig and wiggle and make no fuss about stripping off. There would be no womanly wiles or agonizing afterthoughts. His Salome would probably dance to the music of *the* rock band of the sixties, the Beatles. But this project which he pondered during his first months in California apparently did not develop very far.

At Santa Barbara Basil dined from time to time with Hugh Kenner and his family. One of Kenner's small daughters thought that Basil who was 'trim and twinkling-eyed, with a white moustache' really looked like a poet.[3] Her father, however, suspected that 'she was projecting on his features the undoubted fact that he *sounded* like a poet'.[4] He was a wonderful teller of tales. He told story after story: Persian stories, secret service stories, dog stories and camel stories.

At Christmas that year he entertained a still younger person, his granddaughter Monica, the three-year-old child of his younger daughter Roudaba. Basil was sufficiently in funds at that time that he could send them their air tickets for their flight to California. Roudaba was then training as a nurse at the University of Honolulu. With an interracial marriage and family she found it easier to live in Hawaii than in Wisconsin. She and Monica spent nearly three weeks with Basil in his small flat near Santa Barbara. They all had a good time even though the visitors found California very cold after Hawaii. Roudaba was surprised to find that her father was not the wild Bohemian cape-swirling poet that her mother had so often described but instead a more conventional figure, quiet, gentle and professorial.

In March 1967 as his first academic year approached to its end he travelled across the United States attending a succession of poetry gatherings. He went first to an Ezra Pound conference in Texas where, he reported, the Texans tried to drown him in Bourbon. Ezra Pound himself preferred to remain at his home in Italy and did not attend. But Basil met and greatly liked Ezra's daughter Mary de Rachelwitz. However, he found the conference proceedings plodding and humourless; he did not like to see Ezra and the *Cantos* being embalmed and treated as museum material.

His next stop was New York where he had been invited to share a platform at the Guggenheim Museum with some other poets including Robert Creeley and Allen Ginsberg, both of whom he found extremely kind. Basil read *Briggflatts*, interlarding the movements with passages from Scarlatti. On stage he was accompanied by a beautiful young girl, his *sakki*, who poured his claret while he read. Robert Creeley concluded that no one would ever read in New York again 'without a chick on the platform'. At the end of Basil's reading Ginsberg led the large audience in clapping, jumping and yelling.

But the visit to New York City was not an entirely happy one. Basil had looked forward to a reunion with Louis Zukofsky but his meeting with his old friend, colleague and mentor did not live up to his expectations. Louis still had not enjoyed any great success or fame and seemed to resent Basil's. In a letter to Tom Pickard Basil wrote that he had found Louis 'very bitter and, strangely, very jealous'.[5] They had passed a 'painful hour' together. In old age Louis was increasingly prone to hypochondria and he refused to go to the Guggenheim Museum to hear Basil read insisting that there would be 'drafts' there. Basil left New

York saddened by this rift with Louis for whom, he thought, he ranked 'as his oldest friend'.

Then it was on to Harvard where Basil had a quieter but still most enjoyable time. His hosts drove him around the nearby countryside and showed him Concord and Gloucester. When he did his reading the reception was less noisy than in New York but revealed, he thought, a more convincing appreciation of his work. Back in California he continued his burgeoning career as a performance poet, giving readings in Santa Barbara and San Francisco. In the latter city he met the Beat poet Lawrence Ferlinghetti, recently returned from a trip across Siberia, a journey which, Basil sensed, had bleached out all the red that ever was in him.

In May 1967 Basil underwent a successful operation on the cataracts in one of his eyes. He reported to Dorothy Pound that he had become blinder and blinder. He could only read books that were in reasonably large type and then with the help of a strong light. Though he could see the moon he had not been able to see the stars for three years. His eyesight was barely sufficient to enable him to cross the road safely; but he could still make out and enjoy girls' legs if not their faces.

After his operation he prepared to travel east again in June 1967. His daughter Maria, now aged seventeen and the possessor of a brand new driving licence, had flown out from England and now drove him across America to Bourtai's house near Madison, Wisconsin. Basil's eyesight was not yet sufficiently recovered that he could undertake such a drive on his own. By the end of June father and daughter had reached Aspen, Colorado, where Basil renewed his friendship with Jonathan Williams who was then scholar-in-residence at the Aspen Institute.

Whilst summering in Wisconsin, Basil, together with Bourtai and Maria, visited a poet he greatly admired, Lorine Niedecker, who lived not far away on Blackhawk Island near Fort Atkinson. Lorine's husband, a backwoodsman, odd-job man and house painter was prone to both drink and jealousy. He had no great respect for his wife's literary achievement. Bourtai remembered that, when Lorine opened the wooden box containing her poems, a gun could be seen on top of the manuscripts. However, it was a visit that gave intense pleasure both to Basil and to his hostess.

Towards the end of the summer Basil, Bourtai and Maria and Bourtai's son Ahab set off for Montreal. It had been decided that Ahab, close to

Maria in age, should sail back to England with her and spend a year at Wylam. Before the two young people embarked, the whole party visited Expo '67, then being held in Montreal. At their hotel Basil was robbed of a considerable sum of money. Bourtai, very left-wing in her views, suggested to her father that this was a necessary act of redistribution. But Basil, now far more conservative than he had been forty years before at the time of the General Strike in Britain, angrily contradicted her.

They drove back through Ontario and Michigan to Wisconsin. Knowing that her reputation as a radical and an activist made it difficult for her to find work in her home state Bourtai, who was now a single parent, decided to travel west with her father, settle in California and seek employment there. She took her eldest son Gideon to his father in Chicago and left her next eldest son Saul with her mother in Madison so that he could finish high school there. Then she packed all her possessions into Basil's car and with her youngest sons, Fenris aged fifteen, Todd eight and Colin seven, set off on the long drive west. Basil sat beside her and served as navigator. They stopped at the Mesa Verde and at the Grand Canyon. Basil was expert at keeping his three grandsons on the backseat entertained. As they crossed the California desert, where Basil insisted that Bourtai did not drive too fast, he organized a very successful game, pretending they were crossing the vast Sahara desert and could only have their rations of dates and water at fixed intervals.

Bourtai and her sons stayed with Basil some months in his apartment at Isola Vista, Goleta, California. It was a happy time for them all with Basil's enjoying sitting out, sipping wine and reading Wordsworth in preparation for his classes. Finally Bourtai found a job as a social worker in the Florence district of Los Angeles just north of Watts. She did well at her job and was quickly promoted. She frequently travelled up the coast to stay with her father.

In early summer 1968 when his appointment at Santa Barbara came to an end Basil returned to England and accepted the position of Northern Arts Literary Fellow at the Universities of Newcastle and Durham. Basil spent a very quiet term at Durham but when the Professor of English at Newcastle died Basil was persuaded to take over some of the professorial responsibilities. For the first and only time in his life Basil functioned as an orthodox academic preparing and delivering lectures to undergraduates. He found the necessary background reading very time-consuming but he also enjoyed it. He found himself re-reading such varied texts as *Beowulf, Sir Gawain and the Green Knight* and the poems of Wyatt and Spenser.

His fame as a poet continued to grow. Fulcrum published his *Collected Poems*. He made a recording of *Briggflatts*. The BBC made a film about him. In Lexington, Kentucky, Jonathan Williams published *Descant on Rawthey's Madrigal*. During the New Year holiday in 1969, whilst Basil and Sima were entertaining Gael Turnbull and his wife at Wylam, Basil was considering an invitation from the Poetry Society to take part in their grand poetry festival at the Royal Albert Hall in February. He felt doubts about appearing with Establishment figures such as the Poet Laureate but he finally accepted and enjoyed an enthusiastic reception.

In the late summer Basil was back in London. He was delighted that his son Tom had passed all his O-level examinations and, as a reward, took him to London for a week while Sima was away with friends on a caravan holiday in Scotland. Basil and Tom stayed with Stuart and Deirdre Montgomery of the Fulcrum Press. Father and son enjoyed various excursions. They sailed down the Thames to Kew and also visited a controversial Pop Art exhibition. When they returned to Wylam nineteen-year-old Maria kept house for them.

During 1969 Basil bought himself a second-hand car, a Ford Zodiac, one of the largest and most prestigious cars in the Ford range in Britain at that time. He knew that it was heavy on petrol but it was in prime condition. And, as in his poverty-stricken days in Rapallo when he travelled first class on the train, he always plumped for luxury when it was at all possible.

One of his first trips in the new car was to the village of Hope just south of Shrewsbury where Peggy Greenbank still lived. Basil had persuaded his childhood sweetheart to alter her decision of four years before and to see him again. In December 1969 he told Denis Goacher in a letter that he had spent two days with Peggy, presumably in her husband's absence, and that it had been 'very satisfactory'. They seem to have continued for a while as lovers with no further thought of running off together. Some time later Peggy decided that in fairness to her husband, Edward, she should terminate the renewed affair.

So Basil's life continued to be anchored in the ménage at Wylam which, with the arrival of the Ford Zodiac, had started to appear quite properous. He and Sima rarely took their large car into Newcastle because of the difficulties of parking there. Instead they shopped in the ancient, fortified market town of Hexham which was nearer and smaller. But Basil still kept his bank account in Newcastle. He feared that if he transferred to a closer branch the ups and downs of his financial record might be looked at askance. For all his new eminence in the world of letters he felt that he was no more likely to impress bank managers than were the unconventional young poets with whom he kept company.

Basil's close friendship with the owners of Fulcrum Press enabled him to get the work of some of his friends published. After decades of suffering as a literary outsider, Basil was starting to wield influence in the world of English poetry. In 1967 Stuart and Deirdre Montgomery at their new headquarters at 20 Fitzroy Square had brought out Tom Pickard's first volume of poems, *High on the Walls*, with a preface by Basil in which he describes his young friend as a man who 'has escaped education' and who has 'fresh eyes, a fresh voice and the skill to keep the line compact and musical'. Basil concludes that 'Tom's work to date has already earned him a place in any competent lyric anthology.' In 1971 Fulcrum published Tom Pickard's second volume, *The Order of Chance*. The previous year the Montgomerys had published another of Basil's young friends, Omar Pound, with a collection of translations entitled *Arabic and Persian Poems* and again Basil contributed an admiring preface. It must have been a great pleasure, when the book was being prepared in 1969, to be able to boost the work of the son of the man who had done so much for him. Omar, Basil claims, has broadened our understanding of Moslem poetry. The translations flash 'a momentary light on many poets, tracing another hue in the web'. Omar makes the poetry credible and he makes it a pleasure; he selects and translates the lines which match what Basil identifies as the young man's 'urbane, ironic manner'.

Earlier that year, 1969, Omar's mother, Dorothy Pound, now for ever estranged from Ezra whom she had married more than half a century before, had been a very welcome guest at Shadingfield. Basil and Sima enjoyed showing her Northumberland. Dorothy took a special interest in the great flaming steel mill at Consett, and did paintings of the spectacular sunset there after the burning ash had been emptied from the furnaces.

Sima took a strong liking to Dorothy. But this was not true of all the many people who now came to Wylam to call on Basil. Some of his literary admirers she considered dirty and disreputable. She felt they got Basil to drink too much and exploited his good nature. Often when the conversation was becoming overheated Sima would go into the kitchen and, without their knowing, water the Scotch. Some of the visitors were the cause of angry quarrels between husband and wife. But one of Basil's most outrageous friends charmed Sima with the power of his exuberance and bawdiness. This was the great Scots Marxist poet with the fine head of silver-grey hair, Hugh MacDiarmid. At the local pub he had said to the pretty landlady one winter's night, 'Put your legs around my throat, lassie, I'm frozen.' He also alarmed the other drinkers in *The Boatman* by announcing that he was going to murder Basil so that he could sleep undisturbed with Sima. The landlord's wife was slow to accept Sima's repeated assurances that this was just a joke. And once when Dr Gael Turnbull was a fellow visitor at Wylam, MacDiarmid beckoned him into an adjacent room asking for a medical check up. When MacDiarmid emerged he declared to the household that the presciption was fourteen different women per week.

In the autumn of 1970 Basil joined a more sedate group of people when he returned to North America to take up a position in the English department at the University of British Columbia in Vancouver. Along with my colleague Peter Quartermain I was instrumental in getting him the job. I remember that when Basil's letter of application arrived the department head, a Chaucerian, asked my advice. A keen admirer of Basil's work, I was delighted that he might come and strongly urged the appointment. I left the head's office and he picked up Basil's letter to read again. As I walked down the hall, the head, a rather prim and starchy American conservative, hurried after me crying, 'Hey, did you know that this guy has been in jail?'

I think Basil quite enjoyed his time in Vancouver. There was a large and very enthusiastic audience for poetry there at that time. As a result of the activities of the critic Warren Tallman and his wife Ellen the department had strong connections with the Black Mountain poets in the United States. Charles Olson, Robert Duncan and Robert Creeley all spent time on the campus. Basil was by now a close friend of Robert Creeley who always visited him when he travelled to Britain.

Basil had a small, simple apartment not far from the sea in the Kitsilano area of the city. He enjoyed the restaurants, especially those in Japanese town. He was very active on the campus. On one memorable occasion on 20 November, he read *Briggflatts*, accompanied by yet another beautiful *sakki*, to an enthusiastic audience of more than five hundred in the music auditorium. Another evening he sat and answered questions put to him by a large gathering of students and younger professors. His manner was a compound of quiet dignity, wit and friendliness.

One of Basil's students in Vancouver in 1970 was Susan Swanson who late in 1997 talked to me about what it had been like to be taught by him. She remembered, above all, the great courtesy with which he treated the students and the beautiful way in which he read poetry aloud. This was his principal mode of teaching. His reputation was such that his courses, all for undergraduates, were oversubscribed. Numerous students who could not get into his lecture room would silently stand or sit in the corridor outside, straining to hear him.

At the end of term Basil took the train across the wintery landscape of the Canadian Rockies and prairies to Winnipeg and then flew from there, in a blizzard, to Chicago and then on to Madison to spend Christmas with Marian and Roudaba. The visit was not a happy one. Marian, who had continued to hope that Basil might still return to her, declared that she now felt spurned by him. She became extremely upset, storming out of the house and destroying her Christmas presents.

Early in the New Year Basil travelled to the State University of New York at Binghamton where he had agreed to teach for the first three months of 1971. He told Dorothy Pound that he felt both bored and lonely during this time but had a project which gave him pleasure. He was making an act of homage to Ford Madox Ford by preparing a selection of his old mentor's poems. The book was to be published by Pym-Randall Press of Cambridge, Massachusetts. Though granting Ford's limitations as a poet, Basil in his preface noted certain strengths, particularly the way Ford in his poetry added the rhythms of conversation to conversational diction. This was something, added Basil, which was 'rare in 1910, almost unknown'. It was also, of course, something that was present in Basil's own poetry from its very beginnings.

While he was at Binghamton Basil was invited by Penguin Books to do another poetry selection with a preface, but their list of possible poets included no one that he could interest himself in. He said he would have taken on Wordsworth or Spenser or Wyatt because they deserved it, or Swinburne or Charles Churchill because they suffered from undue neglect. But he could not bear to re-read Tennyson for any money that Penguin could pay.

Except for the work on Ford Basil was not content at Binghamton. He was beginning to weary of teaching; he felt that it got in the way of his writing. So he was relieved when the time came for him to return to

England in the early summer. In London in July he read at the Third International Poetry Festival and then he travelled north to be reunited with Sima who had been very much enjoying her own life and having a good deal of success at tennis. Eddie Kahn had just set up his own architectural practice and drove a glamorous sports car, a Lotus Elan. One day the expensive car spontaneously combusted at the level crossing just below the house. With a touch of malicious glee in his letter Basil described to Dorothy Pound how the fire reduced the Lotus to little more than a metal shell.

Basil's grandson, Roudaba's son Finn, also lived at Shadingfield that summer. A memorable experience for them all in August was a trip to the source of the River Coquet. Basil was intrigued to hear the water 'singing away' under the mountains. The Coquet was the inspiration for one of the finest of his late lyrics, 'Stones trip Coquet burn', in which the pursuing of the course of the upper reaches of the river is delicately metaphorized as the chase after a girl. It is an infectious statement of pleasure in nature and sensuousness.

Around this time Tom Pickard was charged with helping to transport a large amount of marijuana. Entirely loyal to his friend Basil appeared before the judge as a character witness. Presenting himself in his best squadron-leader fashion Basil made an excellent impression and Tom was finally released. When the judge asked Basil, in an upper-class man to man way, whether he, Basil, was not surprised that a friend of his should possess marijuana, Basil, very well acquainted with the opium culture of Iran, replied that he would have been surprised if a young man of Tom's age had *not* on occasion possessed marijuana.[6]

In September, after being made an honorary D.Litt. by Newcastle University, Dr Bunting set off again to Canada to earn money from university teaching. This income greatly enhanced his standard of living. He was able, for instance, to continue to maintain his large Ford Zodiac car and he bought 150 shares in ICI. This time his academic destination was the University of Victoria on Vancouver Island. He was not happy there, telling Dorothy Pound that it was 'a foul place'. He came into prolonged and acrimonious conflict with a colleague in the English department who resented Basil occupying a post teaching poetry whilst maintaining the view that poetry could not be taught. Basil did, however, take pleasure in meeting again old friends from his time at the University of British Columbia, especially Peter Quartermain whom he saw often during these months. Also, Roudaba and her family had moved to nearby Seattle and it was easy for him to take the ferry and visit them.

Nevertheless he was glad when his appointment at the University of Victoria came to an end in April and he could return to Wylam. He travelled on the P&O liner *Canberra*. It sailed from Vancouver to San Francisco and then to Los Angeles, Acapulco, the Panama Canal, Miami, the Bahamas, Bermuda, Cherbourg and finally Southampton. On board the ship he had an experience that led him to think he might be able to begin a new sonata. One warm night in the tropics as he was walking on the deck he saw the delicate crescent sliver of a beautiful new moon. Then, immediately afterwards, he saw a beautiful young girl, 'slim, graceful, blonde'. When he spoke to her, he learned that her name was Linnaea and that she was a descendant of Linnaeus 'who named all the flowers'. This conjunction of experiences lingered in Basil's mind and moved him to write thirty lines of a new long poem. He sent them to Victoria Forde, one of the first critics who planned to write a book about his work.[7] But, as far as is known, the new sonata did not proceed any further.

The language in the three ten-line stanzas that constituted Basil's last venture into the long poem are verbally even denser and richer than most passages in *Briggflatts*. There are subtle and surprising transitions and a considerable number of Northumbrian dialect words: haugh, kerf, goaf, foss, shammy. He included such vocabulary because a leading theme of the poem was to have been the north of England or 'Men of the north' along with other themes such as transience, weather, old age and mortality. Here are the thirty lines which, Basil told Sister Victoria Forde, were a '*First* draft' with 'many errors and clumsinesses to be cut out or changed'.[8]

> Such syllables flicker out of grass:
> 'What beckons goes'; and no glide lasts
> nor wings are ever in even beat long.
> A male season with paeonies, birds bright under thorn.
> Light pelts hard now my sun's low,
> it carves my stone as hail mud
> till day's net drapes the haugh,
> glaze crackled by flung drops.
> What use? Elegant hope, fever of tune,
> new now, next, in the fall, to be dust.

179

Wind shakes a blotch of sun,
flatter and tattle willow and oak alike
sly as a trout's shadow on gravel.
Light stots from stone, sets ridge and kerf quick
as shot skims rust from steel. Men of the north
subject to being beheaded and cannot avoid it
of a race that is naturally given that way.
'Uber sophiae sugens' in hourless dark,
their midnight shimmers like noon.
They clasp that axle fast.

Those who lie with Loki's daughter,
jawbones laid to her stiff cheek,
hear rocks stir above the goaf;
but a land swaddled in light? Listen, make out
lightfall singing on a wall mottled grey
and the wall growls, tossing light,
prow in tide, boulder in a foss.
A man shrivels in many days, eyes thirst for night
to scour and shammy the sky
thick with dust and breath.

The subject of the north of England introduced into the fragment was one that was very much in Basil's mind in his later years. Perhaps his many enforced absences in North America had made him all the more attached to his native place and its history. In the 1970s he spent considerable time in the Literary and Philosophical Society in Newcastle researching the rising of the men of the north against Queen Elizabeth in 1569. 'The Land of the Prince Bishops', the County Durham border signs proudly declare, recalling the near independence of this part of England after the Norman Conquest. Whether he was lecturing abroad or doing research at home Basil, towards the end of his life, continued to ponder and inform himself about this Northumbrian aspiration for independence that had recurred over the centuries.

Not long after his return to Wylam from Canada Basil was honoured by being made President of the Poetry Society. But a few months later an event in the world of poetry brought him great sadness. On 1 November 1972 his great friend and sponsor of nearly fifty years, Ezra Pound, died in Venice. Despite the many differences that had emerged in the 1930s and recurred over the years, Basil felt a great respect for Pound and mourned his loss. Basil wrote an appreciation for the *Sunday Times* and, together with Tom Pickard, arranged a memorial concert at Newcastle University. Before a large audience the Northern Sinfonia Orchestra played Vivaldi because, as Basil reported to Dorothy Pound, 'Ezra took so much part in bringing Vivaldi back into favour'. Basil, Tom Pickard and other northern poets read from Pound's *Canots, Propertius* and *Cathay*. There was a dramatic performance of Pound's version of *The Women of Trachis*. A BBC television crew was present to film the occasion.

In the summer of the following year, 1973, Basil helped to commemorate another of the great poets he had known. He crossed over to Ireland and gave a talk, which he later published under the title 'Yeats Recollected', to the Yeats International Summer School in Sligo. The talk contained anecdotes about Yeats and an admiring though not reverential assessment of his poetry. As a man now in his seventies Basil could especially appreciate the generosities that Yeats in old age had extended to him as an outspoken young man. Yeats, he said, 'put up with the presence of Antheil or myself at times when he must have found us intrusive, merely because the young learn from the old and the old must let them. Now that I am old myself I realise how much kindness was necessary to show such tolerance.'[9]

After his return to Britian came yet another honour; Basil became President of Northern Arts, one of the regional branches of the Arts Council of Great Britian. Also in 1974, along with Hugh MacDiarmid and Gael Turnbull, he gave a reading to a large and appreciative audience at a modern British Poetry conference at the Polytechnic of Central London. MacDiarmid's red-haired wife Valda Trevelyan was, as I remember, in very good spirits, shouting encouragement from the audience to her husband. Basil read forcefully but quietly and provoked no such loud responses.

At this time and during the following year Basil was working on his edition of *Selected Poems* by the Northumbrian collier poet Joseph Skipsey who had been a friend of his father, Dr Thomas Bunting. In his preface Basil was writing very much of his own roots. His admiration for the courage and endurance of the Northumbrian pitmen he had known in his boyhood continues undiminished. And he commends the literary dedication and achievement of Joseph Skipsey, the self-taught pitman poet. For despite his 'lapses into Wardour Street English', 'Skipsey still has the

power to please and to move, sometimes, as Rossetti told him, as
powerfully as anything in the language.' 'Skipsey is the most impersonal
of poets, very close indeed to the anonymous ballad singers and folksong
singers, yet with his own voice and his own manner, holding a place of
his own between them and such poets as Burns. The best of his work is
utterly convincing, even when its faults are obvious.' [10]

In the spring of 1976, the year in which this book was published,
Basil set off on a reading tour in the United States which took him from
coast to coast. On 6 April he read at Harvard, then two days later he
gave a reading at the University of Maine at Orono. Then came Yale and
after that the Poetry Center in new York City. Next he travelled south
to Davidson College in North Carolina for a one night stand before
proceeding to St Andrew's College at Laurinburg in the same state where
he remained for nearly a week. For his appearances in America Jonathan
Williams and Tom Meyer helped produce an eight-page programme. It
contained a poem written by Jonathan Williams after musing in the
garden with Basil following one of the many Sunday morning Quaker
meetings at Briggflatts at which he and Tom Meyer encountered Basil
during this period. 'My poem', Williams notes is obviously 'his' as well.
The poem addressed to 'My Quaker-Atheist Friend' shows something of
Basil's religious attitudes at this time in his life. The answer to the
question 'what do you do anything for?' is

> you do it
> for what the mediaevalists would call
> something like
> the Glory of God

After Laurinberg Basil was off west, first to Buffalo, then to Madison,
Wisconsin and finally to San Francisco where he did a reading in the
Museum of Art. Such a concentrated amount of work and travel took its
toll; he returned to England extremely tired.

In Madison Basil had met Barbara Lesch, a graduate student who was
writing her doctoral dissertation on Basil and his career. She entitled it
'Basil Bunting: A Major British Modernist'. They wined and dined
together and Basil supplied her with some interesting observations on his
career. He rejected many of the statements he had made in the 1920s and
1930s saying that at that time he was merely 'echoing Pound's ideas',

ideas which he, Basil, had long since abandoned. Pound, he said, was 'a little overwhelming. He was the one who had done all the things you had wanted to do, before you ever got around to doing them . . . He'd done everything he wanted to do and I should think that Zukofsky, as well as I, had considerable pondering to do before we could see where we went from that'.[11] Basil went on to specify some of the literary differences which, he came to realize, separated him from Pound. He said that 'Pound's reading was as opposite from mine as it could be. All my life the most important English poet for me was Wordswoth, whom Pound despised. He had no use for Spenser, with whom I think he is entirely parallel, perhaps because Spenser provided the framework for many generations through his poems and Pound was trying to produce a new framework.'[12] In that interview of 1976 Basil also spoke to Barbara Lesch about his shorter poems. he said that his odes were called odes 'because Horace called his odes'. He went on to note that 'An ode is essentially a sonnet to be sung, not all of mine are meant to be sung; most of them are.'[13]

The following year Basil completed a long poem which in a note to the work he indicates he had begun forty years before. It is a children's poem entitled 'The Pious Cat' and he had started it the year after Marian had left him taking the two children with her. 'The Pious Cat' is a highly successful work of its kind, as one might expect from a writer who had such a liking for children and took such an interest in them. The poem is a narrative of exactly two hundred lines followed by a four-line coda in which Basil disclaims authorship and attributes the story to the fourteenth-century Iranian poet Obaid-e Zakani. His adaptation has the gentle, agreeable humour that we find in such classic works for children as Lewis Carroll's 'The Owl and the Pussycat' and Rudyard Kipling's *Just So Stories*. Perhaps Basil might also have intended to emulate T. S. Eliot's *Old Possum's Guide to Practical Cats*. Basil's cat is Tibbald who eats a drunken mouse that has insulted him and then, seemingly, has a crisis of conscience and repents, declaring that in future he will eat only 'lettuces and things like that'. The mice are much impressed and bring him presents to congratulate him. He bids the gift-bearers approach and, when they do, eats most of them. The King of Mice is now persuaded to declare war on Tibbald and the mice manage to tie the cat up. But whilst the mice devote themselves to developing legal procedures for his trial and punishment, Tibbald bursts his bonds, eats the mice's Lord Chief Justice, while the other mice scamper hurriedly away.

Part of the pleasure afforded by 'The Pious Cat' is the element of seriousness in it. Tibbald is a force of nature and the mice are like self-deluding, self-destroying twentieth-century human beings. On one occasion Basil's humour departs from the genteel nursery language of Lewis Carroll and Rudyard Kipling. When the mice call upon Tibbald to surrender this is how the titanic cat replies.

> Now stop your ears, maid, matron, bride!
> Switch off your hearing aids and hide
> your faces in your wraps and shawls,
> for Tibbald answered roughly *.

A footnote explains that the asterisk stands for 'a word in cattish language meaning "Oh dear me, *what* nonsense!"' Beside the violent, amoral Tibbald the mice are ludicrously inadequate. They get drunk, boast, strike committees, hold parades, delude themselves about their ability to impose justice and finally pay the price of their own folly. Their story is related in such a way as to bring to mind the tribulations of humanity during the two world wars. But this is just hinted at; the poem is for the most part a pleasing children's entertainment with some wonderfully outrageous rhyming. Here is how a mouse observes Tibbald's supposed repentance.

> A mouse had hidden behind the pulpit
> He heard Tib's sob and watched him gulp it.

The response of the other mice is given in rhyming that is far from the finely crafted rhyming of *Briggflatts*.

> So all the mice cried: 'Halleluia!'
> 'You don't suppose he'll relapse though, do ye?'

'The Pious Cat' is a charming addition to Basil's oeuvre and a good expression of one aspect of his personality.

In 1977, the year that he completed this poem, Basil was the recipient of a Festschrift organized by his friends Jonathan Williams and Tom Meyer. *Madeira and Toasts for Basil Bunting* had been scheduled to appear in time for his seventy-fifth birthday, but problems with the printing and distribution delayed its publication. Jonathan Williams had planned on having seventy-six contributors, one for each year and one for luck, but in the event there were many more. They included D. G. Bridson, the Northumberland novelist Sid Chaplin, Robert Creeley, Cid Corman, Donald Davie, Roy Fisher, Allen Ginsberg, Hugh Kenner, Stuart Montgomery, Edwin Morgan, Constance Pickard, Omar Pound, Tom Rawarth, Tom Pickard, Colin Simms, Gael Turnbull, and Celia and Louis Zukofsky.

A year later it was Basil's sad duty to write a tribute to his great friend Hugh MacDiarmid who died in 1978. In his obituary Basil recalled an incident that had occurred whilst he was driving MacDiarmid home to Biggar in Strathclyde after a visit to Wylam. When they stopped at a pub in Moffat for a sandwich and some Scotch to wash it down, a group of working men approached them asking, 'Is it no the grreat poet Hugh MacDiarmid?' The men then insisted on buying the drinks for MacDiarmid and Basil. Each of the men bought a round and MacDiarmid, hardened drinker though he was, became affected. But as Basil recollected, 'Luckily the road from Moffat to Biggar carries no traffic whatever much of the year, so that I got him home dazed but safe and Valda had a word or two to say about it.' Basil was much impressed by the way these uneducated men could quote from MacDiarmid. It said something about his poems. 'Their candour, their lack of side, the feeling that he meant what he said, with or without occasional stumblings of technique, these carried through the printed page to the least literary of men.'[14]

Basil's own audience was continuing to expand. Fulcrum Press was by now no longer in operation, and his works, like those of his fellow Fulcrum author Roy Fisher, were taken over by Oxford University Press in 1978. An exhibition was held in Oxford to mark the launch of the new edition of Basil's *Collected Poems*. The exhibition then moved on to the Northern Arts Gallery in Newcastle-upon-Tyne where it attracted a large number of people.

But whilst Basil's literary reputation continued to grow during these years his domestic situation deteriorated. Sima became increasingly annoyed by some of the literary people Basil brought to Shadingfield. She disliked their lack of personal hygiene and she thought some of them dishonest. As a woman in her mid-forties she was often impatient with her husband, now approaching his eightieth year. Sima was physically very fit and much stronger than Basil. He confessed to friends that he was often afraid of her. Quarrels intensified. The climax came one winter's day early in 1979 when after an extended row with Sima Basil left the house at Wylam and sought refuge in a draughty holiday chalet in one of the Northumberland coastal resorts. He and Sima would never live together again.

Basil subsequently moved from the chalet to a very cold and damp cottage on the coast opposite to Lindisfarne. When Michael Shayer and other friends visited him there they feared that he might not be able to survive the terrible physical and psychological conditions in which he was living. The midwinter cold was excruciating on the bleak nothern coast. His friends consulted urgently with other members of the arts community in the north east to try to get him out of danger and to find him a warmer and more suitable home.

Sixteen
The Last Years
1979–1985

His friends soon achieved their objective. Not long after he moved out of the house at Wylam, Basil went to live south of the River Tyne near the old mining town of Washington in what had once been County Durham but which was now incorporated into the newly devised industrial county of Tyne and Wear. He settled himself into a small house belonging to the Northern Arts Council in the Blackfell area of Washington. Blackfell was one of several 'new towns' created in Britain during the 1960s. The estate on which he lived was unfinished and raw. In a letter to Bourtai of March 1980 he called it 'a preplanned slum' and one which housed very few solid citizens. 'Quite a noticeable proportion of my neighbours are burglars by trade, and a very large proportion are out of work. Some of them have been out of work for years, discouraged and restless.' Basil was not at all happy at Blackfell; he longed for a cottage in the country. His only consolation in this ugly new town was the number of children. He told Bourtai, 'New Towns are the only places in the North where newly married couples can hope to rent a house. Then they breed. This town was re-founded thirteen years ago (it will be complete in two more years) so the percentage of children under the age of thirteen is enormous.' The children were much intrigued by the distinguished looking, well-spoken old man in his late seventies and he happily welcomed them into his home, keeping 'crayons and paper for them to draw in my living room on a wet day'.

Basil was especially interested in the young girls of twelve to fourteen, just as he had been throughout all his adult life. Some of them assumed that such an old man was 'a safe playmate' but a few treated him as a younger man. He was shocked a little by the earthy language they used but enjoyed them as 'pretty ornaments in the house'. He was especially taken by the 'artfulness with which they manage to exhibit their legs and other charms without seeming to intend to . . .'[1]

One of these young girls would continue to maintain a relationship with Basil for the remainder of his life. This was Tanya Cossey, who was from a working-class family living nearby. Basil was very much attracted to her and they became close. One visitor recalls the door being opened by the pretty Tanya wearing only her underwear. Basil was impressed by Tanya's ability as an artist and was keen to help her financially in obtaining some training at art school. He did not want her to have to settle for the dull, reductive life of a factory girl which would otherwise be her lot. When more and more he read his poetry in public and on television Tanya served as his *sakki*.

Welcome visitors to Blackfell shortly after Basil's move there were his daughter Roudaba and her family. Before reaching Northumberland they had toured Wales in a gypsy caravan and had many stories to tell. Basil enjoyed showing his visitors from Seattle some of the historic sites of the north-east. He very much liked his granddaughter Monica whom he thought of as 'a grand lass' and to whom he inscribed a copy of his *Collected Poems*. Roudaba was pleased to meet other family members including Sima and Basil's sister, Joyce, whose career as a doctor had ended with her retirement some years before. Roudaba was shocked but then entertained by Joyce's great wit which was regularly employed against Basil and irritated him greatly.

Basil resumed some degree of contact with his second family. His son Tom was studying mathematics at Newcastle University and his daughter Maria had married a young lawyer, John Halliday, who would join a legal practice in Newcastle. Basil became a grandfather yet again when Maria and John had a son, Jonathan. Basil's relationship with Sima improved greatly after they had finally agreed to divorce. With the money that came from the settlement she realized her long-standing ambition of buying a bungalow. It was far better situated than Basil's new home, for Ovingham was a most attractive village, with an ancient church with a Saxon tower, beside the Tyne a few miles west of Wylam. She had an immense garden which she delighted in tending. By 1980 she and Basil were on sufficiently good terms that every ten days or so he would go over to Ovingham for a meal. In March that year Sima was one of the twenty guests at his eightieth birthday party held at a continental restaurant in Newcastle. Unfortunately, she declared the soup cold and the rest of the food unimpressive, and announced her intention of protesting strongly to the waiters. Basil begged her not to spoil his occasion by doing this. Reluctantly Sima agreed, but when Basil proposed leaving a tip of ten pounds, she became combative again and insisted that he did not.

Basil had Christmas dinner that year at Sima's bungalow together with Tom, Maria, John and grandson Jonathan. He was especially grateful for Sima's attentions to him because, not long before, he had become slightly incapacitated by a minor stroke. It left his right arm and hand a little numb so that, as he told Bourtai, he no longer dared to offer to hold a baby. But he could still drive the small car, a Daf which Sima had passed on to him, and he was often shocked to discover, when his mind had been on other things, how fast he had been going.

Basil's friend had always had to brace themselves for his wild driving. Tom Pickard remembered a particularly unnerving experience from the time when Basil still had his large Ford. They were driving down the motorway together at great and illegal speed and suddenly Basil lost control of the steering. The vehicle spun around terrifyingly, completing more than a 360-degree turn and halting all the other drivers on the motorway.

One of the many visitors to Blackfell had a memorable experience of this fast and fearless driving when Basil, overtaking, faced down a large oncoming truck. Carroll F. Terrell, a professor of English from the University of Maine and managing editor of *Paideuma*, the journal of Pound scholarship, suddenly realized that 'we were playing chicken and heading straight for the other world'.[2] But Basil prevailed. He had driven his American visitor over from Blackfell to Corn Close near Briggflatts, the home of his close friends Jonathan Williams and Tom Meyer; it was a sixteenth-century stone cottage which they had modernized and extended. From here they all drove the short distance to the Quaker meeting house. On the way back to Corn Close, as Basil opened the succession of gates on the farm road, Terrell noticed that Basil's eyes seemed watery. Later after an excellent dinner, a stew made with Polish sausage and winter vegetables accompanied by a bottle of red wine especially chosen to please Basil, a Bulgarian Cabernet Sauvignon, Basil explained why earlier he had been close to tears. Opening and closing those farm gates had made him remember doing the same thing, many years before, for 'a certain woman who meant much to him'.

At home at Blackfell Terrell found Basil to be a most gracious host. When he arrived from London Terrell saw that much thought and preparation had gone into receiving him. First there came a lunch of English meat pie with 'wonderful green salad'. Some hours later Basil laid on a dinner of 'broiled mutton chops, brussel sprouts, potatoes, salad, a sweet, and cheese' and, as on that other occasion, a bottle of red wine. Basil allowed his visitor to give him only minimal assistance in the cooking and serving of the meal. There was a lot of good talk about poetry and literary and intellectual history.

Terrell was also impressed by Basil's friendly relationship with a neighbour who dropped in to see him, a much younger man of about thirty-five who came to report on the condition of his wife who had just had a problematical Caesarean delivery. Basil chatted easily with the new visitor, finding no difficulty in turning from the literary conversation with Terrell to talk about 'sport, favourite athletes, local politics, Margaret Thatcher, and so on'. For a man of his years Basil had immense sociability and vitality. But Terrell noticed that certain things defeated him badly. He could get very depressed when the Daf, the little Dutch car that Sima had given him, failed to function properly. Basil also admitted that with the coming of his eightieth year he was prone to sudden and devastating losses of energy. In fact, on the way back from Briggflatts, the point came when he felt he could not go on. In order that Terrell might keep to his tight schedule, Basil dropped him off at Hexham station to catch a train that would allow him to make his connection to London in Newcastle. Urging his host to come and visit him in America, Terrell ran down the small platform to jump on the little local train that was just departing.

Basil had two trips abroad in the latter months of 1980. In August he met Terrell again when he flew to America to attend a literary conference organized by the National Poetry Foundation at Orono, Maine. Bourtai travelled east to see him and stayed in the same house as Hugh Kenner and his wife. Bourtai was astonished to see the reverential attitude which the participants in the conference took towards her father. Basil travelled on west and went to see Roudaba in Seattle. He also made a return visit to nearby Vancouver where he stayed with Peter Quartermain and his wife Meredith. This was the last time I talked to Basil. Accompanied by my wife and our three-year-old daughter, Miranda, I went over to Peter's house and we had a most enjoyable afternoon. Basil did not look his years; he was lively and entertaining. He used a set of dominoes to play 'shop' with Miranda and made wonderful owl noises which pleased her greatly. When the conversation turned to espionage and the name Kim Philby was mentioned, Basil was pointedly silent. He was more ready to talk about literature. He was about to go to Paris and the writers he had known there almost half a century before were much in his mind. He spoke at some length of his tolerance and affection for Ford and his intense dislike of Hemingway.

In October Basil travelled to France on a tour chiefly organized by his French translator, Jacques Darras, whose version of *Briggflatts* had appeared in *Po&sie* 7 in 1978. Basil found that his French admirers were numerous and extremely enthusiastic. 'They never left me alone for a moment', he told Bourtai, adding 'nothing is so tiring as perpetual conversation.' He returned to England exhausted. But he was compensated by the respect and deference with which he was treated in France; he enjoyed 'much more consideration than a mere poet could expect in England or America'. For instance, Basil let it be known that he would like to see a certain painting in Paris. When it was discovered that the museum was closed that day, 'The ministry recalled staff from its holiday, guards, elevator men, even the director of the museum to show me round.' On the other hand, when he travelled to Amiens, 'they *closed* the cathedral, on a Sunday afternoon! so that I could be shown round by the expert without being elbowed by tourists or worshippers.' In Paris Basil received an admiring message from the now highly respected veteran surrealist Philippe Soupault. He had collaborated with André Breton on one of the founding documents of surrealism, *Les Champs Magnétiques*, published in 1920. Based on a systematic arrangement of pieces of automatic writing, it long pre-dated Yeats's *A Vision* which had similar foundations. Soupault in 1980 said he remembered Basil well at the time he had been the protegé of Pound and Ford in Paris in the 1920s but Basil confided to Bourtai that he 'hadn't been quite sure that I had ever met him'.[3]

Honour and recognition in Paris contrasted markedly with the depression, the social and physical squalor of Blackfell New Town. About this time Jacques Darras brought a French television crew from Amiens to make a film about Basil. In the filmed interior Basil complained that he merely 'existed' in Washington. He was demoralized by the low standard of living of his fellow tenants, especially by their furniture which was shoddy and falling to bits. One slight consolation was that his house, unlike most on the estate, did not have cockroaches.

However, there was a more positive side to this conversation. As in other television interviews, Basil commented extensively on the importance of Quakerism in his life and his poetry. To Darras he spoke at some length about the role of silence in both Quaker meetings and in *Briggflatts*. He explained how Quakerism was informed by the same reverence for everything in creation, even those things at first sight might seem unpalatable, disgusting, horrifying. An example he cited was the dance of the maggots in *Briggflatts*.

But clearly his reverence did not extend to the surroundings in which he presently found himself. At times he was extremely miserable at the thought of being 'left to die here in Washington'. Friends tried to help. Jonathan Williams persuaded a number of Americans to contribute to a fund with which to rent a cottage for Basil in the country. They actually found a suitable place close to Hexham in Northumberland. But when the owner discovered that Basil was eighty, he had second thoughts. 'The owner declined to let it to me because I was TOO OLD! He said he might want to use the cottage himself in a few years, but would have a bad conscience about turning such an old man out. So he just didn't let the old man in.'[4] As he went on into his eighties Basil experienced similar difficulties in obtaining motor insurance for the Daf. Painfully aware of his age and deeply disappointed by being refused the cottage, Basil had to reconcile himself to living on in Blackfell New Town where, he feared, he would have to end his days.

The poem beginning with the line 'Now we've no hope of going back' which Basil datelined 1980 and allowed to stand as the last ode in the *Second Book of Odes*, his final collection of shorter pieces, is a grim, unflinching statement of the experience of knowing life to be close to ending and of waiting for death to come. It remembers, tacitly, the way others have faced death. Although he chose as epigraph the words from Guido Cavalcanti, 'Perche no spero' ('Because I do not hope'), to which T. S. Eliot alluded at the opening of 'Ash Wednesday', Basil's poem has none of Eliot's religious hope. Basil's central metaphor is a nautical one that brings to mind Tennyson's 'Crossing the Bar' but there is none of the Victorian poet's rhetoric and self-indulgence. Basil's final lyric is a quiet, lonely meditation founded on a stoical response to the prospect of the imminent ending of his life. The closing lines he presented to his readers run:

> We have no course to set,
> only to drift too long, watch too glumly, and wait,
> wait.[5]

In the event Basil was to be spared to live a few more years in much pleasanter physical circumstances. Towards the middle of 1981 a country cottage was at last found for him. It was in the tiny remote hamlet of Greystead on the road that leads north-west from the little Northumbrian market town of Bellingham to what is now the Kielder Dam. The area was an ancient settlement known as Tarset which in the thirteenth century had had a castle. But over the years the place dwindled and was virtually abandoned. When Basil arrived there were just a very few old houses, a vicarage and a small Regency Gothic church. Some miles to the south lies the confluence of the two rivers, the North and the South Tyne, from where the Tyne itself flows eastward to Newcastle and the North Sea. From his cottage Basil could look across the narrow main road and glimpse and hear the movement of the North Tyne. His cottage was surrounded and sheltered by large, old trees; an enormous ash grew right beside his chimney. He was delighted by his new home in the depths of the country. His close neighbour at Greystead was Colin Simms, naturalist and poet who had much to tell Basil about the animals and birds of Tarset. The two men were also regular drinking companions.

Some six months after moving into his cottage Basil travelled to London to meet a literary admirer of long standing. Sister Victoria Forde, who wrote her Ph.D. dissertation on Basil's poetry in 1970 at the University of Notre Dame, had corresponded with him with increasing regularity throughout the 1970s. During this period she was developing her thesis into a book. She now wrote to say that she was coming to London to assist with the University of Notre Dame's Junior-year-in-England programme. Basil swiftly set up some poetry readings in London so that he could afford to go south to meet her. The arrangements for the readings were made by Tom Pickard who frequently served as Basil's agent in organizing such occasions. Tom was very effective in obtaining good fees for him. Sister Victoria arrived in Britain in January 1982 and stayed for four months. After they met Basil regularly took her along to his readings. At Wentworth Place, Keats' house in Hampstead, the room was packed and people stood outside in the cold winter drizzle hoping to be let in. When Basil read in a much larger room in the Riverside Studios at Hammersmith the audience again overflowed. Only after the intervention of Sister Victoria was Basil's son, Tom, allowed to squeeze his way in to hear the reading.

While in London Basil stayed with two of his admirers, Mr and Mrs Michael Henshaw who lived near Regent's Park. In the evenings they arranged gatherings at which he might meet some of the growing number of people who appreciated his literary achievement. By day Basil went about London with Sister Forde introducing her to publishers and trying to interest them in her book about him. After a publisher's lunch lasting three hours at an expensive French restaurant, the two of them headed up Charing Cross Road for Foyle's bookshop. On their way they stopped at other bookshops and Basil enquired about his sales. When they finally arrived at Foyle's Basil suddenly felt exhausted and required a taxi to take him back to the Henshaws.

When the time came for him to return to Greystead, he and Sister Victoria agreed that she should come and stay with him there in March. The Henshaws escorted him back to Northumberland and stayed for a couple of days in the cottage with him. It was very cold and Basil, utterly tired out by London, was slow to recover, but the spring approached and he was delighted by the hundreds and hundreds of crocuses that appeared around his cottage. He wrote vividly to Sister Victoria about a wild pheasant crowing on the garden walk and two bedraggled peacocks from a nearby farm strutting down the main road holding up the traffic.

But the pleasures of spring at Tarset were disrupted when a film crew arrived to make a documentary about Basil's life. He did an extensive filmed interview and also read from his poetry. Looking at this tape, which was produced by Northwest Films and directed by Peter Bell, one is struck by the two public voices that Basil used. In answering the interviewer's questions he employs the standard English of any educated member of the middle class. But when he begins to read from *Briggflatts* he assumes a strong and resonant Northumbrian accent; his speaking also becomes slower, more deliberate, more emphatic, bardic. In the interview Basil talked at some length about his belief in pantheism. He again recalled his sympathy with the Quaker view of the world and he commended the Quaker commitments to peace and to pacificism. But he also conceded that there was violence in his poems. He talked for some time about his view of poetry. As with other interviewers he insisted that poetry cannot exist unless it has music; poetry and music are the twin daughters of one of the defining activities of human kind, the dance.

The filming tired him out. However, when Sister Victoria came to stay at the end of March she found Basil a very energetic host and keen to show her around his native region. She was touched to learn that Sima had driven over to Greystead to prepare her room and make it attractive for her. The two women did not meet but Sister Victoria often saw Maria who assisted with some of the many excursions Basil had planned for the visitor. They drove to the Roman Wall, to Lindisfarne and, of course, to Briggflatts. At Hexham Abbey Basil persuaded a senior church official to open up the crypt so that Sister Victoria might see one of the great jewels of Northumbrian architecture, the seventh-century vaulted underground chamber built by the Saxons using Roman stones, many of them carved with ornaments or inscriptions.

Back at the cottage, during one of their many literary conversations, Basil showed his visitor a treasured gift, a Canto of Ezra Pound in the author's handwriting. Basil had kept it carefully wrapped up in a newspaper and string. When the time came for Sister Victoria to return to London, they had their photograph taken together against the background of the great dark trees which in March had yet to come into bud. Quite bald now but with a full and robust grey beard and moustache, Basil confronts the camera with an assured expression, his arm thrown affectionately around the shoulders of his smiling young guest.

After Sister Victoria's departure Basil was worried that his tenancy of the cottage might be discontinued by his landlord who made known his concern about allowing a man of such advanced years to live on his own in such a very remote place. Basil was also painfully short of money. Well-off people in the continuing stream of visitors that came his way offered to help him. But he was too proud to let them. He would only accept gifts, preferably Scotch. But some who came to the cottage did, 'accidentally', leave money behind. Nevertheless, his financial difficulties continued to plague him. He felt compelled to accept all fee-paying invitations to literary occasions, however arduous the travelling. One especially lucrative offer was to serve as one of the judges, along with Stephen Spender and Adrian Henri, in the Arvon International Poetry Competition for 1984. This meant a long journey south to Devonshire where the judges were to assemble as guests of Ted Hughes. There were 33,000 poems of which Basil had to read 1,800. It was a demoralizing experience. He didn't find a single good one and finished his stint exhausted. However, the pay was sufficiently good that for a while he felt financially secure.

Returning north through London at the time of his eighty-third birthday, he stopped off to stay with the Henshaws and went on to a party given for him by his old friends of Fulcrum days, Stuart and Deirdre Montgomery. There was a lot of wine and reminiscences and laughter and Basil did not return to his hosts' house until around two in the morning.

A few months later, on 1 July 1983, Basil was the subject of a programme entitled *A Measure of Words* broadcast by Tyne Tees Television. It began with an interview by the presenter Tony Bilbow. Stoically Basil reflected on the lack of material rewards poetry had brought him.

He also described the 1980s as most reactionary times influenced by forces as bad as those which had emerged in the 1930s. He singled out for criticism Prime Minister Margaret Thatcher and Mrs Mary Whitehouse, the leader of the campaign against blasphemy and obscenity on radio and television. The latter he deplored for attempting to introduce censorship into Britain.

After the interview Basil gave a reading before the cameras. It was an occasion on which Tanya served as his *sakki*. She sat at his feet, her legs trailing along the platform. She wore ankle socks and a cotton dress and a rather large jacket that seemed intended to bring some formality to the occasion. A very pretty girl, with short dark hair and a fringe, she had deep set eyes, a slightly pouting mouth and full cheeks. Basil introduced her, explaining the role of *sakki* as winepourer and also commending Tanya's skills as an artist. She steadily poured from the bottle of red wine as Basil read ringingly from his poems. He paused often to sip pleasurably from the wine.

But less happy experiences awaited him. Not long after his return to Greystead, his worst fears were realized when he was required to leave his cottage. He had nowhere to go; he was a homeless old man. He stayed briefly with a succession of friends and for a short while with Maria. When the cold Northumbrian winter began late in 1983 he went for a while into lodgings in Bellingham. He was very miserable. In selecting the epigraph to this biography I have intended to suggest a similarity between Basil's stance towards life and that of King Lear in the final act of the play. Both sought to stand outside of mundane experience and to view it as 'God's spies'. In his eighty-fourth year Basil resembled King Lear in other respects; the proud old man who had known a life of luxury in Teheran was now homeless, well nigh penniless and seemingly unwanted, in the midst of a bleak northern winter.

Eventually his son-in-law, John Halliday, found him another cottage. But it had to be bought, not rented. So with various guarantors to help him, Basil, as he approached his eighty-fourth birthday, took out a mortgage. His new home did not please him as much as Greystead but it was in the countryside and similarly remote. Fox Cottage, in fact a 1950s bungalow, is in the tiny village of Whitley Chapel about eight miles south of Hexham. Just a few yards away is the pub, the Fox and Hounds; the visiting drinkers, parking right outside Basil's door came and went noisily.

On a winter's day in early 1984 the Canadian scholar Jenny Penberthy visited Basil at Whitley Chapel. She went with Peter and Meredith Quartermain who were staying in Hexham in order to have access to Basil. The trio took with them as a present one of Basil's favourite treats and a local delicacy, a Bellingham pie. When Basil opened his door to them, he quickly seized Jenny Penberthy, an attractive woman in her early thirties, in an embrace that lasted longer, much longer, than was socially appropriate. It was clear to her that he had an intense need to hold a woman in his arms. Then they all sat down in the bleak, sparsely furnished sitting-room with its unpainted grey cement walls, and chatted pleasantly. But when Jenny told Basil that the subject of her research was the work of Lorine Niedecker he ceased being charming and gallant. He contemplated the future editor of the *Collected Poems of Lorine Niedecker* with suspicion. After a while he growled, 'Be sure you do your best by her.' The strength of his admiration and protectiveness towards Niedecker was unmistakeable.

Jenny Penberthy was struck by the bitter cold and the comfortlessness of the cottage. When later she visited Briggflatts, it occurred to her that the cottage had the same radical austerity in its interior as the Quaker meeting house. Basil had had to pay for extensive repairs to the run-down bungalow in order to obtain a mortgage. These had put him into debt again, so once again he looked to readings. In 1984 he participated in his last major poetry reading. This was at the Albert Hall and the programme was organized and chaired by Allen Ginsberg. Other poets taking part were Roy Fisher, Liz Lochhead and Gregory Corso. Roy Fisher remembered that the audience in the large hall that night was rather thin. The attendance and zeal that marked the poetry readings of the 1960s had clearly diminished. Basil looked tired and drawn. He had to sleep for some time before his reading and then again immediately afterward. He could not stand to speak his poems; an armchair had to be brought on to the stage for him.

After he returned to Whitley Chapel he admitted to Sister Victoria that this last trip to London exhausted him 'beyond reason'. Around this time he decided that he had to give up driving. He accepted that he was becoming a danger on the roads and he gave the little Daf car to the Cossey family.

This was the time of a bitter nationwide strike by the National Union of Miners organized by their left-wing leader Arthur Scargill. In the 1970s the Conservative government of Edward Heath had fallen in great part because of a successful strike by the miners. In the 1980s Margaret

Thatcher was determined that her Prime Ministership should not be similarly endangered. The strike was lengthy, grim and often violent. Basil resumed the sympathies he had learned from his father in his youth and strongly supported the miners and their cause. He and Colin Simms were accustomed to drinking in various pubs in and around Hexham and Basil would express his support for the NUM vociferously. The consequence was that a number of landlords banned the two poets from their pubs.

That same winter he worried a good deal about money, the cost of the central heating in the chill bungalow being an especial anxiety. But for his eighty-fifth and last birthday so many people brought him bottles of Scotch that he thought of bathing in it and warming up that way.

Basil had just over six weeks to live. Among the last people to visit him in his cottage at Whitley Chapel were the Americans Jennifer Moyer and Britt Bell who ran Moyer Bell, a small but very enterprising publishing company in the United States. They were about to take over the American rights to Basil's work from Oxford University Press and would manage them very successfully. When they came to see Basil ten days before his death, they agreed that one more lyric should be added to the *Second Book of Odes*. This was 'Now we've no hope of going back' which Basil datelined 1980, five years earlier. In adding this piece to the other forty-eight odes Basil brought his nearly sixty-year career as a lyric poet to a conclusion.

Early in April, over in the state of Washington where she and her husband had a farm, and were involved in a hectically busy lambing season, Roudaba had a sudden, powerful intuition that if she wanted to see her father living, she must go to him now. She flew from Chicago on 14 April. When she finally arrived at the remote cottage she had to share a room with Tanya Cossey. Basil appeared to be in good form; he took pleasure in declaiming, from memory, some of the works of the early Scots poet Gavin Douglas. There came a time when Roudaba was alone with her father. She reached out her arms to hold him. In what seemed to her a very British way he seemed shy; he retreated from her. But she persisted and took him in her arms and told him that she loved him. The eighty-five-year-old man and his fifty-one-year-old daughter had some minutes of quiet and calm together. The following day Michael Shayer, an old friend from Migrant days, also arrived; he had to make do with sleeping on the couch in the living room.

Michael Shayer was the last writer to visit Basil and to have a literary conversation with him. One of the authors they talked about in what proved to be Basil's final hours was his favourite writer, Jonathan Swift. In a poem about Basil's death Michael Shayer remembered that Basil spoke of the Struldbruggs, the immortal beings who figure in 'A Voyage to Laputa, . . .', the third book of *Gulliver's Travels*. Basil admired the way Swift described the increasing distaste which these deathless beings felt for themselves and for others as the years went on. In one place Swift writes that after living on beyond their mortal span the Struldbruggs 'find themselves cut off from all possibility of pleasure; and whenever they see a funeral, they lament and repine that others are gone to a harbour of rest, to which they themselves never can hope to arrive.' Given such a vision Basil was happy to accept his mortality. In his poem Michael Shayer reports him saying: 'Look at the description of/the Struldbruggs, Mike,/ . . . accurate in every detail.'

That evening, 15 April, Basil and his various visitors spent a very convivial time at the Fox and Hounds, staying up into the early hours of the morning, drinking and talking and singing songs and bawdy ballads. Tanya Crossey wearing black leather was a most attractive figure whom, Michael Shayer remembered, he and Basil 'were both proud to accompany at one of the bars'.[6]

This was the last social occasion of Basil's life and it was fitting that this great connoisseur of wine, women and song should have hugely enjoyed himself as at so many similar gatherings over past decades. But the next morning he was ill. His stomach was painfully upset. Roudaba, as an experienced nurse, feared for him and urged him to summon a doctor. At first he would not hear of such an idea. Stubbornly he insisted that he could doctor himself with lime water. But finally he went along with Roudaba's wishes. When the doctor arrived, he immediately ordered an ambulance to take Basil to the General Hospital in Hexham where he was straight away taken to the Intensive Care ward. Roudaba was not allowed to stay with him as she wished. Just as she was leaving, the man in the bed next to her father's fell on to the floor with his bedpan. Basil complained reproachfully, 'See what happens in hospital?' But when they reminded him that there were compensations, for instance many pretty nurses and attractive young women doctors, this only brought out Basil's ribald pessimism. 'All they want to do is poke their fingers up my arse', was his response.

The following morning, 17 April, Maria drove over to Whitley Chapel to pick up Roudaba so that they could go together to visit their father.

Just as they were setting off at about ten o'clock, a nurse telephoned from the hospital to say that Basil had just died. After an exercise walk down the hall with one of the nurses, he had returned to his bed, lain down and died quietly and peacefully. The cause of death was officially reported as mesenteric adenitis.

Basil was cremated with just a few people present for the brief ceremony. There were four close relatives, his sister Joyce, Sima (who had been visiting relatives in Los Angeles and flew back immediately when notified of his death) and his daughters Roudaba and Maria. His son Tom was out of England at the time, travelling the Canary Islands. Only two non-family members were at the crematorium, Tanya Cossey and Colin Simms.

Basil's passing was widely noted in the press. There were obituaries in numerous provincial papers particularly in the north-east. But the national papers also devoted considerable space to an assessment of his career and achievement. These lengthy obituaries are a clear indication of the literary standing which Basil enjoyed at the time of his death. The *Daily Telegraph* observed that with the publication of *Briggflatts* Basil Bunting was 'recognised as being among the top six poets of the century'. The *Telegraph* echoed other papers in lamenting the fact that his work had for a long time been 'spectacularly undervalued'. In the *Guardian* of 19 April the obituary began by declaring Basil was 'acclaimed as one of the greatest poets of this century'. The most carefully formulated evaluation of Basil's life and work appeared on the same day in *The Times*, the newspaper for which Basil had worked off and on over a number of years. This obituarist noted that 'Basil Bunting was a poet uncompromisingly married to the modern movement as that movement had first defined itself in the poems of Pound and Eliot in the 1920s'. 'However', the writer continued, Bunting 'had brought the sometimes facile eclecticism of his masters under dour North Country control, and discovered in his native place a local habitation and a name for what is often in Pound and Eliot a spiritual expression of a sense of exile.' The obituarist recalls and endorses Cyril Connolly's judgement that *Briggflatts* was 'the finest long poem to have been produced in England since *Four Quartets*'. *Briggflatts* is particularly commended for its 'lyric intensity that achieves maximum effectiveness where a certain Northumbrian roughness or looseness of speech-texture is allowed to poke through'. The writer concludes that the poem is 'Absolutely modern, it is also local; that is its rarity'.

Family members decided that Basil's ashes should be strewn in the location that had been of such prime significance in his life and art. Three days after the cremation the ashes were taken to Briggflatts. A group of people had gathered there, awaiting the ceremony of the scattering. They were mostly poets. Roy Fisher was there together with Tom Pickard, Michael Henshaw, Michael Shayer, Gael Turnbull and Tom Raworth. Roy Fisher remembered how they all stood beside the Quaker meeting house waiting for the women of Basil's family to arrive with the urn. Down the lane on which the mourners fixed their eyes, the ash trees were in bud on that spring day. At last Roudaba came into sight carrying the urn under her serape. She was followed by Joyce, Maria and Sima who was lamenting miserably that she had been away in America when Basil died.

The waiting poets stepped forward towards the cemetery but Tom Raworth recalled that the Quakers 'would let only the immediate family into the burial ground'. So the Bunting women sheered off through the entrance gate leaving the male poets standing outside. In his poem recalling the occasion Michael Shayer spoke sadly of this awkwardness. he regretted that there was

> no member of the
> Meeting to quieten the
> confused silence or
> speak what was to be
> witnessed.

Roudaba and her companions scattered the ashes on the earth that had been for Basil the place of first love. Peggy Greenbank was not present that day, though she knew of Basil's death. She would survive him by a few years, dying a widow in a nursing home in the small Shropshire town of Bishop's Castle. On the day of the scattering of his ashes she remained in the distant hamlet of Hope in the quiet hill country of south-west Shropshire where for years she had served as schoolmistress. Yet she it was, Basil's first love and muse, who drew them all there to Briggflatts that day, family womenfolk and poets alike, she who at the time of his death had 'been with' him seventy years.

Notes

Chapter 1: Family and Boyhood

1. Cited in Williams, *Descant on Rawthey's Madrigal*.
2. Bunting (ed.), Joseph Skipsey, *Selected Poems*, p. 9.
3. Briggs, *Victorian Cities*, pp. 366–7.
4. *Descant on Rawthey's Madrigal*.
5. *Come In: A Measure of Words*, an interview with Tony Bilbow, Tyne Tees Television, 1 July 1983.
6. Letter to Zukofsky, 16 Sept. 1964, Humanities Research Center, University of Texas.

Chapter 2: Leighton Park and Prison 1916–1919

1. Williams, *Descant on Rawthey's Madrigal*.
2. Victoria Forde, in *The Poetry of Basil Bunting*, reports that Basil discovered the Whitman volume at Leighton Park and that Whitman's English friend, the social reformer Edward Carpenter, rode thirty or forty miles from Sheffield on his bicycle in order to congratulate the young author. It seems more likely that the essay was written at Ackworth which is roughly that distance from Sheffield. Leighton Park is some two hundred miles away, surely too much of a bike ride even for the energetic Carpenter, then in his seventies.
3. These details of Basil's first experience of imprisonment come from a conversation held with and reported by Peter Quartermain in 1984.

Chapter 3: The First London Years 1919–1923

1. The history of this pub, so important in the history of the arts in London in this century, has been written by Papa Kleinfeldt's granddaughter who was born in the Fitzroy. See Sally Fiber, *The Fitzroy*.
2. Fiber, p. 17.
3. Reagan, 'An Interview with Basil Bunting', p. 75.
4. Robbins, *Autobiography of an Economist*, pp. 74–5.
5. ibid., p. 87.
6. Basil also told Jonathan Williams that as a result of his experiences in jail as a conscientious objector, he had been able to supply 'some footnotes' to a book on imprisonment by Wallas. I have been unable to trace such a book.
7. Robbins, p. 76.
8. Reagan, p. 73.
9. Terrell (ed.), *Basil Bunting: Man and Poet*, p. 38.
10. Lesch, 'Basil Bunting: A Major British Modernist', p. 36.

Chapter 4: Paris 1923

1. Antheil, *Bad Boy of Music*, pp. 7–8 (spelling uncorrected).
2. Carpenter, *A Serious Character: The Life of Ezra Pound*, p. 391.
3. Ezra Pound, *The Spirit of Romance*, p. 169.

4. ibid., p. 173.
5. ibid., p. 177.
6. Terrell (ed.), *Basil Bunting: Man and Poet*, pp. 41–2.
7. Smith, *Peter Warlock: The Life of Philip Heseltine*, p. 45.
8. Quoted in Hall, 'Basil Bunting Explains How a Poet Works', p. 7.
9. Hamnett, *Laughing Torso*, pp. 223–4.
10. Williams, 'Eighty of the Best', p. 121.
11. Loeb, *The Way It Was*, pp. 188–9.
12. Bowen, *Drawn from Life*, pp. 166–7.
13. Poli, *Ford Madox Ford and the Transatlantic Review*, p. 29.
14. Cited in Judd, *Ford Madox Ford*, p. 350.
15. Ludwig (ed.), *Letters of Ford Madox Ford*, pp. 160–1.
16. Bowen, p. 116.
17. Judd, p. 351.
18. Bunting (ed.), Ford Madox Ford, *Selected Poems*, p.ix.
19. Hemingway, *A Moveable Feast*, p. 83.
20. Williams, *Descant on Rawthey's Madrigal*.
21. ibid.
22. Ford, *It Was the Nightingale*, p. 284.

Chapter 5: To Rapallo and Back to London 1924–1928

1. *Rapallo Past and Present*, pp. 112–113.
2. Bowen, *Drawn from Life*, pp. 145–6.
3. *Rapallo Past and Present*, p. 20.
4. Baker (ed.), *Ernest Hemingway: Selected Letters 1917–1961*, p. 112.
5. Terrell (ed.) *Basil Bunting: Man and Poet*, p. 43.
6. Lesch, 'Basil Bunting: A Major British Modernist', p. 29.
7. Ahearn (ed.), *Selected Letters of Ezra Pound and Louis Zukofsky*, p. 71.
8. Cox, 'A Commentary on Bunting's "Villon"', p. 36.
9. Letter to Zukofsky, 7 Sept. 1964, Humanities Research Center, University of Texas.
10. Letter of Feb. 1926, cited in Caddel and Flowers, *Basil Bunting: A Northern Life*, p. 31.
11. Letter to Ezra Pound dated 21 Feb. 1934, cited by Quartermain in *Disjunctive Poetics*, p. 139.
12. Bunting, 'What Are We Coming To?', p. 520.
13. Bunting, 'Lydia Sokolova', p. 127.
14. Bunting, 'Chamber Orchestras', p. 676.
15. Bunting, 'Medium Calibre', p. 620.
16. Bunting, 'Gurrelieder', p. 140.
17. Bunting, 'Liszt', p. 701.
18. Bunting, 'Beethoven's Quartets', p. 786.
19. Bunting, 'Gurrelieder', p. 140.
20. Bunting, 'Committing Musical Archaeology', p. 595.

Chapter 6: Patronage and Marriage 1928–1930

1. Lamson, *Roger Baldwin: Founder of the American Civil Liberties Union*, p. 74.
2. Wilson, *The Thirties*, p. 692.
3. Fiber, *The Fitzroy*, p. 25. Donald Calthorpe starred in the first 'talkie' ever made in Britain. This was the film *Blackmail*, directed by Alfred Hitchcock.
4. Letter to Ezra Pound, 29 April 1926, Yale University Library.

5. Letter to Harriet Monroe, 20 Nov. 1933, University of Chicago Library.
6. Letter to M.D. Zabel, 24 March 1933, University of Chicago Library.
7. Letter to Ezra Pound, 8 Feb. 1934, Yale University Library.
8. Wade (ed.), *The Letters of W.B. Yeats*, p. 759.
9. Bunting, 'Yeats Recollected', p. 42.
10. ibid.
11. Antheil, *Bad Boy of Music*, p. 228.
12. 'Yeats Recollected', p. 41.
13. ibid., p. 44.
14. Bunting, *A Note On Briggflatts*, (unpaginated).

Chapter 7: Rapallo Again 1931–1933

1. Letter to James G. Leippert, 30 Oct. 1932, J. Ronald Latimer Collection, University of Chicago Library.
2. The photograph album is in the possession of Bourtai Bunting Hargrove to whom I am most grateful for permission to make a copy.
3. Cited in Makin, *Bunting: The Shaping of his Verse*, p. 65.
4. Carpenter, *A Serious Character: The Life of Ezra Pound*, p. 481.
5. Letter to Zukofsky, Sept. 1932, Humanities Research Center, University of Texas.
6. Letter to Zukofsky, 3 Nov. 1948, Humanities Research Center, University of Texas.
7. Cited in Makin, pp. 38–9
8. Letter from Marian Bunting to Karl Müller, 25 Oct. 1973.

Chapter 8: The Canaries and Hampstead

1. Makin, *Bunting: The Shaping of his Verse*, p. 74.
2. Unpublished essay cited in Forde, *The Poetry of Basil Bunting*, pp. 73–4.
3. Letter from Marian Bunting to Karl Müller, 25 Oct. 1973.
4. Jonathan Williams, US poet and publisher, was a keen reader of the older generation of modernist poets and met Basil on a 1963 research trip to England, interviewing him at length in 1966 for *Descant on Rawthey's Madrigal*, which was the first extended account of Basil's life.
5. Quartermain (ed.), 'Three Essays', p. 46.
6. Anthony Blunt's career in espionage, unlike Basil's, was to have a sensational conclusion; decades later he was, to much public shock and outrage, revealed to be the 'fourth man' in a spy ring headed by Kim Philby that had worked for the KGB for years.
7. Bunting, 'The Roots of the Spanish Revolt', p. 138.
8. Bunting, 'Butler', pp. 411–12
9. Guedalla, *Basil Bunting: A Bibliography of Works and Criticism*, p. 79.

Chapter 9: The Years at Sea 1937–1942

1. Williams, *Descant on Rawthey's Madrigal*.
2. That Basil offended Anne in some way is suggested by a letter he wrote to her mother ten years later, on 28 Aug. 1948. At the end of the letter he sends his regards to Anne 'if she will receive them'.
3. Quoted by Gail Roub in Penberthy (ed.), *Lorine Niedecker: Woman and Poet*.
4. Letter to Ezra Pound, 7 Nov. 1938, Humanities Research Center, University of Texas.
5. Williams, William Carlos, *Autobiography*, p. 264.

6. Forde, *The Poetry of Basil Bunting*, p. 96.
7. Caddel and Flowers, *Basil Bunting: A Northern Life*, p. 41.

Chapter 10: A Very Good War and a Lively Peace 1942–1950

1. Cooper, *Grass*, p. 37.
2. ibid., p. 137.
3. ibid., pp. 188–9.
4. Bullard, *Letters from Teheran*, p. 201.
5. Maclean, *Eastern Approaches*, pp. 213–21. In a letter to Dorothy Pound, 30 October 1949, Basil maintained that Maclean's story was a fabrication and that the kidnapping had been done by someone else who went on to become a vicar in Wales.
6. Payne, *Journey to Persia*, p. 205.
7. Makin, *Bunting: The Shaping of His Verse*, p. 104.
8. Williams, *Descant on Rawthey's Madrigal*.
9. Forde, *The Poetry of Basil Bunting*, p. 47.
10. This story was related by Tom Pickard in conversation with the author, 16 May 1997.
11. Unpublished letter to Dorothy Pound 8 Jan. 1947.
12. King (ed.), *Curzon's Persia*, pp. 126–7.
13. Makin, p. 108.
14. In a letter of 26 Nov. 1970 in the Bunting Archive in Durham University Library.
15. Forde, p. 49.
16. ibid., p. 141.
17. ibid., p. 124.
18. Unpublished letter dated 18 Jan. 1949.
19. Letter to Zukofsky, 28 July 1949, Humanities Research Center, University of Texas.
20. Richard Caddel includes five more translations from Manuchehri in the *Complete Poems*, 1994.
21. *The Times*, 30 Jan. 1950, p. 5.

Chapter 11: Italy and *The Spoils* 1950–1051

1. Letter to Dorothy Pound, 10 Dec. 1946, Lilly Library, University of Indiana.
2. Herodotus, *The Histories*, p. 80.
3. Forde, *The Poetry of Basil Bunting*, p. 178.
4. ibid., p. 205.

Chapter 12: Paradise Regained and Lost 1951–1952

1. Clucas, 'Basil Bunting: A Chronology', p. 71.
2. Lapping, *End of Empire*, p. 212.
3. Payne, *Journey to Persia*, p. 12.
4. ibid., p. 246.
5. ibid., p. 205.
6. ibid.
7. Unpublished letter, 17 Dec. 1951.
8. Unpublished letter, 14 April 1952.
9. Woodhouse, *Something Ventured*, chs. 8 and 9.

Chapter 13: Flight into Poverty 1952–1957

1. Unpublished letter, 1 Aug. 1952.
2. Letter to Margaret de Silver, 1 Oct. 1952, Mountjoy Collection, Durham University Library.
3. Letter to Margaret de Silver, 27 Sept. 1952, Mountjoy Collection, Durham University Library.
4. Letter to Ezra Pound, 9 July 1953, York University Library.
5. Letter to D. G. Bridson, 23 Aug. 1955, Lilly Library, University of Indiana.
6. Forde, *The Poetry of Basil Bunting*, p. 55.
7. Williams, *Descant on Rawthey's Madrigal*.
8. Mottram, 'MacSweeney', p. 22.
9. Turnbull, 'Resonances and Speculations, p. 25.

Chapter 14: The Years of Obscurity 1957–1965

1. Pickard, 'Serving My Time to a Trade', p. 156. Much of the following detail about the first Bunting/Pickard meeting is taken from this essay. In a letter to Dorothy Pound Basil himself gives a slightly different account of this important first meeting with Tom Pickard.
2. Tom Pickard in conversation with the author, 16 May 1997.
3. Reported by Roy Fisher in conversation with the author, July 1996.
4. Gael Turnbull in a letter to the author, 12 Oct. 1996.
5. Bunting, *A Note on Briggflatts*.
6. Basil did not always regard the Four Quartets as a 'mash'. He first read them just after the war and wrote about them admiringly to Zukofsky. From Teheran he asked his friend, 'Have you read Eliot's Four Quartets? I did in Cairo on my way here . . . The verse is exceedingly skilful – few Eliotisms. I was impressed, am hard to impress nowadays.' Letter to Zukofsky, 5 May 1947, Humanities Research Center, University of Texas.
7. 'Basil Bunting Talks about Briggflatts', *Agenda* 16, no. 1, spring 1978, pp. 9–10.

Chapter 15: The Years of Eminence 1965–1979

1. Michael Shayer in conversation with the author, 14 May 1997.
2. Letter to Dorothy Pound, 11 June 1965, Lilly Library, University of Indiana.
3. This perception together with the anecdote about the Wordsworth class derive from Hugh Kenner in Terrell (ed.), *Basil Bunting: Man and Poet*, p. 64.
4. ibid.
5. Quoted in Makin, *Bunting: The Shaping of his Verse*, p. 324.
6. Tom Pickard in conversation with the author, 16 July 1997. Tom was very much aware that the day of our conversation was the day after the thirty-second anniversary of the completion of *Briggflatts*.
7. Forde, *The Poetry of Basil Bunting*, pp. 243–4.
8. ibid., p. 244.
9. Bunting, 'Yeats Recollected', p. 42.
10. Bunting (ed.), Joseph Skipsey, *Selected Poems*, pp. 13–14.
11. Lesch, 'Basil Bunting: A Major British Modernist', pp. 12–13.
12. ibid., p. 25.
13. ibid., p. 36.
14. Bunting, 'Hugh MacDiarmid Lost', p. 81.

Chapter 16: The Last Years 1979–1985

1. Letter to Bourtai Hargrove, 14 March, 1980.
2. Terrell, 'Basil Bunting in Action', p. 71.
3. Letter to Bourtai Hargrove, 19 Dec. 1980.
4. ibid.
5. In an earlier version published in *Agenda* in spring 1978, the last line had three extra words, 'like the proud'. Their subsequent deletion enhances the poem immensely.
6. Michael Shayer in a letter to the author, 25 Sept. 1996.

Bibliography

Ahearn, Barry (ed.). *Selected Letters of Ezra Pound and Louis Zukofsky*, New Directions, New York, 1987.

Aiken, Conrad. 'Review: Active Anthology', *Poetry* 44, Aug. 1934, pp. 276–9.

Alexander, Michael (ed.). *The Earliest English Poems*, Penguin Books, Baltimore, 1966.

Alldritt, Keith. *Eliot's Four Quartets: Poetry as Chamber Music*, Woburn Press, London, 1978.

—— *Modernism in the Second World War*, Peter Lang, New York, 1989.

—— *W.B. Yeats: The Man and The Milieu*, John Murray, London, 1997.

Antheil, George. *Bad Boy of Music*, Doubleday Doran and Company, Garden City NY, 1945.

Apel, Willi. *Harvard Dictionary of Music*, Harvard University Press, Cambridge MA, 1947.

Arberry, A. J. *Classical Persian Literature*, Macmillan, New York, 1958.

—— (ed.) *Persian Poems: An Anthology of Verse Translations*, Dent, London, 1954.

Atkinson, James (trans.). *The Shah Nameh of the Persian Poet*, Routledge, London, 1892.

Bacigalupo, Giuseppe. *Ieri A Rapallo*, Campanotto Editore, Pasian di Prato, 1992.

Baker, Carlos (ed.). *Ernest Hemingway: Selected Letters 1917–1961*, Charles Scribner's Sons, New York, 1981.

Bell, Clive. *Art*, Putnam's, New York, 1958.

Bergin, Thomas G. *Dante*, Orion Press, New York, 1965.

Bersihand, Roger. *Japanese Literature*, trans. Unity Evans, Walker, New York, 1965.

Binns, A. L. *The Viking Century in East Yorkshire*, East Yorkshire Local History Society, York, 1963.

Blunt, Wilfrid. *Isfahan: Pearl of Persia*, Elek Books, London, 1966.

Bowen, Stella. *Drawn From Life*, Collins, London, 1941.

Briggs, Asa. *Victorian Cities*, Penguin, Harmondsworth, 1968.

Brower, Robert and Miner, Earl. *Japanese Court Poetry*, Stanford University Press, Stanford CA, 1961.

Browne, Edward G. *Literary History of Persia*, Cambridge University Press, Cambridge, 1928–30.

Bullard, Reader. *Letters from Teheran: A British Ambassador in World War II Persia*, I. B. Tauris & Co Ltd., London and New York, 1991.

Bunting, Basil. 'Beethoven's Quartets', *The Outlook*, 10 Dec. 1927.

—— *Briggflatts*, Fulcrum Press, London, 1966.

—— *Briggflatts*, *Poetry* 107, Jan. 1966, pp. 213–37.

—— *Briggflatts*, Stream Records P1205, 1968.

—— *Briggflatts*, tape recording with Scarlatti sonatas, University of British Columbia, 20 Nov. 1970.

—— *Briggflatts*, LP record with Scarlatti sonata in B Minor, L.33, 15 April 1977, Bloodaxe Books YRIC 0001, Newcastle-upon-Tyne, 1980.

—— *A Note on Briggflatts*, Basil Bunting Poetry Archive, Durham University Library, 1989.

—— 'Butler', *New English Weekly* 9, no. 25, 1 Oct. 1936.

—— 'Chamber Orchestras', *The Outlook*, 19 Nov. 1927.

—— 'Chinese Lyrics and Some Greek Poems of Love and Beauty', *Criterion* 17, April 1938, pp. 557–9.

—— Chomei at Toyama I–VII, *Poetry* 42, Sept. 1933, pp 301–7.

—— *Collected Poems*, Fulcrum Press, London, 1968.

—— *Collected Poems*, Fulcrum Press, London, 1970.

—— *Collected Poems*, Oxford University Press, London, 1978.

—— *Collected Poems*, Moyer Bell, New York, 1985.

—— *Complete Poems*, associate editor Richard Caddel, Oxford University Press, London and New York, 1994.

—— 'Committing Musical Archaeology', *The Outlook*, 12 May 1928.

—— 'Directory of Current English Authors', *Front*, April 1931, pp. 217–24.

—— 'Eheu Fugaces, Postume, Postume', *Agenda* 8, Autumn–Winter 1978–79.

—— 'English Poetry Today', *Poetry* 39, Feb. 1932, p. 251.

—— 'Ezra Pound', *New English Weekly* 1, 20 May 1932, pp. 137–8.

—— 'Fearful Symmetry', *Poetry* 39, Feb. 1932, p. 251.

—— 'Gurrelieder', *The Outlook*, 4 Feb. 1928.

—— 'Hugh MacDiarmid Lost', *Agenda* 16, no. 3, autumn–winter 1978–79.

—— 'Liszt', *The Outlook*, 26 Nov. 1927.

—— *Loquitur*, Fulcrum Press, London, 1965.

—— 'Lydia Sokolova', *The Outlook*, 23 July 1927.

—— 'Medium Calibre'. *The Outlook*, 5 Nov. 1927.

—— 'The Poet's Point of View', *Arts Diary*, Northern Arts, April–summer 1966.

—— *Redimiculum Matellarum*, Milan, 1920.

—— 'The Roots of the Spanish Revolt', *Spectator*, no. 5639, 24 July 1936.

—— (ed.). Joseph Skipsey, *Selected Poems*, Ceolfrith Press, Sunderland, 1976.

—— (ed.). Ford Madox Ford, *Selected Poems*, Pym-Randall Press, Cambridge MA, 1971.

—— *The Spoils*, Morden Tower Book Room, Newcastle-upon-Tyne, 1965.

—— 'The Spoils', *Poetry* 79, Nov. 1951, pp. 84–97.

—— 'Thanks to the Guinea Worm', *Agenda* 8, autumn–winter 1970, pp. 117–21.

—— 'Villon', *Poetry* 37, Oct. 1930, pp. 27–30.

—— 'What About Herbert Read?', *Agenda* 7, spring 1969, pp. 41–5.

—— 'What Are We Coming To?', *The Outlook*, 15 Oct. 1927.

—— 'Yeats Recollected', *Agenda* 12, no. 2, summer 1974.

Caddel, Richard and Flowers, Anthony. *Basil Bunting: A Northern Life*, Newcastle Libraries and Information Service, Newcastle, 1997.

Carpenter, Humphrey. *A Serious Character: The Life of Ezra Pound*, Faber & Faber, London, 1988.

Catullus, Gaius Valerius. *The Poems of Catullus*, trans. Peter Whigham, Penguin Books, Baltimore, 1966.

Clancy, Joseph P. *The Odes and Epodes of Horace*, University of Chicago Press, Chicago, 1960.

Clark, Thomas. 'New Lines', *Poetry* 109, Nov. 1966, pp. 110–12.

Clucas, Garth. 'Basil Bunting: A Chronology', *Poetry Information* 19, autumn 1978.

Cole, Thomas. 'Bunting: Formal Aspects', *Poetry* 128, Sept. 1951, pp. 366–69.

Connolly, Cyril. 'Critics Choice of the Year', *Sunday Times*, 3 Dec. 1967.

—— 'Out of Northumbria', *Sunday Times*, 12 Feb. 1967.

Cooper, John Xiros. *T.S. Eliot and the Ideology of the Four Quartets*, Cambridge University Press, Cambridge, 1995.

Cooper, Merian C. *Grass*, Putnam, New York and London, 1925.

Cox, Kenneth. 'The Aesthetics of Basil Bunting', *Agenda* 4, no. 3, autumn 1966, pp. 20–8.

—— 'Basil Bunting', *Scripsi* 3, nos 2 and 3, August 1985, pp. 1–5.
—— 'A Commentary on Basil Bunting's "Villon"', *Agenda* 16, no. 1, spring 1978, p. 20–36.
Creeley, Robert. 'A Note on Basil Bunting', *Agenda* 4, no 3, autumn 1966, pp. 18–19.
—— *A Quick Graph: Collected Notes and Essays*, Four Seasons Foundation, San Francisco, 1970.

Davie, Donald. *Ezra Pound: Poet as Sculptor*, Oxford University Press, New York, 1964.
—— *Under Briggflatts: A History of Poetry in Great Britain 1960–1988*, Carcanet Press, Manchester, 1989.
Digard, Jean-Pierre. *Techniques des nomades baxtyâri d'Iran*, Editions de la Maison des sciences de l'homme, Paris, 1981.
Driberg, Tom. *Ruling Passions*, Jonathan Cape, London, 1977.
Duberman, Martin. *Black Mountain: An Exploration in Community*, Anchor Books, Garden City, New York, 1973.

Faranda, Lisa Pater (ed.). 'Selected Letters of Lorine Niedecker to Cid Corman', *Conjunctions* 5, 1985, pp. 137–72.
Fiber, Sally. *The Fitzroy: The Autobiography of a London Tavern*, Temple House Books, Lewes, 1995.
Figgis, Sean and McAllister, Andrew. 'Basil Bunting: The Last Interview', *Bête Noire*, 2 and 3, spring 1987, pp. 22–51.
Ford, Ford Madox. *It Was the Nightingale*, Heinemann, London, 1936.
Forde, Victoria. *The Poetry of Basil Bunting*, Bloodaxe Books, Newcastle-upon-Tyne, 1991.

Gallagher, Dorothy. *All the Right Enemies: The Life and Murder of Carlo Tresca*, Rutgers University Press, New Brunswick and London, 1988.
Goodwin, K. L. *The Influence of Ezra Pound*, Oxford University Press, London, 1966.
Gordon, David. 'A Northumbrian Sabine', *Paideuma* 9, spring 1980, pp. 77–87.
Guedalla, Roger. *Basil Bunting: A Bibliography of Works and Criticism*, Norwood Editions, Norwood PA, 1973.
—— 'Basil Bunting: A Bibliography of Works and Criticism', *Poetry Information* 19, autumn 1978.

Hall, Anthea. 'Basil Bunting Explains How a Poet Works', *The Journal*, 17 July 1965, p. 7.
Hamburger, Michael. *The Truth of Poetry: Tensions in Modern Poetry from Baudelaire to the 1960s*, Harcourt Brace Jovanovich, New York, 1969.
Hamnett, Nina. *Laughing Torso*, Constable, London, 1932, reprinted Virago, London, 1984.
Hemingway, Ernest. *A Moveable Feast*, Charles Scribner's Sons, New York, 1964.
Herodotus. *The Histories*, trans. Aubrey de Selincourt, revised with introduction and notes by A. P. Burn, Penguin, Harmondsworth, 1983.
Heyward, Michael. 'Aspects of *Briggflatts*', *Scripsi* 1, nos 3 and 4, April 1982.
Heyward, Michael and Craven, Peter. 'An Interview with Basil Bunting', *Scripsi* 1, nos 3 and 4, April 1982.
Hoffa, William W. 'Ezra Pound and George Antheil: Vorticist Music and the *Cantos*', *American Literature* 44, March 1972.
Hooker, Denise. *Nina Hamnett: Queen of Bohemia*, Constable, London, 1986.

Judd, Alan. *Ford Madox Ford*, Collins, London, 1990.

Kenner, Hugh. 'Never a Boast or a See-Here', *National Review*, 19 Oct. 31, 1967.
—— *The Poetry of Ezra Pound*, Faber & Faber, London, 1951.
—— *The Pound Era*, University of California Press, Berkeley, 1971.
—— 'A Resurrected Poet', *Poetry* 78, Sept. 1951.
—— *The Sinking Island: Modern English Writers*, Knopf, New York,1988.
King, Peter, (ed.). *Curzon's Persia*, Sidgwick & Jackson, London, 1986.
Kleinzahler, August. 'Remembering Bunting', *Scripsi* 3, nos 2 and 3, Aug. 1985.
Kosciuszko, Jaroslav. 'Four Bottles of Glenfiddich and a Curry', *Bête Noire* 2 and 3, spring 1987.

Lamson, Peggy. *Roger Baldwin: Founder of the American Civil Liberties Union*, Houghton Mifflin, Boston, 1976.
Lapping, Brian. *End of Empire*, Granada, London, 1985.
Lesch, Barbara. 'Basil Bunting: A Major British Modernist', dissertation, University of Wisconsin, Madison, 1979.
Loeb, Harold. *The Way It Was*, Criterion, New York, 1959.
Ludwig, Richard M. (ed.). *Letters of Ford Madox Ford*, Princeton University Press, Princeton, 1965.

McIlhany, William H. *The ACLU on Trial*, Arlington House Publishers, New Rochelle, New York, 1976.
Maclean, Fitzroy. *Eastern Approaches*, Jonathan Cape, London, 1951.
Makin, Peter. *Bunting: The Shaping of his Verse*, Clarendon Press, Oxford, 1992.
Mottram, Eric. 'Conversations with Basil Bunting on the Occasion of his 75th Birthday', *Poetry Information* 19, autumn 1978.
—— 'MacSweeney', *Poetry Information* 18, spring 1977–78.

Nelles, Walter. *A Liberal in Wartime: The Education of Albert De Silver*, W. W. Norton and Company, New York, 1940.
Niedecker, Lorine. 'The Ballad of Basil', *Stony Brook*, nos 3 and 4, 1969.

Osborne, John & Woodcock, Bruce. 'Bunting, Olson and Modernism', *Bête Noire* 5, spring 1988.

Paige, D. D. (ed.). *Letters of Ezra Pound: 1907–41*, Harcourt Brace & Co., New York, 1950.
Payne, Robert. *Journey to Persia*, Dutton, New York, 1952.
Penberthy, Jenny (ed.). *Lorine Niedecker: Woman and Poet*, The National Poetry Foundation, Orono, Maine, 1996.
Pickard, Tom. *High on the Walls*, preface by Basil Bunting, Fulcrum Press, London, 1967.
—— 'Serving My Time to a Trade', *Paideuma* 9, no. 1, spring 1980.
Poli, Bernard J. *Ford Madox Ford and the Transatlantic Review*, Syracuse University Press, Syracuse, 1967.
Pope, Arthur Upham. *An Introduction to Persian Art Since the Seventh Century A.D.*, Peter Davies, London, 1930.
Pound, Ezra. *ABC of Economics*, Faber & Faber, London, 1933.
—— *ABC of Reading*, Routledge & Kegan Paul, London, 1934.
—— (ed.). *Active Anthology*, Faber & Faber, London, 1933.
—— *The Cantos of Ezra Pound*, Faber & Faber, London, 1975.
—— *Guide To Kulchur*, Faber & Faber, London, 1938.
—— *The Spirit of Romance*, New Directions, New York, 1968.

Pound, Omar. *Arabic and Persian Poems in English*, preface by Basil Bunting, New Directions, New York, 1970.

Quartermain, Peter. *Disjunctive Poetics: From Gertrude Stein and Louis Zukofsky to Susan Howe*, Cambridge University Press, Cambridge, 1992.
—— (ed.). 'Three Essays', *Sharp Study and Long Toil*, Durham University Press, Durham, 1995.
Quinn, Terry. *Bygone Scotswood*, Newcastle-upon-Tyne City Libraries and Arts, Newcastle-upon-Tyne, 1991.

Rapallo Past and Present, Reynaud Illustrated Guide Books, Turin, 1925.
Read, Herbert. 'Basil Bunting: Music or Meaning?', *Agenda* 4, no. 3, autumn 1966.
Reagan, Dale. 'An Interview with Basil Bunting', *Montemora* 3, spring 1977.
Robbins, Lionel (Lord). *Autobiography of an Economist*, Macmillan, London, 1971.

Schafer, R. Murray (ed. with commentary). *Ezra Pound and Music: The Complete Criticism*, New Directions, New York, 1977.
Sheard, Charlie. 'Basil Bunting and Music', *The Present Tense* 3, autumn 1982.
Smith, Barry. *Peter Warlock: The Life of Philip Heseltine*, Jonathan Cape, London, 1934, reprinted Oxford University Press, London, 1994.
Stock, Noel. *The Life of Ezra Pound*, Pantheon Books, New York, 1970.
Suter, Anthony. 'Time and the Literary Past in the Poetry of Basil Bunting', *Contemporary Literature* 12, autumn 1971.
Swann, Brian. 'Basil Bunting of Northumberland', *St Andrew's Review* 4, spring/summer 1977.

Terrell, Carroll F. (ed.). 'Basil Bunting in Action', *Paideuma* 9, no. 1, spring 1980.
—— *Basil Bunting: Man and Poet*, National Poetry Foundation, Orono, Maine, 1981.
—— *Louis Zukofsky: Man and Poet*, The National Poetry Foundation, Orono, Maine, 1980.
Tomlinson, Charles. 'Experience into Music: The Poetry of Basil Bunting', *Agenda* 4, no. 3, autumn 1966.
Turnbull, Gael. 'An Arlespenny: Some Notes on the Poetry of Basil Bunting', *King Ida's Watch Chain: A Moving Anthology: Link One*, Morden Tower Bookroom, Newcastle-upon-Tyne, 1964.
—— 'Resonances and Speculations, upon Reading Roy Fisher's *City*', *Kulchur* 7, New York, autumn 1962.
—— 'Then is Now: Meeting Basil Bunting', *Scripsi* 3, nos 2 and 3, Aug. 1985.

Wade, Allan (ed.). *The Letters of W.B. Yeats*, Rupert Hart-Davis, London, 1954.
Walton, George. *Bygone Throckley*, Newcastle City Libraries and Arts, Newcastle-upon-Tyne, 1994.
Wilhem, J. J. *Ezra Pound: The Tragic Years 1925–72*, Pennsylvania State University Press, 1990.
—— *Ezra Pound in London and Paris 1908–1925*, Pennsylvania State University Press, 1990.
Williams, Jonathan. *Descant on Rawthey's Madrigal: Conversations with Basil Bunting*, Gnomon Press, Lexington Kentucky, 1968.
—— 'Eighty of the Best', *Paideuma* 9, no. 1, spring 1980.
—— (ed.). *Madeira and Toasts for Basil Bunting's 75th Birthday*, Jargon Society, Highlands NC, 1977.
—— (ed.). 'A Tribute to Basil Bunting', *Conjunctions* 8, 1985.

Williams, Jonathan and Meyer, Tom. 'A Conversation with Basil Bunting', *Poetry Information* 19, autumn 1978.

Williams, William Carlos. *The Autobiography of William Carlos Williams*, New Directions, New York, 1967.

Wilson, Edmund. *The Thirties*, Farrar, Strauss & Giroux, New York, 1980.

Woodhouse, C. M. *Something Ventured*, Granada, London, 1982.

Woolf, R. S. 'Basil Bunting's Poetry', *Stand* 8, no. 2, 1966.

Wylie, Andrew. 'Basil Bunting', *Agenda* 7, spring 1969.

Zukofsky, Louis. *Prepositions: The Collected Critical Essays of Louis Zukofsky*, Rapp and Carroll, London, 1967.

Index

BB refers to Basil Bunting. Page numbers in **bold** refer to the main analysis of BB's poetry

Ackworth School xv, 11, 13–14
Adams, J. J. 37, 39, 49, 70
Agenda 167
Anglo-Persian Oil Company 101, 119
Antheil, George 34–5, 63, 181
Arvon International Poetry Competition 195
Astor, Colonel John 168
Auden, W. H. 58

Bacigalupo, Massimo xiii–xiv
Bakhtiari tribe 101–104, 109
Barnes, Harry 29
Barney, Natalie 33
Bartok, Béla 68
Bax, Arnold, *Fantasy Sonata* 52
Beat Generation 149
Beecham, Sir Thomas 54
Bell, Britt 198
Bell, Peter 194
Berlin 57–8
Bilbow, Tony 195
Bird, William 33
Black Mountain poets 176
Blackfell New Town 187, 191
Bloomsbury group 24–5
Bomberg, David 51
Bowen, Stella 40–2, 45
Brancusi, Constantin xiv, 33, 35–6
Breton, André 191
Bridson, D. G. 143, 185
Briggflatts 11–12, 201
British Intelligence 63, 105–6
British Poetry conference 181
Bullard, Reader 103
Bunting, Annie (mother of BB) 3, 97, 168
  and grandchildren 90
  marriage 5
  in Rapallo 63, 72
  in Throckley 116, 140, 148
Bunting, Basil
  appearance 168

boyhood 3, 5–14
British Intelligence 63, 105–6, 111–12
British Vice-Consul at Isfahan 107–10
character 16
conscientious objector 20–2
death 200–1
education 10–14
  Ackworth School 11–14
  Leighton Park School 15–20
  Royal Grammar School 11
Festscrift 184
filmed interview 194
friendship with Ford 40–3
friendship with Pound 27, 31–43, 46–7, 80, 94–5
friendship with Yeats 63–5
friendship with Zukofsky 67
literary education 7, 19
London School of Economics 26–8
Madeira and Toasts for Basil Bunting 184
marriage 67
music critic 52–4
Northern Arts President 181
The Outlook 50–4
Persian language 62–3
POETRY
  'A Song for Rustum' 141–2
  'A thrush in the syringa sings' 167
  'Attis: Or, Something Missing' 73–5, 84, 167
  'Aus Dem Zweiten Reich' 58, 75, 167
  'Birthday greeting' 167
  Briggflatts xiv, 12, 23–4, 39, 57, 82, 152–64, 167, 191, 200
    A Note on Briggflatts 66, 152, 159
    in French 191
    readings 171, 176, 194
    recording 174
    reviews 169
  Caveat Emptor 81
  'Chomei at Toyama' 60–2, 75, 167

215

Collected Poems **58**, 73, 77, 118, 150, 174, 185, 188
'The Complaint of the Morpethshire Farmer' 60
The First Book of Odes **60**, 117, 167
'Gin the Goodwife Stint' 60
'I am agog for foam' 51
'Keep Troth' 19
'Lament' 115
'Let them remember Samangan' 92
'Mesh cast for mackerel' 75
'Not to thank dogwood' 55, 93
'Nothing/substance utters or time/ stills' 60, 73
'Now we've no hope of going back' 192, 198
'On The Fly-Leaf of Pound's Canto' 117
'The Orotava Road' 58, 84
'The Passport Officer' 75
'The Pious Cat' 183–4
'Poems 1950' 120, 133
Redimiculum Metallanum 66
Second Book of Odes 167, 198
Shah na Meh **89–90**
'Shall I sulk because my love has a double heart?' 118
'The Song of the Ackworth Clock' 14
The Spoils 58, 82, 90, 99, 104–5, 121–31, 150–1
'Stones trip Coquet burn' 178
'They Say Etna' 7, 49
'Two Photographs' 75
'Under sand clay. Dig, wait' 58
'Verse and Version' 77
'Vestiges' 72, 75
'Villon' 44, 47–8, 72, 77, 95, 167
'The Well of Lycopolis' 84–6, 167
'What the Chairman Told Tom' 167
'You idiot! What makes you think decay will/never stink from your skin?' 167
poetry and music 27–9, 78, 194
Poetry Society President 180
political beliefs 7, 17, 49, 87–8
Quakerism 11, 65, 191, 194
RAF service
    in balloon ships 97–100
    as interpreter in Iran 103–4
    in Italy and Sicily 106–7
    promotion 109
    in western desert 104–5

sight 172
Throckley 116, 140, 145
TRAVELS
    Berlin 57–8
    Canary Islands 80–4
    Iran 63, 101–19, 133–7
        expulsion from 138–40
    Italy 121, 131–2
    London 23–30, 90–1
    New York City 67–9
    Norway 25
    Paris 31–44
    Rapallo 45–8, 59, 70–9
    United States 182–3
    Venice 59–60
unemployed 140–3
university teaching 170–1, 173, 176, 178
Villon 33–5, 37
war service 97–109
writing 13, 76, 87, 150, 166–7
Wylam 146
Bunting, Bourtai (daughter of BB) xiii, 80, 90, 113, 166, 169–70, 188
    birth 72
    children 172–3
    in Wisconsin 94, 112
Bunting, Elizabeth (aunt of BB) 49
Bunting, Hettie (aunt of BB) 4, 48, 146
Bunting, Joseph (grandfather of BB) 4
Bunting, Joyce (sister of BB) 6, 10, 48, 142, 188, 200
Bunting, Marian (wife of BB) 68, 94, 120, 169
    children 71–2, 81, 91
    BB visits 177
    divorce 97
    marriage 67, 80–1, 83–4, 90–1
    meeting 59–60
Bunting, Roudaba (daughter of BB) xiii, 90, 94, 113, 141, 169, 177, 188, 190, 198–201
    birth 81
    family 171, 178
Bunting, Rustam (son of BB) 91, 120, 141
Bunting, Sallie (aunt of BB) 4, 48
Bunting, Sima Maria (daughter of BB) 118, 121, 138–9, 168, 172, 188–9, 194, 199–200
Bunting, Sima (wife of BB) xv, 141, 147, 166, 168, 174–8, 194, 200

children 118, 142
divorce 188
in Italy 121, 132
leaves BB 185–6
leaves Iran 138–40
marriage 113–16
returns to Iran 144
Bunting, Thomas Faramy (son of BB) 142, 168–9, 174, 188–9, 193, 200
Bunting, Thomas Lowe (father of BB) 4–11, 16–17
death 48
marriage 5
medical career 8
Butts, Mary 73

Caddel, Rick xiv, 99
Calthorpe, Donald 59
Canary Islands 80–4
Carrington, Dora 25
Chaplin, Sid 185
Cheesman, Annie see Annie Bunting
Cheesman, Annie (grandmother of BB) 3
Cheesman, Isaac (grandfather of BB) 3–5
Clarke, Michael 135
Cleaners' Press 120
Cockburn, Claude 79
Cocteau, Jean 33, 40
Connolly, Cyril 169, 200
Conrad, Joseph 32, 43
Cookson, William, Agenda 167
Coppard, A. E. 41
Corman, Sid 185
Corso, Gregory 197
Cossey, Tanya 187–8, 196, 198–200
Cowley, Malcolm 68
Cox, Kenneth 48
Creeley, Robert 170, 171, 176, 185
Crowley, Aleister 24
Culver family 70–1
cummings, e. e. 149

Daily Telegraph 200
Darras, Jacques 12, 191
Davie, Donald 185
Davies, Fred xv
de Rachelwitz, Mary 171
de Silver, Albert 55–6
de Silver, Anne 93
de Silver, Margaret 93, 114, 117, 119, 142

allowance to BB 56–7, 59, 66–7, 69, 80–1
death 148
Deakin, Ralph 116, 136–7, 140
Dillabough, Dave xv
Dixon, Thomas 8
Doolittle, Hilda 32
Douglas, Gavin 198
Drerup, Carlos 81, 94, 109
Duncan, Robert 176

Echanges 68
Eliot, T. S. 49, 73, 76, 130
'Ash Wednesday' 192
Criterion 89, 92
Four Quartets 152, 154, 200
Little Gidding 121, 164
modernists 110, 151
Old Possum's Guide to Practical Cats 183
and Pound 32, 33, 81
'Preludes' 27–8
referred to 120
The Waste Land 33, 127
English Review 32, 49

Faber & Faber 49, 76, 81, 120
Fabian Society 23, 26
Fellowes, Dr Edmund 10
Ferlinghetti, Lawrence 172
Firdusi, Shah na Meh 62–3, 76, 81, 89, 157
First World War 14, 20–1
Fisher, Roy xiv, 151, 185, 197, 201
Fitzroy Tavern 23, 28, 29, 50, 59, 155
Flowers, Anthony 99
Flynn, Dallam 120
Four Pages 120
Ford, Ford Madox xiv, 31, 40, 50, 76, 177
BB in jail in Genoa 46
editor of English Review 32
friendship with BB 32, 40–3, 190
Some Do Not 41
The Good Soldier 40, 43
The Outlook 50
transatlantic review 40–1
Forde, Sister Victoria 179, 193–5, 197
Fry, Roger 24
Vision and Design 25
Fulcrum Press 167, 174, 185

Gaudier-Brzeska, Henri 24, 27, 70
Geddes, Patrick 5
General Strike 49
Gertler, Mark 25
Ginsberg, Allen 167, 171, 185, 197
Goacher, Denis 151, 166, 174
Gonne, Maud 33
Gray, Cecil 28–9
    Survey of Contemporary Music 28
Greenbank, Jean 12
Greenbank, John Allen 11–13, 20
Greenbank, Peggy 12–13, 152, 165–6,
    174, 201
Greene, Graham 87
Guardian 200
Guedalla, Roger 81

Haas, Eugen 76
Halliday, John (son-in-law of BB) 188,
    196
Hamilton, Richard 151
Hamnett, Nina 24, 27, 29–30, 31, 38–9,
    51
    death 144
Hardy, Thomas 32
Hauptmann, Gerhart 75
'HD' 76
Heifetz, Jascha 40
Hemingway, Ernest xiv, 33, 42, 76,
    190
    A Moveable Feast 42–3
    BB in jail in Genoa 46
Henri, Adrian 195
Henshaw, Michael 193–5, 201
Herman, Leopold 136
Heseltine, Arthur 37
Heseltine, Philip *see* Peter Warlock
Hogarth Press 25
Horace 38
Hughes, Richard 87
Hughes, Ted 195

Il Mare 71, 76, 78
    Supplemento Letterario 76
imagism 32, 72
International Poetry Festival 178
Iran 63, 101–19
    Bakhtiari tribe 101–4
    Isfahan 107–9
    politial situation 133–7
Isherwood, Christopher 58

James, Henry 32, 43
Jockey Club 40
John, Augustus 24
Jones, David 151, 161
Joyce, James 31, 32, 33, 76
    Ulysses 82

Kahn, Eddie 148, 178
Kenner, Hugh 169, 170, 185, 190
Keynes, Maynard 25
Kiki 40
Kleinfeldt, Papa Judah 23, 155

Larkin, Philip 149
Laughlin, James 78
Lawrence, D. H. 32–3, 49–50
    Women in Love 29
Le Rougetel, Sir John 112
Leighton Park School 15–20
    Leightonian 18, 21
Les Champs Magnétiques 191
Lesh, Barbara 28, 182–3
Lewis, Wyndham 32, 51, 70
L'Indice 71
Lochhead, Liz 197
London Society, *London Squares and How to
    Save Them* 50

McAlmon, Robert 73
MacDiarmid, Hugh 151, 176, 181
Maclean, Fitzroy 103
MacLeish, Archibald 76
MacNeice, Louis 87
MacSweeney, Barry 144
Malherbe 38
Man Ray 40
Manuchehri 117–18
Marsh, Edward, *Georgian Anthology* 28
Masoliver, J. R. 76
Maupassant 38
Messer, Andrew 49
Meyer, Tom 182, 189
    Festschrift for BB 184–5
Migrant Press xiv, 151
modernist movement 32, 110, 151
Modigliani 24, 39
Monotti, Francesco 71, 76–7
Monroe, Harriet 61
Montgomery, Stuart 167, 174–5, 185,
    195
    Fulcrum Press 167, 174–5
    Loquitur 167

Moore, Helen 27, 51
Moore, Marianne 110
Morden Tower Bookroom 150–1, 167
Morgan, Edwin 185
Mossadeq, Mohammed 101, 133–7
Moyer Bell 198
Moyer, Jennifer 198
Muggeridge, Malcolm 88–9
Mullett, Peggy 51
Münch, Gerhart 78
Musical Times 54

National Poetry Foundation 190
The New Age 28, 76
New Directions publishing company 78
New English Weekly 76, 89
New York Sun 76
New York Times 71, 135
Newcastle 7–8
    Central High School 11
    Literary and Philosophical Society 7–8,
        33, 148, 180
    Royal Grammar School 11, 168–9
Newcastle Daily Journal 143–4
Newcastle Evening Chronicle 147
Niedecker, Lorine 93–4, 172
    Collected Poems 197
North Mail 20
Northwest Films 194

Oakshot, Ronald 113
objectivism 72
Olson, Charles 151, 176
Orage, A. R. 28, 76
Orwell, George
    Down and Out in Paris and London 67
    Homage to Catalonia 88
The Outlook 50–4

Paris Tribune 776
Payne, Robert 134–5
Penberthy, Jenny xv, 196–7
    Collected Poems of Lorine Niedecker 197
Penguin Books 177
Perse, St John, *Anabase* 89
Persia *see* Iran
Philby, Kim 190
Pickard, Constance 185
Pickard, Tom xiv, 149–50, 167, 178,
    185, 189, 193, 201
    Eruption 149

High on the Walls 175
Pound's memorial concert 181
The Order of Chance 175
Plomer, William 87
Poetry 61–2, 71, 72, 76
Pope, Arthur Upham 134
Pound, Homer and Isobel 78
Pound Conference in Texas 171
Pound, Dorothy
    correspondence with BB 94, 106, 110,
        114, 119, 135, 168, 170, 172,
        177–8
    food parcels 111
    guest in Northumberland 175
    marriage 32
    in Paris 33
Pound, Ezra xiv, 27, 31–3, 49, 59–69,
    130, 142, 149, 151
    anti-semitism 94
    arrested by Italians 107
    death 180–1
    Eliot's *The Waste Land* 33
    in France 33, 37, 43
    friendship with BB 31–43, 46–7, 80,
        94–5
    imagism 32
    in Italy 33, 44–7, 59–76
    memorial concert 181
    in mental hospital 110, 117, 120
    modernist movement 31–2
    The Outlook 50
    Villon 35
    vorticism 72
    WORKS
        A Lume Spento 32
        ABC of Economics 95
        Active Anthology 81
        Cantos 32, 33, 44, 63, 68, 75, 76,
          166, 181, 195
        Cathay 181
        Guide To Kulchur 95–6
        Homage to Sextus Propertius 27, 31, 32
        Le Testament de Villon 33–4
        'Malatesta' cantos 87
        Pisan Cantos 110
        Propertius 181
        The Spirit of Romance 35
        The Women of Trachis 181
Pound, Omar 112, 119, 185
    Arabic and Persian Poems 175
Pritchett, V. S. 87, 175

Private Eye 79
Pym-Randall Press 177

Quakers 11–12, 65, 191, 194
Quartermain, Peter xiv, 176, 178, 197

Rabelais 38
Racine 38
Rakosi, Carl 73
Rapallo 44–6, 106
Rawarth, Tom 185, 201
Read, Herbert 169
Reading, Leighton Park School 15–20
Reid, Marjorie 41
Rexroth, Kenneth 73
Reznikoff, Charles 73, 94
Rhys, Ernest 8
Rhys, Jean 40–1
    Wide Sargasso Sea 41
Robbins, Lionel (Lord Robbins) 26–7
Roberts, Michael 76
Roosevelt, Kermit 137
Rubinstein, Artur 39
Rudge, Olga 34, 45, 76, 78, 106, 119,
    190
Russell, Peter 120, 133
    Nine 120

Schnabel, Artur 53
Schoenberg, Arnold, *Gurrelieder* 53, 160
Schumann, Elisabeth 53
Scotswood-on-Tyne 3
Scott, William Bell 8
Serly, Tibor 68
Shakespear, Dorothy 32, 63
Shakespear, Olivia 32, 63
Shayer, Michael xiv, 151, 166, 198, 201
Simms, Colin 185, 193, 198–200
Simpson, Dallum 120
Skipsey, Joseph 8, 182
    Selected Poems 181
Society of Friends *see* Quakers
Sokolova 51–2
Soupault, Philippe 191
Spectator 87
Spender, Stephen 195
Stein, Gertrude 31, 33
Stendahl, *De L'Amour* 38
Stephenson, Ernest Cooper Apperley
    13–14, 21
Stokes, Adrian 87, 134
Strachey, Lytton, *Eminent Victorians* 25

Surrealists xiv, 38–9, 191
Swanson, Susan 177
Swift, Jonathan, *Gulliver's Travels* 199
Swinburne, Algernon Charles 9

Tallman, Warren and Ellen 176
Tarset 193–4
Tate, Allen 76
Taupin, René 68, 94
Terrell, Carroll 28, 46, 189–90
    Paideuma 189
Thatcher, Margaret 196
Theiss, Otto 50, 56
Thomas, Dylan 24
Three Mountains Press 33
Throckley 116, 119, 140, 145
The Times 54, 57, 116, 118, 119, 135–7,
    140, 158
transatlantic review 40–2
Tresca, Carlo 56
Turnbull, Gael xiv 145–6, 167, 174, 176,
    181, 185, 201
    Migrant Press 151
    and Northern Arts Council 169
    and Peggy Greenbank 165–6
Tyne Tees Television, *A Measure of Words*
    195
Tzara, Tristan 38, 40

Villon 33–4
vorticism 72

Wallas, Graham 6, 26
Walter Scott Company 8
Warlock, Peter 28–9, 37
    Capriol Suite 29, 52
    The Curlew 29
Watson, R. S. 8
Wells, H. G. 25
western desert 104–5, 122
Whitehouse, Mary 196
Whitman, Walt 27, 149
    Leaves of Grass 19
Whittaker, William 9
    North Countrie Ballads 9
Williams, Carlos 110
Williams, Jonathan xv, 26, 40, 43, 150,
    172, 182, 189, 192
    Descant on Rawthey's Madrigal 174
    Festschrift for BB 184–5
    Jargon Press 150
    Rawthey's Madrigal 87

Williams, William Carlos 32, 68, 73, 76, 94, 151
Autobiography 97
Wilson, Edmund 56, 76
Woodhouse, C. M. (Monty) 137
Woolf, Leonard 25
Woolf, Virginia 25
Night and Day 25
Wordsworth, William 9, 152, 170, 183

Yeats International Summer School 181
Yeats, W. B. 29, 32, 33, 50, 110
A Packet for Ezra Pound 63
A Vision 191
At the Hawk's Well 63
Fairy and Folk Tales of the Irish Peasantry 8
illness 64–5
Oedipus at Colonus 63
On Baile's Strand 63
Rapallo 63–5

Zabel, Morton Dawen 61–2
Zahidi, General 103
Zawadowski, Waclow 39
Zukofsky, Louis 67, 72–3, 77, 81, 82, 87, 93, 97, 98, 109, 110, 114, 117, 131, 148, 151, 183
An 'Objectivists' Anthology 73
Festschrift for BB 185
meeting 171
poetry 110
in Rapallo 78